RENWOMEN

What Modern Renaissance Women Have to Teach Us
About Living Rich, Fulfilling Lives

DALE GRIFFITHS STAMOS
& W. SCOTT GRIFFITHS

www.RenWomen.com
www.facebook.com/RenWomen

Cover Design by Debbie Yudkin
Interior and Jacket Design by Alex Espinoza

ISBN 978-0-9976005-1-3
First Paperback Edition
Printed in the United States of America

This book is dedicated to
our loving and supportive spouses:
Greg Stamos &
Loretta Griffiths

CONTENTS

FOREWORD

BY LARRAINE SEGIL

When Dale and Scott asked me to write the foreword of their book *RenWomen: What Modern Renaissance Women Have to Teach Us About Living Rich, Fulfilling Lives*, I said "I am honored but why me?"

"You are the quintessential RenWoman," they assured me. "Please tell our readers about yourself as we know it will entice them to read further and spread the word about the remarkable women in our midst and in our book. RenWomen have been unheralded and criticized for being too 'scattered,' 'unfocused', or even 'not good employees' due to their multiple interests and intense individuality. It is time for them to come into their own."

Ah yes, that definitely rang true for me.

Here is my story.

I immigrated from South Africa to Los Angeles where, after being a high school teacher in Latin and English and a university teacher in Latin, I pursued a career in law. I completed my JD at night in the only school in Los Angeles that paid attention to its night students, Southwestern School of Law, while working all day at various jobs (telemarketing, paralegal, and more). I passed the bar in California (a truly dreadful ordeal) and began the practice of law only to find that I disliked it so much that it made me ill.

The search began for joy in my work life.

I joined with a group of entrepreneurial men (met the organizer at a swimming pool—typical of RenWomen to find opportunity in the strangest places), who were creating a financial services company. From them I learned a great deal about the world of business and loved it! The experience I gained from partnering with eleven large egos in the world of financial services was critical, especially when I moved into a management role in one of their financial services companies. There I learned that it was as important in business to know what NOT to do as it was to understand the fundamentals. With lessons learned, I realized that it was also important to learn the academics of business: accounting, marketing, sales, quality control and more. I obtained an executive MBA from the Presidential Key Executive Program at The Pepperdine Graziadio School of Management.

What a mind stretching experience! This was valuable not only for the quantitative and qualitative knowledge gained, but also for the relationships developed.

Another business opportunity arose in the medical arena and I jumped into that, applying my new-found business knowledge on a daily basis. Raising angel investor capital for the medical business was a challenge—another good lesson learned: don't raise money when you need it; raise it before you do! After a number of years of building the enterprise, the chain of medical clinics was sold.

A new opportunity popped up—an aerospace distribution company in advanced materials used for microchip manufacture—

and I took it. What fun it was to learn about another industry—it never occurred to me that being in an industry where I was a novice could be a problem—whether financial services, health care, aerospace or electronics. Novelty intrigued and fascinated me, and the challenges were stimulating and exciting. To onlookers, it was appalling. Why would I take such risks in three different industries when I could have had a "safe" career practicing law? To me—it was perfect!

I have now learned from the book which lies ahead for you, that I was being a RenWoman—and that was indeed a fine thing to be!

That company was successfully turned around and sold and onward I went!

For those RenWomen reading this, you will recognize that all of this was while I was raising our only child (he is now 44 and a very successful serial entrepreneur in tech) trying to have another, losing five pregnancies, experiencing a failed adoption attempt (the birthmother kept the baby), supporting my husband's career and working really hard to become an integral part of the community—to feed our hearts with arts and music, and our souls with religion while staying healthy and sociable.

I was always a great networker. I created an advisory board of powerful and knowledgeable people for my companies and always joined the trade association for my current industry (with the personal mandate to become its chair or at minimum to become part of its leadership). Along the way I became a member (and board member) of SoCalTen —Southern California Technology Executives Network, a member of The Committee of 200—A Global Group of Women CEO's (and Chair of Foundation and Vice Chair of Governing Board), NACD So Cal—The National Association of Corporate Directors, (board member and Committee Chair), as well as a board member of a Fortune 200 public company, Frontier Communications (NASDAQ: FTR) and a number of private companies. My nonprofit work was wide-reaching: Board of Governors of Cedars Sinai Medical Center, UCLA Entrepreneurs Board of Anderson School of Management, LARTA—Los Angeles Regional Technology Alliance, Southwestern School of Law Board of Trustees and much more.

Because of my extensive network, I built (and sold) the leading global boutique consulting firm in Strategic Alliances, authored six books on Partnering and Leadership, created online education programs (live TV executive education as well as video series and seminars) and taught executive education in Strategic Alliances at Caltech for 24 years. When my grandchildren arrived (four glorious little boys) I wrote songs and books for them and a blog with recipes, publishing on Audible.com to join my novel and business books already there. My hobby is running our Little Farm where we raise Alpine goats, tilapia, turkeys, chickens, quails, rabbits and birds, along with 300 exotic fruit trees. We make cheese, jams and relishes, feeding off our urban farm in the center of a city of 10 million people.

I decided it was time to stop building companies. I chose to make giving back my full time job. I thought long and hard about the direction into which I would focus my dollars and commitment. I wanted to conceptualize philanthropy in a different way. In 2008 with the assistance of the development officers at the three different educational institutions which have added value to my life, I set up endowment funds and created the Larraine Segil Scholars Group (the awardees selected the name).

Annually we choose one woman from Southwestern School of Law, one from the PKE MBA program at The Pepperdine Graziadio School of Management and one 10th grade student from Kingsmead, my former high school in Johannesburg South Africa. There is a financial award, but far more important is how I mentor these women. They range in age from 15 – 55. The selection criteria could well have been written by Dale and Scott as key parts of the definition of a RenWoman. There are 5 criteria:

Women who. . .

1. Are square pegs in round holes
2. Walk the road less travelled
3. Have integrity
4. Are willing to be mentored by me for the rest of my life
5. Are willing to mentor each other and those coming after them for the rest of their lives

There are 14 women in our Larraine Segil Scholars (LSS) group as of the date of publication of this book, with between three and five joining annually (sometimes the candidates are so amazing that we cannot choose and so I double the award). Their stories are remarkable. I meet with them quarterly in person as a group in Los Angeles where most of us live, or by Skype (for the South African high school girls). I help them change jobs, inspire them to greater opportunities, help solve financial, personal and career problems and am on call 24/7 to each of them. I bring the South African girls to Los Angeles upon their high school graduations so that they can discover the huge opportunities offered by our great country. They each spend a day shadowing our other scholars in their businesses.

I believe that these wonderful women give me much more joy than the benefits, introductions and advice I give them, although they have assured me that is not so. What is most joyful of all is that I have seen the arc of life make a full circle. The RenWoman that I have always been now has a way of paying it forward. The Scholars annually interview, evaluate and vote on the new candidates, and the endowments are structured so as to make the program sustainable beyond my life term. The Larraine Segil Scholars can and will support the RenWomen of the future.

I am so grateful to Dale and Scott for putting a name to the phenomenon that is exemplified by the women in this book. It is a Sisterhood of Being Different—yet in so many ways we are the same—as their book clearly defines. In that, I find comfort, as will other RenWomen, their parents, spouses and the children who love them.

Larraine Segil
www.larrainesegilscholar.com
https://en.wikipedia.org/wiki/Larraine_Segil

PREFACE

JILL by Scott Griffiths

My twin sister, Dale, remembers as a fifteen-year-old girl explaining to our mother all the things she wanted to do when she was older. "Darling," Mom said, "you can't do all of that. You have to choose just one." At which point, our mother quoted the often-used phrase: "Jack of all trades, master of none."

Well, I'm happy to say Dale ignored her. She is a produced playwright, screenwriter, and published poet. She speaks several languages, has a master's degree in literature, plays two musical instruments and writes songs, and she is a workshop leader and manuscript consultant/editor. In her personal life, she is married and has raised a son, now in his early twenties, and she has been a caretaker for our elderly parents. Still, for a long time, our mother's admonition lingered like a buzzing insect at the back of Dale's mind. "Am I watering down each skill by pursuing others?" she wondered. "Am I compromising the quality (or at least the quantity) of my work by sometimes needing to put family first? Or am I living a fuller, more interesting life by developing many passions, while still staying true to the caring side of myself?" She came to the firm conclusion that the latter was true, and that, in fact, the apparently disparate parts of her life and varying interests fed and enhanced each other.

For many Renaissance-style women, having multiple passions and life commitments can make them feel scattered, unfocused, and unsure of whether they can be equally competent in them all. They are often stuck on the negative labels they have heard. Labels such as *dilettante*, which implies a person who only dwells on the surface of knowledge, or *dabbler*, with its equally frivolous connotation. They wonder if they have to resist their inner nature and "zero in" on just one thing. But, as Margaret Lobenstein argues in her book, *The Renaissance Soul* "[There is] the idea that expertise is achieved only through exclusivity; that in order to commit to any of our own strong passions, we will have to give up all the other things we love. This is absolutely *not* the case. Not only do Renaissance Souls have loads of interests; they are often capable of bringing a passionate level of intensity to several of them at once."[1]

There are remarkable examples of women today who do just that: who are multi-talented, visionary, and groundbreaking. And they, more than anyone, belie the concept that we can only pursue one thing in life, or that we cannot develop mastery in multiple arenas.

JACK by Dale Griffiths Stamos

My twin brother, Scott, also ignored our mother's advice. He is a visual artist, a marketing and branding expert, an entrepreneur, a CEO, a professor, and has conceived, co-authored, and published numerous books, including several best sellers. His last book, co-authored with Eric Elfman, *Beyond Genius: The 12 Essential Traits of Today's Renaissance Men* (on which I served as editor), was inspired by his very successful current enterprise—the 18/8 Fine Men's Salons. 18/8 seeks to help men be the best they can be in their appearance. Scott began to contemplate the question: what represents man at his best in the more general sense? For him, the answer was: a Renaissance man!

Beyond Genius makes the case that modern Renaissance men, as well as Renaissance men through the ages, share a certain set of traits. These traits in combination are what make these men as remarkable as they are. A Renaissance man:

- Is outstanding in his field and exceptional in many areas
- Is insatiably curious
- Embraces culture
- Merges his left and right brain
- Delights in sharing what he does
- Has the courage to take risks
- Creates
- Perseveres
- Is passionate
- Has vision
- Challenges the status quo
- Shapes the future

In the surveys Scott and Eric conducted for that book, out of curiosity, they asked the question: "Do Renaissance women share the same traits as Renaissance men?" The answer was an overwhelming "Yes." In fact, during the writing and publication of *Beyond Genius*, they were often asked the question: What about the women? Aren't there modern day Renaissance women? And were there Renaissance women in the past?

Interestingly, when Scott searched the words "Renaissance women" on Google, he was surprised to find listings that were predominantly women who *lived* during the Renaissance and only a few scattered modern women who were described this way. That seemed wrong. There were, no doubt, *many* modern women every bit as multi-talented and groundbreaking as the men featured in *Beyond Genius* (such as Elon Musk, Steve Jobs, Steve Allen, and Dave Stewart). And there must have also been Renaissance-style women throughout history, despite societal pressures and patriarchal systems against which they had to struggle.

He also wondered, do these women manifest their "Renaissance-ness" in the same way as the men do? And what can we learn from these extraordinary women?

The idea for a new book had taken hold. Scott decided to discuss the idea with his friend, the multi-talented Barbara Lazaroff, (who would later become our first profile subject). They met up at Spago in Beverly Hills. The inimitable Ms. Lazaroff, beautifully adorned in designer jewelry and a stunning Valentino outfit, sat at a round table toward the rear corner of the restaurant. Although Scott and Barbara had known each other for years, they had not seen each other for a while, so there was a fair amount of catching up to do. Eventually, Scott brought Barbara up to speed on his book on modern Renaissance men, then broached the subject of starting on a book about modern Renaissance women. "Scott," she said, incredulously, "I don't mean to be rude, but you're a man. What entitles you to work on such an important female-centric book?" Without missing a beat, Scott responded that he was very qualified. He had a special understanding of women. In fact, he had spent many months in close proximity to a bright, creative, forward-thinking female. (I'm blushing.) He paused for a moment and then added: "And that was the nine months before I was born." Barbara laughed and cried, "Oh! You have a twin sister! Well, then, you are awash in estrogen. You're OK. Do the book."

Not long afterwards, during the time I was wrapping up the editing on *Beyond Genius*, Scott asked me if I would be his partner on the new book. He knew Barbara was right. The book needed a woman as author. But it also needed a conceptual and marketing thinker like him who could simultaneously appreciate what women bring to the world. Additionally, Scott felt, as twin sister and brother, we would bring a unique and gender- balanced perspective to the subject matter.

RenWomen: What Modern Renaissance Women Have to Teach Us About Living Rich, Fulfilling Lives has been more than two years in the making. For months Scott and I discussed the structure, outline, and tone of the book. We thought about how academic the book should be, how aspirational, and what type of supporting data/research we would need. We also considered how the book would be positioned within the publishing world, in terms of the influence we hoped it would have on women's lives.

We settled on an initial short list of women to begin the interviews. Then, as we looked into other potential subjects, our RenWomen interviewees also began to introduce us to other RenWomen. Our list ultimately became the 16 women you will find in the pages of this book.

Scott and I have enjoyed bringing our diverse but complementary abilities to this collaboration. When it came down to the "heavy lifting" (as Scott puts it) of writing the book, Scott deferred to my talents. He felt that I, as an experienced playwright, have the unique ability to define character and find those narrative threads that make people's stories so fascinating.

As the interviews progressed, it became more and more apparent to us that these women *knew* things. Not just the many skills and careers they had mastered, but things about life, about happiness, and about helping the planet we all live on evolve. To them, living a rich fulfilling life is a multi-dimensional experience that involves mind, heart, and spirit. It is also about pushing past the fears that have stopped so many women in the past, and in the present. It is about saying a resounding "NO" to limits. Their life stories can inspire us all.

We call these exceptional women, "RenWomen™." It is a term we have coined, rather than co-opting the expression so often used for multifaceted men. We do not claim to present a complete list of modern RenWomen, but we have an excellent sampling. We have also primarily focused on women who live in the United States, though there are clearly many international Renaissance-style women.

This book is an exploration and celebration of what these women have to teach, not just to other women, but to everyone, about embracing one's fullest potential and living life expansively and meaningfully.

- Dale Griffiths Stamos
- W. Scott Griffiths

INTRODUCTION

"The purpose of life is to live it, to taste experience to the utmost, to reach out eagerly and without fear for newer and richer experience."
*-**Eleanor Roosevelt***

The world we live in has radically changed. In the 21st century, information is the reigning currency, as we are bombarded from all directions with media, messages, and endless choices. It's hard to believe that the main reason for this, the World Wide Web, was born a mere 25 years ago. In 1989, software consultant Tim Berner-Lee originally hatched the idea of an open computer network, and on Christmas day, 1990, with help from computer scientist Robert Cailliau and others, he set up the first successful communication between a Web browser and a server via the Internet.[2] Today, the Internet is an integral part of almost everyone's life, and with so much so quickly at our fingertips, it feels sometimes like we're moving at the speed of light.

On top of that, the old paradigm of learning one skill well and having only one or two jobs in a single area of expertise for one's entire work life is breaking down. Our rapidly evolving times and the volatility of the job market make it far more likely that an individual will hold numerous jobs in a lifetime. A *Forbes.com* article states, "Ninety-one percent of Millennials (born between 1977-1997) expect to stay in a job for less than three years, according to the Future Workplace 'Multiple Generations @ Work' survey of 1,189 employees and 150 managers. That means they would have 15–20 jobs over the course of their working lives!"[3] And chances are good those jobs will span more than one occupation and will demand different sets of skills. So a person who can flexibly move from one skillset to another, from one discipline to another, who has a broader rather than narrower base of abilities may be better adapted to our modern times. In this world in flux, it seems the old adage "adapt or perish" couldn't be more true.

Renaissance individuals not only have a raging curiosity and a hunger to master many things, but also embrace risk, growth, and transformation. And with the Internet, they no longer need to spend hours in a library poring through books to learn new things. Knowledge is at the click of a mouse.

The bottom line is we need Renaissance people now more than ever.

Women are particularly suited to the Renaissance life. They already wear many hats as mothers, career women, household managers and caretakers. And as more opportunities have opened up for women in the past 50 years, through the women's movement, the advent of the pill, and shifting societal attitudes, women have proven they can excel in every field of endeavor, even those once considered strictly male domains.

It is no surprise that a number of exceptional women have made their mark in not just one arena but many. These are the women who can't imagine being limited to just one expression of themselves. Maya Angelou, the quintessential modern Renaissance Woman, said: "I think you can be a jack-of-all-trades and a mistress-of-all-trades. If you study it, and you put reasonable intelligence and reasonable energy, reasonable electricity to it, you can do that."[4]

An increased lifespan and more years of productivity add even more opportunities for a RenWoman to expand. Here are some striking examples: Maya Angelou was still writing and speaking until her death at age 86. Tao Porchon-Lynch, a professional yogi, who has also been an actress, dancer, and model, set a Guinness World Record at 93 as the world's oldest yoga instructor. She is now 97 and still going strong.[5] Gloria Steinem, journalist, women's rights activist, author, and co-founder of *Ms.* Magazine, is 81 and has no intention of retiring.[6] Jane Fonda, renowned actress and fitness guru, is 76 and embracing a revitalized acting career. The old maxim, "age is just a number," is becoming more and more true, especially for RenWomen!

There are other reasons we are seeing the emergence of more Renaissance women. The role of professional women, particularly in western societies, is growing. Currently, a greater percentage of women (60 percent) than men graduate from our universities.[7] And, although we still have a way to go, women are gaining more positions of power and leadership in business, politics, and the arts.

Studies have shown there are clear advantages that accompany the increased presence of women leaders, managers, and executives. A Pepperdine University study conducted over several years reported high profits in Fortune 500 companies with a strong record of promoting women to the executive suite. The study stated: "The 25 best firms for women outperformed the industry medians, with overall profits 34 percent higher when calculated for revenue, 18 percent higher in terms of assets and 69 percent higher in regard to equity."[8] According to a 2007 study by the consulting firm McKinsey and Company, European firms with the highest proportion of women in power saw their stock value climb by 64 percent over two years, compared with an average of 47 percent.[9] An article in *The Economist* reports, "eliminating the remaining gap between male and female employment rates could boost GDP in America by a total of 9%, in the euro zone by 13% and in Japan by as much as 16."[10] Credit Suisse Research Institute reported that greater gender diversity in a company's management coincides with better financial performance and stock market valuations.[11] MIT found that the most effective and collaborative teams have a greater proportion of women.[12]

Studies, articles, and books also point to the idea that women have a unique management style that can add to the success of an organization. In the article "Why Women Should Lead Boldly," Sharon Hadary and Laura Henderson, authors of the book *How Women Lead*, describe six leadership strengths that women display. They note that women are "1) values-based 2) holistic 3) inclusive and collaborative 4) invest time in consultation 5) create shared visions, values and goals, and 6) generate trust from employees."[13] John Gerzema, co-author with Michael D'Antonio, of the book, *The Athena Doctrine*, conducted a survey of 64,000 people across 13 countries. As Gerzema reports in a *Harvard Business Review* article, two-thirds of survey respondents felt that "the world would be a better place if men thought more like women."[14]

The time is ripe for women to take the lead in a new Renaissance, one that balances feminine values with the prevalent masculine ones and that allows women to live up to their full potential.

The modern Renaissance women we feature in this book—some of whom you have heard of, but others who will, no doubt, be welcome discoveries—are an embodiment of that promise and that potential. Their stories will also serve to inspire those women who want to live a Renaissance life but don't know how.

Who are these RenWomen? They come from all different careers and walks of life. There are, for example, poet, actress and linguist Hélène Cardona; professional explorer, writer and symposium leader Lorie Karnath; and restaurateur, designer, and philanthropist Barbara Lazaroff. There are those who turned tragedy or misfortune into triumphs like Kathy Eldon, whose 22-year-old son was killed in Somalia, and Eva Haller, who barely escaped being killed by fascist forces during World War II. The youngest of our RenWomen, Alexandra Franzen, is an online entrepreneur, coach, and writer; the oldest is eminent thought leader and former CEO of Girl Scouts of America, Frances Hesselbein. There is Lydia Kennard, who led Los Angeles World Airports through the 9/11 crisis, and Bosnian native Marinela Gombosev, who came to America to build an expansive new life. There is former opera singer turned arts organization founder and director, Dale Franzen; therapist, professor, and photographer, Lita Rawdin Singer; and twin sisters Margaret and Christine Wertheim, who work at the intersection of math, art, environmentalism, and women's crafts. And there are the three founders of The MY HERO Project, the multiply-capable Jeanne Meyers, Rita Stern Milch, and Karen Pritzker. All of these RenWomen have forged their own paths, learning lessons along the way. These lessons are evident in both their lives and their words, and form the bedrock of this book.

Our book is divided into three parts. In Part One, we explore what a RenWoman is, look at a number of historical RenWomen, and talk about modern icons like Maya Angelou, Hillary Clinton, and Oprah Winfrey. In Part Two, we feature our profile subjects. At the end of these chapters, we have our "Ren Gems"--quotes from each of the women that will challenge and motivate. In Part Three, we talk about the boons and barriers for RenWomen in today's world, as well as for young women who aspire to a Ren life. We conclude with a summary of characteristics common to all of our RenWomen.

So use this book as inspiration, as a spur, as a roadmap, and most of all, as a torch to light your own Renaissance path.

I

Definition, History, and Icons

1

WHAT IS A RENWOMAN?

Renaissance Women, like Renaissance Men, are driven by a sort of inner compass to push ever outward, to swallow life whole, to challenge themselves to gain mastery in many things because all of those things interest them. These are the women who tackle two degrees at once, who read voraciously and in many subjects, who gain proficiency in a musical instrument or a foreign language, who start their own business, then branch out into speaking and writing, and love to rock climb too. This is not because they feel compelled to prove themselves in a man's world; on the contrary, it is their need to be all that they are and to not feel bound by the limits imposed by their education or by society that motivate them.

During the process of exploring the subject of this book, we spoke not only to the women we profiled, but to other highly successful women—often Renaissance-style women in their own right.

Shari Rudolph is Executive Producer of Gigging & Grubbing, the first TV show about musicians and their favorite places to eat while on tour, and also teaches courses on creativity and advertising. She has been a frequent entrepreneur and an executive and chief marketing officer for numerous consumer, retail, and e-commerce brands. When asked to define what a "RenWoman" is to her, she says: "I think she is an explorer. She is incredibly curious, always pursues new interests, and is not limited by things she was told growing up. I don't believe it's necessarily about fame or fortune, it's much more than that." Dana Manciagli, who has been a corporate executive for more than 30 years and is now an author, blogger, keynote speaker, career coach, and global career expert, comments, "A RenWoman has traits like agility, flexibility, dealing with ambiguity, and she also knows how to face adversity." Tracy Cioffi, VP of Marketing for Sur La Table, and former Head of Marketing for See's Candies, remarks, "A RenWoman is always hungry for more. She has a clear goal and works hard to get there."

How does a RenWoman differ from a Renaissance man? First of all, there are many ways in which the two are alike. As one would describe a Renaissance man as someone who has expertise in a number of areas, so would this apply to a Renaissance woman. And as we mentioned in the preface, they share such common traits as passion, drive, willingness to take risks, curiosity, creativity, and challenging the status quo. But there are often differences in the way women manifest these traits, and there are additional skills that RenWomen bring to the table.

"Everyone talks about how women have a better ability to multitask," Shari Rudolph remarks. "But maybe it's really an ability to move more fluidly from one thing to the next. I think we do that well. I also think there's a level of emotional sensitivity that women have.

Not to say men aren't sensitive at all, but I think women exhibit a different way of being compassionate and empathetic. In other words, women have some very unique strengths and gifts, just as men do."

We also spoke to a special man, a filmmaker who is an advocate of women's role in transforming the world.

Emmanuel Itier, who directed the award-winning documentary *Femme: Women Healing the World,* is passionate about what women bring to the table. His film, which features a hundred women, including groundbreakers like feminist Gloria Steinem, futurist Barbara Marx Hubbard, and Nobel-Peace-Prize-winner Mairead Maguire, is a testament to the value of "feminine" traits like cooperation, collaboration, nurturing, and empathy. "There is an imbalance between the feminine and the masculine in this world," he says. "You push women out of politics, education, and religion, and you end up with a totally unstable world. Until we have that balance between the feminine and masculine, we will go nowhere. Men don't need to give up the power; they just need to share it."

Renaissance-ness implies a different kind of thinker. A RenWoman is someone who moves smoothly between multiple fields, drawing ideas from one to spark discoveries in another. Working in this inter-disciplinary way, she gains insights and finds creative solutions that are not limited to one specialty, but rely on her wide-ranging knowledge base. This is one of the reasons why she is a creative out-of-the-box thinker, making unique and unexpected pairings and connections, challenging the standard thinking around her, and thus urging society forward.

RenWomen, like all women, do not live their work lives in a vacuum but usually have multiple responsibilities outside of work, including children to raise and/or elderly parents to care for. This aspect of their lives, while often creating difficult choices, adds a vital dimension, coloring their priorities and concerns.

In the end, a RenWoman is a woman first. And those societal and family pressures that exist for all women also exist for her. But, as the RenWomen in this book show, when there is commitment, drive, and creativity, it is truly amazing what a woman can accomplish!

2

Everyone has heard of Leonardo da Vinci. But how many have heard of Isabella d'Este? She was an extraordinary multi-talented woman who lived at the same time as da Vinci. She was by any definition a Renaissance woman—not just a woman who lived during the Renaissance—whose grasp of politics, diplomacy, the arts, languages, and much more was exceptional. And she was not alone in history. Renaissance-style women, or female *polymaths*, ("A person of wide knowledge or learning" –*Oxford Dictionaries*) have existed throughout time.

For much of history, being able to have a career outside the home, let alone a substantive education, was very difficult for a woman to obtain, if not impossible. Imagine then, what it must have been like to be a woman who was able to get an education (either on her own or through an enlightened parent) and who was not only accomplished in one area but in many. A woman who could hold her own with the male artists, politicians, or intellectuals of her day. That these women existed at all seems to defy all odds. But exist they did. Some of the names in this section will be ones everyone recognizes: Elizabeth I and Eleanor Roosevelt, most notably. But others will be unfamiliar to most readers. It's important to keep in mind that even though these women have not often appeared in history textbooks, their accomplishments were not any the less remarkable. There is the old saw that you need only look at who writes history to understand who gets included.

Since our book is a celebration of modern day Renaissance women, we want to emphasize that the potential for women to develop into polymaths has always been there. But society's strictures, frequent childbearing, and domestic responsibilities have usually proved potent barriers. So those who "broke through" are even more extraordinary for this. In this chapter, we will look at a representative group of such women, understanding that it is upon the shoulders of women like these that our modern RenWomen stand.

Hypatia c. 360-415 CE

Hypatia lived during the fourth and fifth centuries AD and was a Neo-Platonist who ran a school where she taught philosophy, logic, astronomy, and mathematics. She was also an exceptional orator and spoke publicly to men and women alike. A quote from the 5th-century Christian church historian, Socrates Scholasticus, described her in this way: "There was a woman at Alexandria named Hypatia, daughter of the philosopher Theon, who made such attainments in literature and science, as to far surpass all the philosophers of her own time. Having succeeded to the school of Plato and Plotinus, she explained the principles of philosophy to her auditors, many of whom came from a distance to receive her instructions. On account of the self-possession and ease of manner which she had acquired in consequence of the cultivation of her mind, she not infrequently appeared in public in the presence of the magistrates. Neither did she feel abashed in going to an assembly of men. For all men on account of her extraordinary dignity and virtue admired her the more."[15]

Although no written work of Hypatia's has survived, she is reported to have co-authored or edited with her mathematician father a number of mathematical and scientific commentaries, examining the works of Ptolemy, Euclid, and Apollonius. She is also reputed to have charted the celestial bodies.

Hypatia died tragically at the hands of a Christian mob who falsely thought her entangled in a religious and political feud of the time. There are two vastly different accounts of Hypatia and her death. The first is in the already mentioned *Ecclesiastical History* by Socrates Scholasticus; and the second is in the writings of the 7th century Bishop John of Nikiu. He described Hypatia as a "pagan" who was "devoted at all times to magic, astrolabes, and instruments of music, and she beguiled many people through Satanic wiles." While Scholasticus described her murder as one in which "she fell victim to the political jealousy which at the time prevailed," John of Nikiu claimed that "A multitude of believers in God arose . . . and they proceeded to seek for the pagan woman who had beguiled the people of the city." But in both accounts, she was stoned to death and dragged through the streets by an angry mob. A sad ending to an exceptional life.

A legend of Hypatia began to rise in the 19th century where there were various interpretations of her as everything from a witch to an erotic heroine, and in the 20th century, more scholarly works have explored her life and her contributions. In astronomy, a main asteroid belt and a lunar crater were named for her.

The legacy Hypatia has left is one of a thinking woman who dared to share her knowledge, who had great influence on her times, and who took on near-mythological stature in other eras.

Hildegard von Bingen 1098-1179

Hildegard von Bingen was a medieval nun and mystic who wrote voluminous works on theology, astronomy, medicinal cures, and philosophy. She also founded two monasteries, composed music, supervised illuminated illustrations of her mystical visions; wrote poetry, a morality play, and even cookbooks!

Renewed interest in women of the medieval Church has brought Hildegard more attention in recent decades. She is particularly lauded for her musical compositions, 69 of which have survived to this day. She wrote in the form of the *chant* or *plainsong* of her time, but her music is characterized by soaring sweeps up the octave, uncharacteristic of the more limited range of most plainsong. Each of her compositions was accompanied by her own poetic text, and she was particularly mindful of the relationship between music and words. She wrote the music and the script for the *Ordo Virtutum*, which is now considered the oldest morality play written (meaning she essentially *invented* a form that is associated with the Middle Ages).

Hildegard had visions since childhood. She describes one, at the age of three, as "so great a brightness that my soul trembled; yet because of my infant condition I could express nothing of it."[16] Until the age of 40, she was resistant to sharing them or writing them down, even though she had been told in one vision to do so. But then, she was struck down by illness, and she saw this as a sign of God's disapproval. So she decided to recount some of her visions to her male superior who convinced her to write them down. He then shared them with *his* superiors, who were so struck by them that they declared them prophetic. These writings eventually reached the Pope, who wrote Hildegard a letter asking her to set the visions down in a more systematic way. This she did in three volumes: The *Scivias* ("Know the Way"), *Liber vitae meritorum* ("Book of Life's Merits"), and *De operatione Dei* ("On God's Activity"). She also supervised the beautiful mandala-like illustrations in the illuminated texts. Here is an example of her writing: "[God is speaking:] I, the highest and fiery power, have kindled every spark of life . . . I, the fiery life of divine essence, am aflame beyond the beauty of the meadows, I gleam in the waters, and I burn in the sun, moon, and stars. With every breeze, as with invisible life that contains everything, I awaken everything to life."[Vision 1:2.] What is striking is that the concept of God as present in all things is a pantheistic philosophy expounded later in the 17th century by Baruch Spinoza and reflective of elements of Eastern religious thought.

Hildegard's renown and influence spread wide, and within a few years she was carrying on correspondence with kings, theologians, and scholars, and despite the rarity of public preaching by women, she conducted four preaching tours throughout Germany, denouncing clerical corruption and demanding reform.

Additionally, she wrote two very practical books on medicine. The first, *Physica*, describes the scientific and medicinal properties of various plants, stones, fish, reptiles, and animals. The second, *Causae et Curae*, is an exploration of the human body, its connections to the rest of the natural world, and the causes and cures of various diseases. All of this was, of course, through a medieval perspective and base of knowledge, but she nonetheless covered such topics as human sexuality, psychology, and physiology.

These accomplishments are extraordinary, even seen from a 21st century perspective. And though she called herself a member of the "weaker sex" and an unlearned woman, by insisting all her authority came from the divine,[17] this actually gave her a persuasive voice to speak with when women seldom had that voice. And a little bit of feminist thought crept in when she stated: "Woman may be made from man, but no man can be made without a woman."[18]

Isabella d'Este, 1474-1539

As mentioned before, Isabella d'Este was a contemporary of the quintessential Renaissance man, Leonardo da Vinci. He, in fact, did a sketch of Isabella, with plans (never completed) to do a full portrait.

Precocious from an early age and raised by a father who believed in educating girls, Isabella received a classical education, excelling at history, Latin, and Greek, and by the time she was a teen, she was able to discourse on affairs of state. She was also a talented singer, musician, and dancer.

At the age of 16, she married Francesco Gonzaga, the Duke of Mantua, to whom she was betrothed from the age of six. She admired Francesco and enjoyed his company, and it was, for many years, a happy alliance. Four years into the marriage, she bore a baby daughter, Eleonora, who would be the first of eight children. In 1502, Francesco began what would be a long-standing affair with the infamous Lucrezia Borgia. More sexual in nature than romantic, the liaison was a great source of pain for Isabella.

In 1509, when Isabella's husband was captured and held hostage in Venice, it fell to her to take control of Mantua's military forces, and to hold off its invaders. During those three years, she was a confident and assertive leader, even, at one point, persuading King Louis XII of France not to send troops against Mantua. Her husband, upon his return in 1512, was so humiliated by her superior political skills that their marriage was never the same after, and they began to pursue independent lives. When Isabella was 45, Francesco died, and, as Marchesa of Mantua, she became an official head of state. She took this role very seriously, studying architecture and agriculture, and encouraging the development of the textile and clothing industry, which became one of the key industries of Mantua.

Isabella was a passionate patron of the arts. She collected art and sponsored writers, philosophers, and painters, such as Raphael and da Vinci. She was also a fashion leader, whose style was copied by women throughout Italy and at the French court. She wrote thousands of letters, commenting on everything from politics to war, and her letters are considered to be important historical documents of the times she lived in. During her later years, she established a school for girls and ruled Solarolo, in Romagna.

Isabella was widely admired during her lifetime. Author Matteo Bandello described her as "supreme among women," and diplomat Niccolò da Correggio called her "The First Lady of the world."[19]

Queen Elizabeth I, 1533-1603

Queen Elizabeth I is well known for her political savvy and ability to rule a nation. But perhaps less known is that she could also speak eight languages and was one of the best educated women of her time. She was an avid supporter of the arts, and during her reign, later referred to as the "Elizabethan Era," there was a great artistic flowering, particularly as regards the dramatic arts, exemplified by William Shakespeare. Although we now consider female monarchs to be an entirely typical occurrence, and in retrospect look upon her iconic reign as a highly successful one, at the time of her ascension, women rulers were anything but the norm. It was male heirs, and males only, who were expected to rule. In 1553, however, at the death of the teenage king Edward VI, there were no male heirs in the Tudor line left. Only Edward's two half sisters, Mary Tudor and Elizabeth, could legitimately be considered heirs. Thus, out of this necessity, Mary ruled as queen for five years, before her early death at age 42, at which point, the 25-year-old Elizabeth ascended to the throne.

Both Mary Tudor and Elizabeth I dealt with the attitudes of the time regarding female rulers. Mary was pressured to get married, not only to produce a (male of course) heir but also for other more patriarchal reasons. Holy Roman Emperor Charles V said of the Queen: "It will be necessary, in order to be supported in the labour of governing and assisted in matters that are not of ladies' capacity, that she soon contract matrimony with the person who shall appear to her most fit." Mary later responded with the assurance she would love and obey her husband, but "if he wished to encroach in the government of the kingdom she would be unable to permit it."[20] She ended up marrying King Philip of Spain (an unpopular choice), but the marriage produced no children.

Mary came under severe condemnation from the Scottish Protestant agitator John Knox, opposed to her not only because she was female but also because she was fiercely Catholic and persecuted Protestants under her rule. He described her reign as "monstrous," and claimed that "to promote a woman to bear rule, superiority, dominion or empire above any realm, nature or city is repugnant to nature, contumely to God, a thing most contrarious to his revealed will and approved ordinance, and finally it is the subversion of good order, of all equity and justice."[21]

Interestingly, when Elizabeth came along, Knox, knowing that at least a Protestant now ruled, tried to assuage the queen by writing her that she was the exception to his blanket condemnation. She, however, was not placated and forbid the Scotsman to step foot on English soil.

In other ways, too, Elizabeth was her own woman. Despite similar pressures as those put on Mary, she made the radical choice not to marry. She had numerous suitors, but she stated in 1563, "If I follow the inclination of my nature, it is this: beggar-woman and single, far rather than queen and married." Of course, in this, she was also choosing not to produce an heir. When pressed to name one, she refused. This was a savvy decision. She suspected if she did so, she would be vulnerable to a coup. This was a way to help assure her political security. And indeed, she ruled from 1558 until her death in 1603.

She walked a fine line between asserting her authority as ruler and acknowledging herself as the anomaly that she was, i.e. a female monarch. In her famous speech to the troops in Essex in 1588, during the threat of invasion by Spain, she said: "I know I have the body but of a weak and feeble woman, but I have the heart and stomach of a king."[22]

She was guided by an exceptional self-confidence and strength of mind. "I am your anointed Queen," she proclaimed, "I will never be by violence constrained to do anything. I thank God I am indeed endowed with such qualities that if I were turned out of the realm in my petticoat I were able to live in any place in Christendom." And intelligence and curiosity guided her. In a statement that would still resonate today, she said, "Life is for living and working at. If you find anything or anybody a bore, the fault is in yourself."[23]

Margaret Fuller, 1810-1850

Margaret Fuller was an American author, editor, journalist, literary critic, educator, and women's rights advocate.

Like other Renaissance women in history, Margaret had a father who believed in education for girls, and she was educated at home and at various schools. Much of her learning was also self-taught. She trained herself in the classics and several modern languages, and was an avid reader.

In her twenties, Margaret pursued writing and journalistic work, publishing essays and reviews in several periodicals. When she was only 25, her father died of cholera, which left her bereft. She swore she would financially support her mother and younger siblings. To earn a more consistent income, she began teaching at various schools. In 1839, she initiated what she called her "Conversations." These were discussions among groups of women—with the intention of making up for their lack of access to higher education. They covered topics which included history, mythology, the fine arts, and literature. A number of women who would later become significant in the women's suffrage movement attended these meetings.

In that same year, Ralph Waldo Emerson offered her the job of editor of his new Transcendentalist journal *The Dial*. One of her most important works originally appeared in serial form in *The Dial*. When she expanded it into a book, she named it *Woman in the Nineteenth Century*. Published in 1845, it talked about the role of women in America and became a seminal work in American feminism.

She moved to New York in 1844 and joined the *New York Tribune* as a literary critic. By 1846, she was the newspaper's first female editor. She published more than 250 columns ranging in topics from art and literature to women's rights and the evils of slavery. She also became the *Tribune's* first female foreign correspondent. She was sent to Europe, where she remained for four years, interviewing important literary figures. In all, she sent back 37 reports. There, she met and fell in love with Giovanni Angelo Ossoli, and they had a son, Angelo. But in 1850, on a voyage back to the United States, the ship collided with a sandbar close to the American shore, and a number of people perished, including Fuller and her new family. In 1852, in response to a keen public interest in her life, *The Memoirs of Margaret Fuller Ossoli* was published, edited by Emerson and others. Although much of her story was censored or changed (leaving out mentions, for example, of various lovers), it became the bestselling biography of the time and went through thirteen editions before the end of the century. Two collections of her various writings, *At Home and Abroad,* and *Life Without and Life Within* were published in 1856 and 1858.

What was it about Margaret Fuller's life that made her so compelling to her contemporaries (and to those who still study her)? She was clearly one of our first feminists, and was the first American to write a book about equality for women. She pushed for education for women, followed by political rights. She warned women not to marry before knowing who they were and, once married, not to be dependent on their husbands. She also did not see a clear division between men and women and said, "Male and female represent the two sides of the great radical dualism. But in fact they are perpetually passing into one another . . . There is no wholly masculine man, no purely feminine woman." It's hard to believe these very modern thoughts were conceived by a woman in the 1800's. Margaret Fuller also advocated reforms in the prisons, aid to the poor, and African-American rights.

She was, of course, harshly criticized by a number of her contemporaries, who accused her of being un-female, over-confident, and a radical. But Margaret Fuller held firm to her beliefs, at a time when society did not encourage such a thing in a woman. Like all Renaissance women, she also valued expansion and self-discovery. "Very early, I knew that the only object in life was to grow," she said, and "What concerns me now is that my life be a beautiful, powerful, in a word, a complete life of its kind." For her, this was not a luxury or a privilege, but a necessity. "I am suffocated and lost," she said, "when I have not the bright feeling of progression."[24] This was a woman, in other words, whose most powerful legacy, it can be argued, was giving voice to the intellectual, artistic and socially-conscious strivings of women everywhere.

Eleanor Roosevelt, 1884-1962

Much of course has been written and is known about Eleanor Roosevelt. There is little doubt that she was a Renaissance woman. Not only was she a remarkable First Lady, but she was a campaigner, an author, a diplomat, an advocate of racial, women's and human rights, a U.N. delegate, and a public speaker.

Eleanor Roosevelt redefined what it meant to be a First Lady, refusing to play the traditional domestic role of White House "hostess." During her husband's tenure, she was the first presidential wife to hold her own press conferences, write a syndicated newspaper column, and speak at a national convention. She also continued the public speaking she had begun before FDR's presidency. She earned a good income, comparable, in fact, to her husband's, and donated most of it to charity. As admired as she later became, she was a most controversial First Lady. She sometimes disagreed publicly with her husband's policies (as when, just before he took office, she wrote an editorial criticizing his public spending policies); and she was outspoken in her condemnation of social and racial inequities. Her support of the African American community made her very unpopular among whites in the South. When WWII broke out, she spoke out against anti-Japanese sentiment, another very unpopular stand. She worked hard to convince her husband to allow greater immigration of Jews escaping Nazi occupation, but he chose to restrict immigration, to her deep regret.

Eleanor was a strong advocate for women's rights. For example, she helped women get into top positions in her husband's administration. Because the famous Gridiron Club didn't allow women at its annual dinner for journalists, she held another dinner for women reporters at the White House. She also banned male reporters from her press conferences. In this way, newspapers had to keep women on their staffs if they wanted the conferences covered.

After her husband's death in 1945, Eleanor was appointed by President Truman as a delegate to the United Nations General Assembly. Then in 1947, as chairperson of the UN Commission on Human Rights, she was involved in the drafting and ratification of the Universal Declaration of Human Rights. At a seminal speech in front of the United Nations, she declared: "We stand today at the threshold of a great event both in the life of the United Nations and in the life of mankind. This Universal Declaration of Human Rights may well become the international Magna Carta of all men everywhere."[25]

In the late 1940s, there were a number of Democrats that pushed for her to seek public office, even going so far as suggesting she run for the presidency. She took none of this seriously, however. (Although she might well be proud to see a woman currently running for president.)

Throughout the 1950s, she continued to write her newspaper column, appeared on numerous radio and television programs, and had a very active public speaking life, averaging 150 lectures a year. Since 1937, she had worked on various volumes of an autobiography. In 1961, these volumes were combined into *The Autobiography of Eleanor Roosevelt*, and published that year.[26] At the age of 76, she wrote the wonderful advice book: *You Learn by Living, 11 Keys to a Fulfilling Life.*[27]

What are the elements of Eleanor Roosevelt's character that led her to a life of such high accomplishment and social integrity? Well, in true Renaissance fashion, she embraced life with vigor. "Life was meant to be lived, and curiosity must be kept alive!" she said. "The purpose of life is . . . to taste experience to the utmost, to reach out eagerly and without fear for newer and richer experience." She also knew the importance of facing one's fears: "You gain strength, courage and confidence by every experience in which you really stop to look fear in the face," she said. "You must do the thing you think you cannot do." And she learned to not care what others thought of her, but to follow the urgings of her own heart. As she put it: "Do what you feel in your heart to be right—for you'll be criticized anyway."[28]

Eleanor Roosevelt was a great lady, deeply committed to making the world a better, more just place; and willing to put her whole heart and soul into it.

We have presented in this chapter some particularly remarkable examples of Renaissance women in history. But this is by no means a complete list. From the beginning of recorded time, these extraordinary women have existed. And for those interested in looking further into Renaissance-style women in history, here is a more complete, if still partial list: Assyrian queen Semiramis (9th c. BCE), Theodora, wife of Justinian (5th c. CE), Empress Eudokia Makrembolitissa (1021-1096), Trotula of Salerno (11th c. CE),

Marguerite of France, (1279-1318), Christina, Queen of Sweden (1626-1689), Lucia Galeazzi (1743-1788), Maria Gaetana Agnesi (1718-1799), Abigail Adams (1744-1818), and Ada Lovelace (1815-1852). In the 20th century, perhaps the most surprising RenWoman would be Hedy Lamarr who is well known for being an accomplished and beautiful actress, but who was also mathematically gifted, and who, at the beginning of WWII, helped develop a frequency-hopping invention with the purpose of preventing enemies from detecting American radio-controlled torpedoes. Although the invention was not feasible due to the lack of advanced technology at the time, it played an important role in the U.S. blockade of Cuba in 1962. Later on, it also contributed to technology used in Wi-Fi network connections and wireless telephones.

From the 17th through the 19th centuries, there were also, in parts of Europe, the *courtesans*, who used their beauty (and their bodies) to gain intellectual freedom. And there were patronesses and *salonnières*, who sought artistic and intellectual stimulation through supporting and entertaining the talented men of their times.

All of which is a striking display of the strong driving force within women, as much as within men, to rise up to their full potential, and live an abundant life.

3

THE ICONS

We've all heard of them. So much so that some, like Oprah, need only a single name to identify them. These are our iconic modern Renaissance women—those who have gained much renown and recognition. Some are known for a particular thing, and people may not be as aware of the many other fields they have mastered. Others are like chameleons, pursuing first one thing, then the next, or tackling many fields all at once. All of them represent the highest echelons of the Renaissance life.

In this chapter, we will look at six modern Renaissance icons: Maya Angelou, Hillary Clinton, Jane Fonda, Arianna Huffington, Condoleezza Rice, and Oprah Winfrey. These are women who have continually challenged themselves, choosing to embrace a rich palette of experiences. Much, of course, has already been written about them. But we will focus on their Renaissance-ness—how they have succeeded in not just one area, but in many. And we will look at how the Renaissance nature of their personalities has enhanced their successes, enriched their lives, and widened their influence. *(Note: the quotes in this section will come from the two sites, BrainyQuotes.com and GoodReads.com unless otherwise specified.)*[29]

Maya Angelou

"Love life. Engage in it. Give it all you've got. Love it with a passion because life truly does give back, many times over, what you put into it."

The phenomenal Maya Angelou, who died on May 28, 2014, was the quintessential Renaissance woman. She rose from poverty and racism in the deep South to become one of the most accomplished and influential people of our times. Recipient of over 50 honorary doctorate degrees, Maya Angelou was a singer, dancer, editor, poet, memoirist, educator, dramatist, songwriter, producer, actress, filmmaker, and civil rights activist. And on top of that, she spoke five languages! Among her celebrated books are the autobiographical *I Know Why the Caged Bird Sings, All God's Children Wear Traveling Shoes*, and *The Heart of a Woman*; the collections of essays *Wouldn't Take Nothing for my Journey Now* and *Even the Stars Look Lonesome*; and the poetry volumes *Oh Pray My Wings Are Gonna Fit Me Well, And Still I Rise*, and *I Shall Not Be Moved*. For the inauguration of President Bill Clinton, she wrote and recited the poem *On the Pulse of Morning*, which was so admired that sales of the paperback versions of her books rose by 300–600% the week after Angelou's presentation. The recording of the poem went on to win a Grammy Award for "Best Spoken Word" album.

Maya Angelou also wrote the screenplay and composed the score for the 1972 film *Georgia, Georgia*, the script of which was nominated for a Pulitzer Prize. She acted in a number of television shows and films, including the TV miniseries *Roots* in 1997 and John Singleton's film *Poetic Justice* in 1993. She even directed the film *Down in the Delta* in 1996.

Maya started out, in the 1950s, as a singer and dancer. She danced with Alvin Ailey; she sang and danced Calypso in the iconic San Francisco nightclub, The Purple Onion; she toured Europe with a production of the opera *Porgy and Bess*, and she sang her own compositions in an Off-Broadway revue. In the late 50s, she moved into writing, joining the Harlem Writers Guild. With the help of her friend James Baldwin, she began work on her seminal book *I Know Why the Caged Bird Sings*.

During the early 1960s, Angelou lived for a time in Cairo, where she was the editor of an English-language newspaper; and then in Ghana, where she taught at the University of Ghana's School of Music and Drama and wrote for the *Ghanaian Times*. By 1964 she was back in the States and became active in the civil rights movement, serving, at the request of Martin Luther King Jr., as the Northern Coordinator of the Southern Christian Leadership Conference. She also supported the anti-apartheid movement.

Angelou served on two presidential committees, for Presidents Ford and Carter. She received the Springarm Medal in 1994, the National Medal of Arts in 2000, and President Barack Obama presented her with the Presidential Medal of Freedom, the country's highest civilian honor, in 2010. In the arts, she had three Grammy nominations, two Pulitzer Prize nominations, and a Tony Award nomination.

It is clear Maya Angelou celebrated an extraordinarily rich Renaissance Life! As with the women you will meet in the pages of this book, so many of her astonishing accomplishments were due to her attitudes and approaches toward herself, others, and the world.

She rose above traumatic events in her childhood, transmuting negative experience into sources for her art. Although she suffered a sexual assault at the age of eight and witnessed the rampant racism that permeated her small town of Stamps, Arkansas, she did not believe in self-pity or victimhood. "Don't let the incidents which take place in life bring you low," she said. "You can be brought low, that's OK, but don't be reduced by them." She trusted in the power of the inner self to dream and to make those dreams a reality. "A person is the product of their dreams. Dream great dreams," she exhorted. And she embraced the transformative power of love. "Love recognizes no barriers," she said. "It jumps hurdles, leaps fences, penetrates walls to arrive at its destination full of hope."

Maya Angelou represented the apotheosis of Renaissance-ness. And she did so through belief in herself, a refusal to accept limitations, a voracious desire to express her creativity in abundant ways, an imperative to inspire and help others, and the certainty that truth does indeed set you free. A hole was created in the world when this exceptional woman left us. She was a visionary and a healing presence for all who encountered her. But her influence and her legacy will go on, pointing the way for others to an authentic life of vitality and significance.

Hillary Clinton

"It is past time for women to take their rightful place, side by side with men, in the rooms where the fates of peoples, where their children's and grandchildren's fates, are decided."

As of this writing, Hillary Rodham Clinton is once again campaigning to be the Democratic nominee for the office of the

President of the United States. But Hillary is much more than a politician. She has, in fact, lived a life of intellectual accomplishment, social commitment, women's and children's rights advocacy, and public service.

When only a teenager, Hilary Rodham put together a program to provide babysitting for migrant workers. At her graduation from Wellesley College in 1969, she delivered the commencement speech for her graduating class—the first student to ever do so. She was one of only 27 women in a class of 235 at Yale Law School, and she subsequently did a year of postgraduate study on children and medicine at the Yale Child Study Center. Her first scholarly article, "Children Under the Law", was published in the Harvard Educational Review in late 1973 and has been frequently cited. She was the first female law partner at her firm in Arkansas, and an early advocate for family and child services and for maternal health in areas in the world with high maternal mortality. She was the only woman on the Nixon impeachment legal team. As First Lady, she fought for universal health care in the U.S. before anyone else did. She has devoted significant time and energy to helping girls and women across the globe—giving an iconic speech in 1995 at the United Nations 4th World Conference on Women where she said: "Human rights are women's rights, and women's rights are human rights." And, of course, she has served as a U.S. Senator and as Secretary of State.

What are the reasons behind her dedication and her many accomplishments? Well, for one, Hillary always knew she was more than "the little woman at home." As she said in an interview on ABC's *Nightline* that aired in March of 1992, "You know, I suppose I could have stayed home and baked cookies and had teas, but what I decided to do was to fulfill my profession, which I entered before my husband was in public life." Hillary was clear about who she was, and she saw no reason to act contrary to that.

Hillary Clinton has always embraced ambitious goals and perseverance. "Always aim high, work hard, and care deeply about what you believe in," she has said. "And, when you stumble, keep faith. And, when you're knocked down, get right back up, and never listen to anyone who says you can't or shouldn't go on." She has learned that *how* you encounter a situation is as important as the situation itself. "I think that if you live long enough," she has remarked, "you realize that so much of what happens in life is out of your control, but how you respond to it is in your control. That's what I try to remember."

Hillary has not been one to shy away from confrontation or from standing up for what she believes in. One of those things is women's rights. "Whether I am meant to or not, I challenge assumptions about women," she has said. "I do make some people uncomfortable, which I'm well aware of, but that's just part of coming to grips with what I believe is still one of the most important pieces of unfinished business in human history—empowering women to be able to stand up for themselves." She has also been sympathetic to the plight of the LGBT community, and has supported gay rights. On Dec. 6, 2011, she made the following remarks in Geneva Switzerland in recognition of International Human Rights Day. "To LGBT men and women worldwide, let me say this: Wherever you live and whatever the circumstances of your life, whether you are connected to a network of support or feel isolated and vulnerable, please know that you are not alone."[30]

Importantly, Hillary looks at politics as a means of addressing society's ills, not in a purely pragmatic sense, but in a deeper, more abiding way: "We need a new politics of meaning," she has said. "We need a new definition of civil society which answers the unanswerable questions, as to how we can have a society that fills us up again and makes us feel that we are part of something bigger than ourselves."

As a true RenWoman, Hillary Rodham Clinton has followed her own path, challenged the status quo, explored every avenue in which she feels she can contribute to the world, and fought for the rights of the repressed and under-represented. She has an avid intellect and lively curiosity, and she is passionate about her beliefs.

Jane Fonda

"You can do one of two things; just shut up, which is something I don't find easy, or learn an awful lot very fast, which is what I tried to do."

When people think of Jane Fonda, three Janes come to mind: Jane the actress, Jane the political activist, and Jane the fitness guru. In addition, she has also been a producer, a writer, a philanthropist, and a businesswoman. Oh, and when she was 20, she dropped out of Vassar and went to Paris to study painting. Jane's life has been a constant search for meaning and engagement, both in terms of self and the world she lives in.

Daughter of the famous actor Henry Fonda, Jane knew, when she attended Actors Studio in the late 1950s, that she had to prove herself and that people would be looking for her to fail. So she worked harder than anybody else. As she told Hilton Als of the New Yorker magazine, "Everybody would take one class, I'd take four. They'd work on one scene, I'd work on three."[31]

Despite a very promising start on Broadway in 1960, with the play *There Was a Little Girl*, she was subsequently cast in a number of rather uninspiring conventional films, including *Tall Story*, with Antony Perkins. She decided to go to France where the "New Wave" movement was in full swing. There she worked with, and fell in love with, Roger Vadim who directed her in *La Ronde* and the cult classic *Barbarella*. She married Vadim in 1965. During the 60s, she also starred in the films, *Cat Ballou* (1965) and *Barefoot in the Park* (1967). Both were hits and proved her comedic capabilities.

In 1968, her friend Simone Signoret took her to her first anti-Vietnam rally. She was also reading, at the same time, the book *The Village of Ben Suc*. "And," as she says, "The world changed."[32] This began for her a period of anti-war activism that would result in her trip to North Vietnam in 1972 and her infamous photo on the seat of a North Vietnamese anti-aircraft gun. Although she does not regret her trip, she deeply regrets that photo.[33]

In 1969, Jane returned to the U.S. with Vadim and their baby girl, Vanessa. She starred in two films that demonstrated her true brilliance as a dramatic actor: *They Shoot Horses Don't They*, where she played a desperate Depression-era woman, and *Klute*, where she played a high-class call girl. She was nominated for an Oscar for the first and won an Oscar for the second. Meanwhile, her marriage to Vadim fell apart, and they divorced in 1973. Shortly after, she married activist Tom Hayden, whose life and politics aligned well with her own political and social activism.

During the 70s and 80s, she starred in a number of issue-oriented films, some of which she co-produced through her production company, IPC Films. These include such films as *Julia, Coming Home, The China Syndrome,* and *9 to 5*. During that time, she and Hayden supported various causes that included advocating for Vietnam veterans, Native American rights, and women's rights. In 1976, they founded the Campaign for Economic Democracy, which promoted solar energy, environmental protection, and renters' rights. To help support this organization, she started what would become an incredibly successful enterprise: The Jane Fonda Workout videos. In all, she put out 23 videos, five workout books, and 12 audiobooks. The series is credited with not only changing how women exercised but also in helping create the home-video market.

Jane and Tom divorced in 1990. She married her third husband, Ted Turner, in 1991. During that marriage, she chose to retire from acting and began a focus on philanthropy that continues to this day. Many of the charitable causes she has founded or supported focus on the health and welfare of teenagers. The Jane Fonda Center at Emory University states as its mission "to advance scientific knowledge about adolescence with an emphasis on adolescent reproductive health. We also seek to disseminate information and strategies for risk reduction and healthy transitions to adulthood."[34] She also helped create the Grady Teen Clinic at Atlanta's Grady Hospital, and she donated $500,000 to the Georgia Campaign for Adolescent Pregnancy Prevention.

After her marriage to Turner ended in 2001, Jane, at 64, started a whole new creative chapter in her life. She returned to acting with such films as *Monster-in-Law* and *This Is Where I Leave You*. She also wrote an autobiography, *My Life So Far,* published in 2005 (which the New York Times called "achingly poignant") and the book, *Prime Time: Love, Health, Sex, Fitness, Friendship, Spirit—Making The Most of All of Your Life*, in 2011. In 2009, she made a triumphant return to Broadway in the play *33 Variations* by Moisés Kaufman, for which she was nominated for a Best Actress Tony. She chronicled her experiences with this play in a blog. More recently she has played Leona Lansing in HBO's *The Newsroom*, for which she was twice nominated for an Emmy, and Grace in Netflix's hugely popular *Grace and Frankie*. Jane also completed two films: *Fathers and Daughters* with Russell Crowe, and *Youth*, Paolo Sorrentino's follow-up to *The Great Beauty*.

So, it looks like, even in her late seventies, there's no slowing

Jane Fonda down!

What has motivated Jane's sometimes tumultuous but always fascinating Renaissance life? It seems, for her, it's been all about searching. Searching for self, for meaning, and for continual growth and discovery. "We all wonder what, if anything, we're going to leave behind," she told *DuJour* magazine. "My ability to understand what my life means—to put it in a way that can be meaningful to other people—that's the gift I would leave behind."[35] This search has kept her constantly moving forward. "What matters is realizing you can always get better," she says, "that you have to keep taking leaps of faith."[36]

For Jane Fonda it is also about that recurring RenWomen theme: curiosity. She has been quoted as saying, "Ask questions. Stay curious. It's much more important to stay interested than to be interesting." In this, she does not see age as an issue. And in fact, she feels life can continue to grow and expand as one grows older. In a TEDxWomen talk she did in 2011, entitled "Life's Third Act," she said, "We're still living with the old paradigm of age as an arch. That's the metaphor, the old metaphor. You're born, you peak at midlife and decline into decrepitude . . . I've spent the last year researching and writing about this subject. And I have come to find that a more appropriate metaphor for aging is a staircase—the upward ascension of the human spirit, bringing us into wisdom, wholeness and authenticity."[37] Jane Fonda represents that ascension fully, as her continued growth, self examination and creative explorations fully attest.

Arianna Huffington

"Fearlessness is like a muscle. I know from my own life that the more I exercise it the more natural it becomes to not let my fears run me."

Arianna Huffington is a woman of many varied talents. She has been an author, a political pundit, a syndicated columnist, a media mogul, an actress, even a cartoon character! Born Arianna Stassinopoulus in Athens, Greece, she moved to Great Britain as a teen to attend the University of Cambridge where she earned her masters in economics and was president of their prestigious debate club. (Notice already, the emergence of two different skillsets, the first two of many more.) In 1974, at the age of 23, she wrote her first book, *The Female Woman*, a controversial look at feminism that became an international bestseller. In 1980, she moved to the United States. There, she wrote more books, including *Maria Callas: The Woman Behind the Legend* in 1981, *The Gods of Greece* in 1983, and *Picasso: Creator and Destroyer* in 1988.

In 1986, she married Michael Huffington, and they had two children. In 1994, she added the book *Fourth Instinct: The Call of the Soul* to her growing number of publications. Between 1993 and 1995, her husband was a Republican member of the House of Representatives. He lost, however, his subsequent Senate bid. The two divorced in 1997.

Although Arianna started out as a conservative and a frequent television pundit espousing these views (for example, as the conservative half to Al Franken's liberal for *Strange Bedfellows* on Comedy Central), she eventually embraced a more liberal stance. In 2003, she ran as an independent candidate for Governor in the California recall election. The same year, she published *Pigs at the Trough: How Corporate Greed and Political Corruption Are Undermining America*, which became a *New York Times* bestseller. In 2005, she was a panel speaker during the California Democratic Party State Convention. Five years later, she would become co-host of the radio program *Both Sides Now with Huffington & Matalin*, representing the liberal point of view in debates with conservative Mary Matalin.

In 2005, along with Kenneth Lerer, Arianna launched the blog site *The Huffington Post*, for which she served as editor-in-chief. *Huff Post*, as it is sometimes called, has become an internet phenomenon, with columns, news, and blogs covering a full range of topics from politics to business to quality of life. By 2008, *The Observer* ranked *The Huffington Post* as "the most powerful blog in the world." And in 2009, Arianna Huffington was listed as number 12 in *Forbes*'s "Most Influential Women in Media." In 2014, she was listed by *Forbes* as the 52nd most powerful woman in the world.

In 2011, AOL purchased *The Huffington Post*, making Arianna President and Editor-in-Chief of the Huffington Post Media Group.

During this time, Arianna also published the book *On Becoming Fearless ... in Love, Work, and Life* (2006). From all appearances, she was at the top of her game. However, on the morning of April 6, 2007, Arianna collapsed from exhaustion and woke up on the floor in a pool of blood, having cut her eye and broken her cheekbone. This was a wake-up call. As she writes in the introduction of her book *Thrive: The Third Metric to Redefining Success and Creating a Life of Well-Being, Wisdom, and Wonder*, "Was this what success looked like? Was this the life I wanted? I was working eighteen hours a day, seven days a week . . . In terms of the traditional measures of success, which focus on money and power, I was very successful. But I was not living a successful life by any sane definition of success."[38] In *Thrive*, she defines a "third metric" equally as important as money and power. This added metric consists of four pillars: well-being, wisdom, wonder, and giving. This is something she had instinctively known throughout her life. In her twenties, on the promotional tour for her first book, *The Female*

Woman, she had her first glimpse into the shallowness of just living for money and recognition. But, as she writes: "My journey from that first moment of recognition that I didn't want to live life within the boundaries of what our culture defined as success was hardly a straight line. At times . . . I found myself caught up in the very whirlwind that I knew would not lead to the life I most wanted."[39] It took her fall in 2007 to really awaken to the vital importance of a more dimensional definition of success. *Thrive* was published in 2014, debuting at number one on the *New York Times* bestseller list. It clearly touched a chord in others as well!

Besides Arianna's literary, political, and media life, she has also done some acting. She appeared frequently as "Arianna the Bear," an animated talking bear, over the course of the *The Cleveland Show*'s four-year run (2009-2013). She played herself in a *Family Guy* episode, and appeared in an episode of *The Fran Drescher Show*.

Arianna has brought important qualities to the many paths she has taken in her life. Like the other iconic women in this chapter, she has been bold and fearless in the pursuit of her goals. "Fearlessness," she has said, "is not the absence of fear. It's the mastery of fear. It's about getting up one more time than we fall down." Failure, for her, is a means of growth. As she has put it: "We need to accept that we won't always make the right decisions, that we'll screw up royally sometimes—understanding that failure is not the opposite of success, it's part of success."[40] Spirituality has also been a core value throughout her life. In her autobiographical book *Fourth Instinct: The Call of the Soul*, she wrote: "It is the Fourth Instinct . . . that urges us to exceed ourselves . . . by awakening our intuitive selves, and striving to be all that we were intended to be." She also recognizes the importance of a values-based life. As she puts it, "The journey toward self-discovery and self-knowledge is not only life's highest adventure, but also the only way to transform society from one based on self-centeredness and compulsory compassion to one based on service and mutual responsibility."[41]

Arianna Huffington is a RenWoman who has been a powerhouse communicator with her finger on the pulse of modern life, and who has been willing to share her own process of evolving with others.

Condoleezza Rice

"We need to move beyond the idea that girls can be leaders and create the expectation that they should be leaders."

It is easy to think of Condoleezza Rice only in her most high profile role as the 66th United States Secretary of State during the administration of George W. Bush.

But she is and has been much more. She is a classically trained pianist, a professor, an author, an athlete, a university Provost, and an expert in Soviet affairs who also served under George H.W. Bush. As a musician, Condoleezza has performed in public on many occasions. When only 15, she played Mozart with the Denver Symphony. More recently, she has played at many diplomatic events including a performance, in 2008, for Queen Elizabeth II. In 2002 she performed with Yo-Yo Ma at the National Medal of Arts and National Humanities Medal event, and she played Dvorak at the Aspen Music Festival in 2008.

Condoleezza Rice received her PhD in 1981 in political science from the Joseph Korbel School of International Studies at Denver University. She spent a summer in Moscow learning Russian and from 1980-81, she was a fellow at Stanford University, having won a Dual Expertise Fellowship in Soviet studies and international security. She joined the Stanford faculty as a professor of political science in 1981 and served as Provost there from 1993-1999. From 1989 through March 1991, during the period of the fall of the Berlin wall and the dissolution of the Soviet Union, Condoleezza worked on President George H.W. Bush's National Security Council. She served as Director, and then Senior Director, of Soviet and East European Affairs and Special Assistant to the President for National Security Affairs.

Athletically, as a teen Condoleezza pursued competitive figure skating and became an avid tennis player. Her current passion (which she took up at the age of 50) is golf. She recently became one of the two first female members admitted to Augusta National Golf Club, the home of the Masters Golf Tournament.

That is only one of many "firsts" for Condoleezza Rice. She was the first female, first minority, and youngest Provost in Stanford history. She was the first woman to serve as a National Security Advisor and the first female African-American Secretary of State.

Condoleezza has authored and co-authored numerous books, including two bestsellers, *No Higher Honor: A Memoir of My Years in Washington* (2011) and *Extraordinary, Ordinary People: A Memoir of Family* (2010). In 1991, she co-founded the Center for a New Generation (CNG), an after-school academic enrichment program for students in East Palo Alto and East Menlo Park, California. Since 2009, she has served as a founding partner at Rice Hadley Gates, LLC, an international strategic consulting firm, and she is currently on a number of boards, including Dropbox, the online storage technology company, C3, an energy software company, and the Boys and Girls Clubs of America. Rice is a Fellow of the American Academy of Arts and Sciences and has been awarded eleven honorary doctorates.

Condoleezza's accomplishments are impressive. They are even

more so in light of the world in which she was brought up, one torn apart by racial strife. She was born and raised in Birmingham, Alabama at a time when the South was still segregated. Her mother was a teacher, her father, a Presbyterian minister. She experienced discriminatory laws and attitudes in myriad ways, including being barred from the circus and local amusement park and being told to change in a storage room at a clothing store instead of a dressing room. When she was eight years old, the Sixteenth Street Baptist Church, close to the church where her father preached, was bombed by white supremacists. The attack touched her personally. As she described it in a commencement speech at Vanderbilt University in 2004, "I remember the bombing of that Sunday School at 16th Street Baptist Church in Birmingham in 1963. I did not see it happen, but I heard it happen, and I felt it happen, just a few blocks away at my father's church. It is a sound that I will never forget, that will forever reverberate in my ears. That bomb took the lives of four young girls, including my friend and playmate Denise McNair. The crime was calculated to suck the hope out of young lives, bury their aspirations. But those fears were not propelled forward, those terrorists failed."

Condoleezza's parents instilled in her the determination to rise above the built-in injustices of society, by being twice as good. As she has said, "My parents were very strategic. I was going to be so well prepared, and I was going to do all of these things that were revered in white society so well that I would be armored somehow from racism. I would be able to confront white society on its own terms."[42] And indeed, it is clear from Condoleezza's achievements that she has worked harder, better, and risen above any stereotypes as a consequence. As she told Katie Couric in an article for Glamour Magazine, "The most important lesson I think I could impart is don't let anyone determine what your horizons are going to be. You get to determine those yourself. The only limitations are whatever particular talents you happen to have and how hard you're willing to work. And if you let others define who you ought to be, or what you ought to be because they put you in a category, they see your race, they see your gender . . . [you] shouldn't let that happen."[43]

This overcoming-the-odds and reaching-for-vast-horizons attitude defines Condoleezza Rice as a leader and a RenWoman. In a speech at the 2012 Willow Creek Association Global Leadership Summit, she said, "Great leaders never accept the world as it was and always work for the world as it should be." Additionally, she asserted, "You must be able to motivate people to a common goal. Sometimes that means accomplishing something impossible that now seems inevitable."[44] And her feeling about being a woman leader was summed up in the statement, "If you consistently worry about a glass ceiling you can't break, you will be your own brake."[45] Essential also to Condoleezza is the imperative to encourage the leaders of tomorrow. As she said in a keynote speech at the KPMG inaugural Women's Leadership Summit in June of 2015, "Truly remarkable leadership is not just about motivating others to follow, it's about inspiring them to become leaders themselves and setting the stage for even greater opportunities for future generations."

Condoleezza Rice is a RenWoman whose life and accomplishments have inspired many young women—particularly those of color—to confront and transcend their own barriers.

Oprah Winfrey

"I believe the choice to be excellent begins with aligning your thoughts and words with the intention to require more from yourself."

Oprah Winfrey is a phenomenon. Most everyone knows her story. Born in poverty to an unwed mother, molested by relatives from the age of nine to thirteen, running away from home at 14, and ending up pregnant herself that same year (her baby died soon after birth)—these were ingredients for a dead-end life of despair and failure. But Oprah was a survivor with a spirit that couldn't be crushed. She also had a caring, if tough, grandmother for her earliest years who taught her to read before the age of three. In her mid-teens, she went to live with her biological father in Nashville, who recognized her brightness and imposed a strict and structured environment, expecting her to do her best. She flourished within that structure, becoming an honor student and winning a scholarship to Tennessee State University, where she studied communications and performing arts.

While still in college, Oprah got her first job on air at a radio station in Nashville. This was followed by an anchor job at a local TV station. In 1976, she moved to Baltimore to become a co-anchor on WJZ-TV News. There she co-hosted her first talk show and was subsequently invited to Chicago to host *AM Chicago*, which she soon turned into the hottest show in town. In 1985, it was renamed *The Oprah Winfrey Show* and one year later it went into national syndication, soon becoming the number one talk show in the country (surpassing the very popular *Phil Donohue Show*). The program continued to grow exponentially in popularity and influence until it went off the air in 2011.

Of course, this was just one of the aspects of Oprah's amazing trajectory. Even before her syndicated talk show, she had made her mark in acting in 1985 with her heartbreaking portrayal of Sofia in Steven Spielberg's *The Color Purple*, for which she was nominated for a Golden Globe and an Academy Award. She continued acting in numerous films throughout the years, up to her most recent roles as

Gloria Gaines in *The Butler* and as Annie Lee Cooper in *Selma* (both of which garnered her many recognitions and nominations).

As a savvy business woman and entertainer, she formed Harpo Productions in 1986, first acquiring ownership of *The Oprah Winfrey Show* and then becoming a major player in the production of both television movies and miniseries as well as feature films. A partial list coming out of Harpo Productions includes: *The Women of Brewster Place* (TV miniseries), *Tuesdays with Morrie* (TV movie), *Their Eyes Were Watching God* (TV movie), *The Great Debaters* (feature film), *Precious* (feature film), and *Selma* (feature film).

Meanwhile, Harpo Productions also became a force in magazine publishing and the Internet. It published *O, The Oprah Magazine*, and there is active online content for all things Oprah related at www. oprah.com.

The deepest influence that Oprah has had on the world (and *The Oprah Winfrey Show* has been seen in 140 countries) is as *herself*: the charismatic, folksy, and willing-to-be-vulnerable talk show host whose program evolved from its beginnings of tabloid, celebrity fare to tackling such subject matters as spirituality, books, life improvement, and most importantly, helping others. In fact, Oprah, listed by Forbes as the first black woman billionaire, has also been ranked among the 50 most generous Americans, having donated millions of dollars to multiple causes. She has been an active and involved philanthropist, encouraging her television and online audiences to give through her "Angel Networks" and through other charitable programs. She has raised countless millions and has footed all the administrative costs, so 100 percent of donations go to the intended charities.

Oprah's popularity is so immense that she can make a marked difference in a political campaign (as she did for Barack Obama), her Oprah Book Club picks can send books soaring up the bestseller lists, and she can create careers and television shows for those whose work she admires (think Dr. Phil). Interestingly, even in countries such as Saudi Arabia, she was able to draw record numbers of female viewers for *The Oprah Winfrey Show*.

So what are some of the elements that have turned Oprah into the astounding success story that she is?

Well, first of all, she is guided by the belief that there is a deeper meaning to life and that we all have a reason to be here. As she has explained it, "I've come to believe that each of us has a personal calling that's as unique as a fingerprint—and that the best way to succeed is to discover what you love and then find a way to offer it to others in the form of service, working hard, and also allowing the energy of the universe to lead you." Like her idol and close friend Maya Angelou, Oprah has found ways to rise above a traumatic childhood of poverty and abuse. "Challenges are gifts that force us to search for a new center of gravity. Don't fight them. Just find a new way to stand," she has said. "The great courageous act that we must all do is to have the courage to step out of our history and past so that we can live our dreams."

Like other RenWomen, she has also been willing to venture into the unknown and to embrace failure when it arises. "Do the one thing you think you cannot do," she says. "Fail at it. Try again. Do better the second time. The only people who never tumble are those who never mount the high wire."

It is not because she is fearless that she has succeeded, it's because she has acted *despite* the fear. As she has described it, "The true meaning of courage is to be afraid, and then, with your knees knocking and your heart racing, to step out anyway—even when that step makes sense to nobody but you. I know that's not easy. But making a bold move is the only way to truly advance toward the grandest vision the universe has for you."

A particular crusade she strongly believes in is providing education and opening doors to girls worldwide. Her admonition to girls is: "You are built not to shrink down to less but to blossom into more. To be more splendid. To be more extraordinary. To use every moment to fill yourself up."

And as with all RenWomen, she believes in constant growth, self discovery, and expansion. "I want every day to be a fresh start on expanding what is possible," she says. "Create the highest, grandest vision possible for your life, because you become what you believe."

Oprah is not only a stunning example of a modern Renaissance Woman, but she is a model and an inspiration to those whose lives may have told them No, but whose spirit tells them Yes!

All of the women represented in this Icons chapter are phenomenal examples of modern Renaissance women. Like the RenWomen we will feature in this book, their paths have not always been easy, and some lessons have been hard won, but they have embraced the rich possibilities of life with enthusiasm, passion, commitment, and a clear sense of who they are.

II

RenWomen Profiles

4

"You have to do what you're meant to do."

Actress, poet, linguist (six languages), musician, literary translator, dream analyst, teacher, master's in English & American literature, journal editor, producer

Nineteen-year-old Hélène Cardona couldn't go on. She had tried. Following her father's dreams for her to become a doctor, she had used her formidable skills in math and science to take her through the stringent French school system and into medical school at 17. But all the while her other passions—artistic, linguistic, and literary—had called to her. She longed to continue her piano and dance studies. She wanted to keep up her summer travels to Spain and England to study the languages and literatures of those countries. She hadn't written a new poem in ages. "Study math and science and all doors will open for you," she had been told. But instead, all doors except one had slammed shut. And the one that remained open didn't speak to her heart. She made a decision to leave medical school. But her father, deeply disappointed, pulled all financial and emotional support from his daughter. A profound depression hit. Hélène wanted to die. The climb out of this abyss was painful and fraught with challenge, but it was in this break with what others expected from

*her, and her trust in her own passions, that allowed Hélène to find her
true self.*

Hélène Cardona, the beautiful European-accented actress,
sits sipping tea and talking about her life. Her long auburn hair falls
casually to her slender shoulders. Her arresting green eyes are devoid
of makeup, unlike the various glamour shots of her on red carpets,
sporting fashions from Monique Lhuillier. Hélène is known for
her roles as "Fuffi" in the movie *Chocolat,* the voice of both Adélie
Penguin in the animated film *Happy Feet Two,* and the French Food
Critic in *The Hundred-Foot Journey*, the French Announcer in *Jurassic
World*, the BBC Reporter in both *Dawn of the Planet of the Apes* and
World War Z, as well as many other TV and film roles.

Acting is just one of an astonishing list of Hélène's skills and
accomplishments. Born in Paris to an Irish/Greek mother and a
Spanish father and brought up throughout Europe, she speaks French,
English, Greek, Spanish, German, and Italian. As a teen, she attended
the Music Conservatory in Geneva where she was awarded the second
prize in piano. She later studied piano under Maître Sancan at the
Salle Pleyel in Paris. She also trained as a dancer in Geneva, Paris,
and New York. In high school she focused on math and science, and
then went on to complete two years of medical school. She did two
BAs at the Sorbonne, in English and Spanish. She also received her
master's in American literature from the Sorbonne, where she wrote
her thesis on Henry James ("The Search for Fulfillment in *The Wings
of the Dove*"). During various summer programs, she studied English
Philology and Literature at Cambridge, Spanish at the International
Universities of Santander and Baeza in Spain, and German at the
Goethe Institute in Germany. While still an undergraduate at the
Sorbonne, she attended a year abroad at Hamilton College in New

York, where she was also assistant professor of French and Spanish. To support herself through college, she worked as a translator/interpreter for the Canadian Embassy and the French Chamber of Commerce and later as a translator and language coach for the film and music industry. After her master's, Hélène attended the prestigious American Academy of Dramatic Arts in New York City.

Currently, Hélène is not only an actress, but an award-winning poet, translator of poetry, teacher, editor of literary journals, and even dream analyst. She also co-produced the award-winning documentary *Femme: Women Healing the World,* and is currently co-producing the documentary *Pablo Neruda: The Poet's Calling.*

If this impressive list exhausts you, it's no surprise. Few people come into this world being naturally proficient at so many things and so driven to work at them all. What is fascinating about Hélène's story is that being multiply gifted has been, for her, both a source of great pleasure and the cause of deep suffering.

The Best and Worst of Times

As a child, Hélène's passions were already far-ranging. She attended a provincial French school near the border of Switzerland that gave her full rein to explore her many interests. It was an idyllic time for her. As she explains, "I went to school in a village. But it was very cultural because of the proximity to Geneva, and a lot of people there worked for the UN and for CERN. The teachers were extraordinary. I learned grammar like hardly anyone else. My teachers distilled in me a love for it, a love for language. I grew up with books at home. A ritual would be to go to the bookstore regularly and pick a book. So I was reading constantly. My father is also a poet, and all my parents' friends were basically intellectuals.

"Up until the age of 14," she continues, "the world was my oyster. I was going to school; I was dancing; I was riding horses; I was with animals and loving nature. I started writing poetry when I was ten, I had a predilection for math as well as literature, and I was going to the music conservatory in Geneva. I loved all of it. I could do it all. It was a time where I felt I could do anything I wanted in life. And I was good at everything. So I never thought things would become an issue."

But a rude awakening awaited Hélène at the age of 14 when the family moved back to

"I loved all of it. I could do it all. It was a time where I felt I could do anything I wanted in life."

Paris. The wonderful school where she was encouraged, inspired, and allowed to pursue all her loves was supplanted by the more structured, authoritarian, science-oriented high school system. In French high school, you are required to specialize. You choose, for example, a school for humanities or a school for math and science. Since Hélène was good at everything, the system encouraged her to go into math and science, with the eventual goal of becoming a doctor. "It's the most valued, the most prestigious thing to do," Hélène explains. "The French are very scientific-minded. And because I had this affinity for math—it was a game for me—I thought, sure I'll specialize in math and science. It opens all doors, I was told." Interestingly, because she had not come from a Parisian school but had instead come from the "provinces," when she first arrived at the high school, she was not expected to do well. When, in fact, on her first math test, she scored the highest score along with a Parisian girl, she wasn't told this, and only discovered it afterwards. And when it came to her French classes, she remarks: "The French teacher was puzzled by me. I was my own person. I basically had favorite authors that didn't coincide with hers. And the way I wrote puzzled her too. She just said these really odd things, like she had to give me a high mark, but it was almost in spite of herself, because I wasn't spitting out exactly what she had taught. When I graduated, she told me, 'You're like a wild horse, you can't be tamed.'"

On top of the hours and hours of homework required

"She told me, 'You're like a wild horse, you can't be tamed.'"

("You just go crazy, studying!"), Hélène continued to pursue her many other interests, taking the maximum allowed schedule of three foreign languages, continuing to study piano and dance, and even performing with a dance company at the Théâtre des Champs Élysées.

Breakdown

But in her last year, things began to go awry. "It was very very stressful, keeping it all up. And I started to realize, okay . . . so I graduate with a Baccalauréat Scientifique, which 'opens all doors,' but it doesn't really open all doors, because now I have to continue in the scientific direction. That's what I've worked for. And I was thinking, I'm very artistic, and I love languages, and I spent so many years doing those things. But now here I am, 17 years old, and I'm being told, 'All that is well and good, but it's secondary, what you really need to do with your life is something scientific.'" Still, Hélène wanted to please her parents and do what was expected of her. And she hoped she could find a way to pursue some of her other loves. So at seventeen she started medical school.

And at nineteen, she had a breakdown.

She explains: "I started med school and I realized I really couldn't continue the piano. I couldn't continue to dance. I was still going during the summers to study in England, and nobody else was doing that. Soon enough I realized I couldn't either. So what happened is I made the decision to drop out of med school at 19. The medical world, the way you study there . . . I didn't feel it was about healing. People were numbers . . . few people were there for the right reasons. When I told my Dad, he said to me, 'You're just throwing away your life! At least try to be a dentist!' But I had no interest whatsoever. I didn't want to be an engineer or any of that. I realized what I truly wanted was to be an artist. But I had been brainwashed into thinking math and science were the only things that mattered. The rest maybe could be hobbies, but you didn't *do* that."

"When I told my Dad, he said to me, 'You're just throwing away your life. At least try to be a dentist!'"

Hélène's father, angry at her decision, pulled all financial support from his daughter, which flung her into despair. "My dad didn't want to know me at that point," she says. "I dropped into a terrible depression, where I almost died. I wanted to end my life."

Growing Self Awareness

Hélène recognizes now that she had to go to that dark place to emerge into a greater knowledge of herself. "I had to learn to say no—to a parent, to a teacher, to anyone basically. I had to learn the process of individuation."

Such a process would not be easy. With no financial help from her father, and yet still wanting an academic life, Hélène enrolled at the Sorbonne in Paris and worked simultaneously on two BAs— one in English and one in Spanish. To support herself, she taught at L'Ecole Active Bilingue and worked as an interpreter at the Canadian Embassy. She also earned scholarships to attend summer university programs in Germany, Spain, and England. And she spent her senior year at Hamilton College in the U.S., where she got a scholarship, as well as room and board in exchange for teaching French. There, she took a test to take a Spanish Literature class and got the highest score, which led to an offer to teach Spanish as well.

Continuing to push herself at this intense pace, after receiving her BAs, she moved into a PhD program in American literature. But soon after finishing the master's degree portion of the program, she hit another wall. Not surprisingly, she collapsed from exhaustion. "One day I couldn't get up, and I had a blood test, and most of my red blood cells were missing. I was severely anemic. And the doctor said, 'You have to stop everything,' and I was, like, 'I can't,' and he said, 'No, you have to.' And that's how I took time off and made the decision that I could never fulfill myself as long as I stayed in Paris. There, I was putting pressure on myself to get the next degree. I didn't stop after the BAs; I didn't stop after the master's. Meanwhile, I had been doing theater with the English Department of the Sorbonne, and I had come to know that was something I wanted to do. So for a second time I went to my parents for help, and I remember showing them the medical results, and my dad saying, 'There's nothing wrong with you.' He was clearly in denial. So again I had no support from him. That's when I knew I had to get out of there completely. I had enjoyed my time in the U.S., and I decided to audition for the American Academy of Dramatic Arts in New York." So she traveled there and auditioned. "Despite being a foreigner," she says, "I got in!"

Still the question was how was she going to pay for it, along with supporting herself in a new country? It was her mother who

"And the doctor said, 'You have to stop everything,' and I was, like, 'I can't,' and he said, 'No, you have to.'"

came to the rescue. Her mother, an intelligent woman who'd given up a law career to be with her children, had always sympathized with her daughter. But she had a hard time standing up to her strong husband. This time, however, she went to Hélène's grandmother and asked that the inheritance she was planning to give her granddaughter be given to her now to pay for tuition.

Hélène smiles. "And that's how I got to go to the Academy of Dramatic Arts and start my life over!"

Of course many new challenges faced her in America. She had to, again, work multiple jobs to support herself. She had to get a work permit, then a green card, and eventually citizenship (she is proud to be a citizen of three countries, the U.S., France and Spain). And then there was her accent, a combination of a soft French accent and a British accent, which she needed to Americanize. She worked hard at the Academy, and then trained at the Actors Studio under Sandra Seacat and Ellen Burstyn. Seacat also introduced her to Carl Jung and dream work, something that would become a passion for her as well as a future career.

"That's how I got to go to the Academy of Dramatic Arts and start my life over!"

Notable acting roles began to come. She played "Candy" in the Lawrence Kasdan directed *Mumford*, followed the next year by her role in *Chocolat*. She also got a series about Robin Hood, was cast in a *Law & Order* episode, and landed a couple of soap operas. After that came a number of voice roles including characters in the animated films *Happy Feet 2*, *Muppets*, and *Muppets 2*, as well as the voice of the "French Food Critic" in *The Hundred-Foot Journey*.

But that doesn't mean Hélène gave up her other passions. She dove back into writing and produced seven poetry chapbooks, followed by the publication by Red Hen Press of her book of poems *The Astonished Universe*, and by Salmon Poetry of her latest, *Dreaming My Animal Selves*. *Ce que nous portons*, her translation of Dorianne Laux, was published by Éditions du Cygne in 2014. Her new bilingual poetry collection, *Life in Suspension*, is forthcoming from Salmon Poetry in 2016, and *Beyond Elsewhere*, her translation of Gabriel Arnou-Laujeac, is also forthcoming in 2016 from White Pine Press. She has collaborated with her life partner, poet, and writer John FitzGerald on a screenplay, and she has also penned some children's stories. She co-edits *Fulcrum: An Anthology of Poetry and Aesthetics*, *The Dublin Poetry Review*, and *Levure Littéraire*, and is a contributor to *The London Magazine*. She is producing and co-producing several movies as well. Oh, and then there is the therapeutic work she does as a dream analyst.

It seems, in other words, that she is as busy as she has ever been! But there is something different now. She is calm, centered. The over-extended, overwhelmed place she has been before, when she tried to do everything, is less of a threat now. So what has changed? What lessons has she learned in managing her many passions?

"I've learned to balance," she says, "not to exhaust myself. I love what I do, but I can still sometimes get depleted, when I have months where a lot of events are happening. I'm a member of the British Academy, so I go to many of their events for networking, and also to functions with the French Consulate, and of course there are book readings, and when I put myself out like that, it's draining, energy-wise. So I have to watch my health and balance it with saying no when it's necessary."

She stresses the importance of self-care and proper attitude. "It's really how you live your life; how you treat your body; how you treat yourself. Because you are what you eat, you are what you think, you are what you do, you are all of it. And, importantly, what is your attitude toward others? Are you a good person? All of this is reflected on the face. You can see somebody's face and read their story."

Spirituality has also played a big part in her life. "When I was young, I didn't believe in anything, which is fine for whoever can live that way. My father is like that, and I used to also be very Cartesian. Coming from that scientific background, you think that all you see is all there is. But it didn't serve me; I almost died from it." So Hélène began a process of spiritual

"You can see somebody's face and read their story."

discovery that led her to meditation, dream work, and eventually to Shamanic studies. She trained with Stephen Aizenstat at Pacifica Graduate Institute ("Dream Tending"), with Californian Valerie Wolf, and with Alberto Villoldo, whose specialty is Incan Shamanism.Much of her dream work and spiritual beliefs weave through her poetry, as, for example, in her book *Dreaming My Animal Selves*. In the poem "From the Heart with Grace" are the lines: "I too swim in concentric circles / to find the resonance of my core / and discover that in dreaming / lies the healing of the earth. In dreaming / we travel to a place where all is forgiven. / In dreaming is the Divine created."

Her life partner, John, also has a balancing effect on her life. "Having a partner, somebody who's there with you on the journey, is huge because up until I met John, I was always basically on my own. We are each other's biggest supporter and fan, and I think that's so important."

Gifts from the Hard Times

Hélène does not regret the difficult times she went through or the drive that pushed her in so many directions. In fact, much of it has contributed to her successes today. When referring to her years in the

French school system and medical school, she remarks, "I'm grateful the experience was a bit . . . traumatic. What I learned in those years was the capacity to work like a beast. It gave me the discipline that I ended up needing to pursue the arts. When I went to the Academy of Dramatic Arts, I had to overcome being a foreigner. I had to get my papers. I was working in two restaurants and in a health club. I had no money. I was struggling. Even so, I did all kinds of training and apprenticeships with theaters to learn and see how things worked behind the scenes. Some of my fellow students had parents paying for everything, and you could tell the difference

"What I learned in those years was the capacity to work like a beast. That gave me the discipline that I ended up needing to pursue the arts."

in attitude. After the first year at the Academy, half of the people dropped out, and after the second year, half of the rest didn't continue to try to get a job. You could see people dropping out year after year. I started working as an extra and as a stand-in to make money. I learned a lot. And because of my education and varied background, I felt on equal footing; I felt like I could talk to anyone. I remember when I was in New York, I went to see a play in New Jersey, and on the train was this critic (I forget for which paper), and we started talking. He was so amazed that an actor could have a master's on Henry James, and he was, like, 'Oh my God, how interesting.' I can talk to people from all walks of life because I've had to do all kinds of jobs. I've worked as an interpreter, and I've taught at Hamilton College and Loyola Marymount University, but I've also worked as a waitress and hostess in restaurants, and I've distributed fliers and worked in a health club. I did all the jobs I had to do, and, each one that came my way, I was grateful for it. You meet all kinds of people, and that, I think, is something that enriches the work we do, right?"

She then stresses what was the most important and hard-earned lesson for her: "You have to live your life. You have to do what you're meant to do." And, she explains, it's also about our place in this world. "We want to contribute. We want to connect. It's not just about the isolated things we do. We are all interconnected. It is about respect for life. And respect for the earth. We're guardians of the earth, and we need to be better caretakers of it if we are to survive as a species."

We talk about evolving as a society and how Renaissance women contribute to this evolution. "Yes," she says. "I think we do so because we are not defined by one thing. There is this multiplicity of being. And as women, we are usually more empathetic, more caring and open. We are more willing to work together. On the surface that may appear less useful in terms of immediate success, but the willingness to work together is what is necessary to move us forward in the long run."

> *"You have to live your life. You have to do what you're meant to do."*

Describing an ideal world, she says: "It's a world where the feminine and the masculine are integrated. We are all part masculine and part feminine, but I think in our evolution, we are all going to be more perceptive, which is a feminine quality. The more we are able to be in touch with our intuition, which is also considered a feminine quality, the more we will be able to read people and see when a person does not have our best interests at heart. And those people are not going to be able to hold on to their positions of power. We will see that the emperor has no clothes."

And with this, I regretfully bid adieu to this inspiring and gracious woman of many talents.

> *"I think in our evolution, we are going to be more perceptive, which is a feminine quality."*

Ren Gems

Hélène Cardona

"Be bold and be daring, but with balance."

"The beauty of mystery is in not knowing."

"Find out who you are and be true to that."

"We are consciousness wanting to expand."

"The ultimate aim is reverence for the universe,
love for life, and harmony within oneself."

5

KATHY ELDON

"Do more, be more, experience more, create more."

Journalist, author of 18 books, speaker, film producer, social activist, founder of Creative Visions Foundation and the Dan Eldon Center for Creative Activism

It was the worst news a mother could ever receive. Her son, Dan Eldon, a 22-year-old photojournalist working in the war zone of Somalia, had been stoned to death by an angry mob. It was July 12, 1993, and her son had rushed from his hotel in Mogadishu with four other war journalists to capture the tragedy of a UN bombing gone terribly awry. The UN forces had bombed the Abdi Villa, where their target, the warlord General Aidid, was believed to be meeting with his followers. But Aidid wasn't there. Instead, more than 200 innocent people were killed or wounded in the bombing. By the time the journalists arrived on the scene and began shooting pictures, the crowd there had turned into a furious mob. They set upon the journalists with stones, sticks and pipes. Only one of them, Mo Shaffi, a mentor and friend to Dan, survived. When Kathy received the news, she was overtaken by a searing rage against life and God. She slid to the floor, animal noises escaping her she didn't recognize. It would be a long time before she could accept what had happened. Little did she know in this, her darkest hour, that Dan's life would inspire both her and many others to pursue a calling of giving back and supporting creative ways to transform the world we live in.

Kathy Eldon is a ball of energy. Tall and slender, she is dressed in vibrant colors that highlight her red cropped hair and expressive hazel eyes. She invites me into the light-filled Malibu office of Creative Visions Foundation, housed in the Dan Eldon Center for Creative Activism. Creative Visions is her brainchild, created in 1998 in memory of her son Dan, who was killed in Somalia in 1993. The initial idea for Creative Visions first emerged, however, twenty-five years ago in a prescient dream. It was 1990, and Kathy was living in England at the time. As she told Xenia Shin from The MY HERO Project, who was interviewing her as a subject of their "Women Transforming Media" blog series, she saw "an airy penthouse office that would include an art gallery and center that supported young artists, writers, and cinematographers . . . I had never had a dream like that before . . . I started writing down the notes about what I was supposed to do. I was supposed to create an organization. It had a mission statement: to use the power of media to help people achieve their potential for themselves and the planet. There was a logo: it was the first hexagram of the I-Ching, which is the creative force, a really powerful concept. Eventually, I drew a blueprint of the

"[I saw] an airy penthouse office that would include an art gallery and center that supported young artists, writers, and cinematographers."

organization I was supposed to create."[46] Strangely, this dream came to her when she was living in a cold London flat, divorced and jobless. She put the notes away in a drawer. It seemed like an impossible vision.

But today, Creative Visions Foundation is a thriving organization that supports and encourages "creative activism," a term they coined to describe "an individual who uses media and the arts to ignite social change in the world around them."[47] There are many ways in which Creative Visions promotes and encourages this activism. The Creative Activist Network is a membership-based educational and networking series that includes social get-togethers, panels, and webinars, as well as screenings, festivals, and exhibits. Rock Your World is a school-based program that helps young people learn how to give back by creating media and art campaigns inspired by social issues that are meaningful to them. The Creative Activist Program (CAP) incubates social media and arts projects through curated mentorships, fiscal sponsorship, and a myriad of resources.

Many of the 180 projects initiated and supported through CAP have inspired people worldwide and have brought about significant social impact and policy changes. *Landfill Harmonics* is a documentary film which tells the story of how, in the barrios of Paraguay, musical instruments made from trash enable a youth orchestra to be born and musical dreams to be realized. Local Leaders Global Lens is a program which seeks to change how men of color are perceived in the world of business by offering a college program where black men get opportunities outside the classroom to develop creativity, entrepreneurship and innovation. *An Inconvenient Youth* is a documentary about kids on the front lines of climate change. The Rwanda Film Institute is dedicated to breeding the next generation of Rwandese filmmakers and to further the cultural and economic development of Rwanda. The Markham Summer Camp: "Dare 2 Dream" program addresses the long-standing issue of summer learning loss in the inner cities of America. And these are just a few examples of the many remarkable projects supported and promoted by CAP.

Creative Visions Productions

As early as 1992, using the name she had dreamed about, Kathy created *Creative Visions Productions* with the intention of producing socially conscious narrative and documentary features, as well as video content and shorts. For their first project, they made a narrative feature with the theme of ivory poaching, called *Lost in Africa* (released in 1994). Later, in 1998, the company produced the documentary *Dying to Tell the Story*, about war journalists like Dan Eldon, who put their lives at risk, and in 1999, the documentary *Soldiers of Peace*, about the children's peace movement in Colombia. Both were aired on *CNN Presents*, and *Dying to Tell the Story* was nominated for an Emmy. "I'm also really proud of our documentary *Global Tribe*," Kathy says, "which was co-created and presented by my daughter Amy when she was 26. It was the first film on grassroots social entrepreneurs. And more recently we have done *Extraordinary Moms* with Julia Roberts, Hillary Clinton, Rosie O'Donnell, and Christiane Amanpour, about the power of mothers to transform the world around them." She is excited about a project in development, a series called *Best Care Possible*, based on the award winning book *The Best Care Possible: A Physician's Quest to Transform Care Through the End of Life* by Ira Byock, MD. "It's about, how do we want to die?" Kathy says. "We want to live fully until the end, and then we want to go peacefully."

Another long-held vision has been to make a film about her son, Dan. "It's been a long slog, but we now have the funding in place to be able to make this film! It's an incredible group of people who are involved. We couldn't be more excited." Principal shooting for the film, entitled *The Journey is the Destination*, began in October 2015 and, as of this writing, is in post production.

The Call of Africa

A good portion of Kathy's life was spent in Africa. She first traveled there as a teenager. "When I was sixteen I was sent to South Africa as an exchange student, and at that time that was perceived as risky," she explains. "There were riots in South Africa. Nobody in my home town of Cedar Rapids, Iowa knew where South Africa was. I certainly didn't. The truth is, when I got there, it was pretty boring and annoyingly suburban." She had been assigned to an all-girl Afrikaans-speaking school in the city of Bloemfontein. "I had to learn Afrikaans. That was very tough, but I was living with a perfectly lovely family in a house with a swimming pool. It wasn't like I was on the edge of anything. But to have that experience of going off to the unknown, to have that opportunity, I was really lucky."

While living in this pristine environment, however, she got her first lesson in the racial system of apartheid. As she writes in her memoir, *In the Heart of Life*, "Black Africans seemed to be almost invisible in 'Bloem.' Unless they were working in white households, black servants had to live in distant townships. When I asked my Boer friends why that was, they patiently explained that God had ordained that blacks and coloreds were inferior and must remain separate from superior 'Europeans' (whites) under apartheid."[48] Despite this troubling system, Kathy found herself entranced by Africa, by its stunning landscape and diverse peoples, and she vowed to return.

> "My Boer friends . . . patiently explained that God had ordained that blacks and coloreds were inferior and must remain separate from superior 'Europeans' (whites) under apartheid."

A Restless Spirit

Ever since she was a young woman, Kathy had the feeling she needed to do something important in the world. As she puts it, "I always felt this sense of urgency and pressure. I wanted to change the world! Perhaps as a product of this, I went to Wellesley College, which was a college of driven young women. Hillary Clinton was a year behind me, and Diane Sawyer was a year ahead of me. I think that we were drilled that we *could* do something great, and indeed we must. I had been brought up that way by my parents but it was intensified there." This sense of urgency Kathy describes in her memoir as a need "to do more, be more, experience more, and create more."[49]

After graduating from Wellesley College, Kathy applied to the Peace Corps, seeing this as one way to get back to Africa. She had been dating an Englishman named Mike Eldon, whom she had met while he was on an internship in the U.S. When she finally heard from the Peace Corps, she also received a proposal from Mike. She chose to say a reluctant no to the Peace Corps and a happy yes to Mike, and moved with him to London. There she struggled to find work (there were few opportunities for American women), eventually finding a job in a gift shop. Their son Dan was born a little over a year later. His sister, Amy, came along when Dan was almost four. Although Kathy adored her family, that feeling of the imperative to do something important never left her.

In 1977, her husband received a job offer to work in Nairobi, Kenya. Though Kathy knew little about Kenya, she was thrilled to return to her beloved Africa. As she recounts in her memoir, Nairobi immediately fascinated her with its "expansive avenues lined with exotic plants . . . the sidewalks alive with people who reflected the unique blend of nearly forty-six ethnic groups . . . and the 'Kenya

Cowboys,' as some people dubbed the handsome, often extroverted and noisy whites who ran safari camps and resorts."[50] She was also immediately struck by the sheer beauty of the Kenyan landscape, with its sweeping vistas, startling light, and piercing blue sky. Though work was hard to come by, she eventually got a job writing food columns for the English-language newspaper *The Nation*. Over time she was able to pursue investigative pieces for the paper, and this is when her life as a journalist really began. She sought out fascinating individuals and gripping stories in the complex African world around her. She wrote about such groundbreakers as Dr. Michael Wood, who founded East Africa's first "Flying Doctors Service," Michael Werikhe, a Kenyan who traveled all over talking about the extinction of the rhino, and Joan and John Karmali, a bi-racial couple who started the first interracial elementary school in Kenya.

Kathy found herself attracted to the dangerous side of being a journalist in Africa. As she says, "I liked pushing the envelope; I liked being on the edge. As a young journalist in Nairobi, sometimes I drove too fast, or I was in places maybe I shouldn't be—in the wrong part of town or interviewing people who were a bit dodgy. I understood the other journalists there. I understood the adrenaline rush. There was a group of journalists called 'The Bang Bang Club.' They were *real* adrenaline junkies! They were great journalists doing great

"I liked pushing the envelope; I liked being on the edge. As a young journalist in Nairobi, sometimes I drove too fast, or I was in places maybe I shouldn't be."

work, but they were perceived as being more interested in that kind of high you get from danger. They were operating in very dangerous situations. And I got totally hooked on that feeling you get when you are pushing against boundaries and barriers."

Dan's Story

Her children, Dan and Amy, took completely to life in Africa, exploring the bush, making friends with natives, learning Swahili. Dan was particularly gregarious and adventurous, able to disarm others easily. His was a childhood far flung from his contemporaries back in London or the States. "Dan was brought up with this heightened sense of awareness," Kathy says. "He was brought up with journalists wandering through the house at all times and with friends who liked to explore. At sixteen they drove all by themselves down to South Africa. It was not like crazy edgy stuff; it was just that if you lived in Africa, it was not like being in Iowa. It was different, and so he wasn't more risk-taking than his friends who were brought up in a similar way." Dan also displayed, early on, a desire to help others. As his bio on the Creative Visions website recounts: "When he was 14, he started a fund-raising campaign for open-heart surgery to save the life of Atieno, a young Kenyan girl. Together with his sister and friends, he raised $5,000, but due to neglect by the hospital, Atieno died. When Dan was 15, he helped support a Maasai family by buying their handmade jewelry and selling it later to fellow students and friends.

"At sixteen, they drove, all by themselves, down to South Africa. It was not like crazy edgy stuff; it was just that if you lived in Africa it was not like being in Iowa."

"During Dan's high school years," the bio continues, "he held many charity fund-raising dances in the 'Mkebe,' a large tin shed in the backyard of the Eldon home. There, scores of students gathered, paying an entrance fee, which went towards Dan's latest charity. Always looking for a way to raise funds, he also produced colorful tee shirts of his own design, and even launched a collection of brightly printed boxer shorts."[51]

While attending college at UCLA, Dan's commitment to helping continued. He set up a charity called Student Transport Aid, and together with fifteen friends, they raised $25,000, met in Nairobi, and traveled thousands of miles in three vehicles to a refugee camp in Malawi. There, they donated one of their vehicles to the Save the Children Fund, and gave money for three wells and for blankets to a children's hospital.

While still in his teens, Dan had begun joining Kathy on a number of her journalistic assignments. He took photos, many of which were used in local newspapers. After college, he continued as a photojournalist. In 1992, the famine in Somalia was raging. He flew there and shot some of the first shocking pictures of the tragedy. Picked up by Reuters, many of his photos landed on the pages of major magazines, bringing the plight of the Somalis to the attention of millions, something which helped spur the initiation of aid programs from the UN and the United States. When war broke out, Dan felt compelled to stay on in Somalia to capture the violence and horror.

On July 12, 1993, Dan and three of his colleagues heard about the bombing of what was thought to be General Aidid's headquarters. It was believed that Aidid was holding a meeting with his followers. But, as Kathy sadly remarks, "The irony is there *was* a meeting there, but it was a *peace* meeting. It was not a war meeting! These were Somalis who were tired of war. They had a 93-year-old grandma there, and children! It was a total injustice. Helicopters came out of the sky. And they even shot out the staircase, so people couldn't get down the stairs. And not only did they do that, but they mortared the villa for 45 minutes, and as the survivors crawled out, the UN forces came down on ropes, still shooting, and photographing the dead. They were trying to see if they had got General Aidid."

It is not surprising, then, although heartbreakingly tragic, that the survivors, in a fury, turned on the journalists who were just trying to tell the story,

"The UN forces came down on ropes, still shooting, and photographing the dead. They were trying to see if they had got General Aidid."

and clubbed and stoned four of them to death. Among them was Dan Eldon, the young man of 22 who only wanted to help others.

The World Turned Upside Down

When Kathy heard the news, her world collapsed. As she relates in her memoir, "A wail escaped me in a tone I didn't recognize . . . The room blurred before me. I slid to the floor, and I howled like an animal, clawing at my face and hair."[52]

It would take a long time before life would feel anything close to normal again. But strangely, in the midst of all this grief, Dan appeared to be contacting her! As Kathy tells it, "Three months after Dan was killed, a friend came to me very excitedly saying that she had been to a medium, Mollie Martin, to talk about her love life, and immediately this medium had said, 'Oh my goodness me, this boy has come in, and he was the youngest of a group, and there were three others, and they were killed suddenly. . . . ' and she described him very accurately.

"So I went to see her. I booked under a false name, and I was presented with almost a shopping list of things I had to do by this spirit who sounded an awful lot like Dan. He made puns. He talked about the fact that there were two memorial services, one for friends and one for distinguished colleagues and industry leaders. He told me that I needed to start a foundation in his name to help others, and he wanted a film done. But not to make him a hero. And that I would be speaking all over and talking to decision makers and influencers and helping them understand the importance of a way of living that he felt was important." Soon after this, there was also an old friend of Dan's who went to a medium, Brenda Lawrence, to connect with his uncle, and, as Kathy says, "In bounded Dan!" So she also visited this medium. Kathy describes the experience: "She told me, 'There's so much to do.' I asked, 'Why does he think I can do it?' and she said, 'He's right there, as close as if he was perched on your shoulder. Most people have to live through their children, but he has to live through you.' So that was the beginning of this belief that I'm not doing it by myself and that I would be helped."

Still it wouldn't be easy. "Knowing that I couldn't do all of it then, because I was too battered, I tackled bits of it over time and eventually managed to tick off everything on the list, except the film—that is, until now, when we are finally in production."

> *"She said, 'He's right there, as close as if he was perched on your shoulder. Most people have to live through their children, but he has to live through you.'"*

Not only has Kathy done everything on that daunting list, she has done more. Along with the documentaries that she has executive produced, Dan's journals that she edited and got published (*The Journey is the Destination: The Journals of Dan Eldon*), and the extraordinary work that she does through Creative Visions, Kathy has found countless other avenues for her boundless creativity and energy. She has written 18 books, which include her stirring memoir *In the Heart of Life,* as well as *Angel Catcher, Soul Catcher,* and *Love Catcher*—a series of popular self-guided journals written with her daughter Amy Eldon Turteltaub. She has also written cookbooks, eating-out guides and children's social history books.

Additionally, Kathy is the co-founder of Sanctri, a new Facebook application to help people remember and celebrate the lives of those who've passed on. She has been profiled in a number of books, including Katherine Martin's *Those Who Dare: Real People, Real Courage*, Nancy Alspaugh, Marilyn Kentz, and Mary Ann Halpin's *Fearless Women*, and Arianna Huffington's *On Becoming Fearless*.

Honors have included a Euro-American Women's Council Artemis Goddess Award for her work with young creative activists, a Civic Ventures Purpose Prize Fellowship, a grant of $25,000 after being named the winner of the Unite4Humanity's Inspiration Award in the Arts (at a ceremony in the presence of President Bill Clinton), and being named one of MSN's "10 Amazing Women You Have Never Heard Of." On Nelson Mandela's Birthday in 2013, she was nominated by his grandsons, Kweku and Ndaba Mandela, for the George H.W. Bush "Points of Light" award.

Kathy has also been featured on a number of television and radio programs, including several appearances on Oprah and a segment on Oprah's "Producer's Favorites."

The "F" Word

In addition, Kathy is an inspiring speaker. She has spoken to numerous organizations, including Forbes Women Summit, TEDx Talks, TEDx Teens, and the Conference on Volunteering and Service. Her speeches are passionate, thought-provoking, and moving. One of her talks, presented to TEDx Orange Coast in 2013, is a powerful recounting of how she was ultimately able to forgive the people who had killed her son. When she and her daughter Amy were making their film, *Dying to Tell the Story*, about the dangers war journalists face, they returned to the site in Somalia where Dan was killed. It was a very painful moment, and the rage that she had felt since his death seared through her once again.

She told the TEDx audience, "Desmond Tutu once said, 'Not to forgive is like drinking poison and waiting for your enemies to die.' I knew that held a message for me, but I was not prepared to listen to it at the time."[53] Then came the night of the film's opening, in November of 1997. It was premiering at the United Nations. She describes in her TEDx talk that when she and Amy got in the taxi to head

"Desmond Tutu once said, 'Not to forgive is like drinking poison and waiting for your enemies to die.'"

to the UN, they were shocked to discover that the cab driver was Somali! After taking this in, Kathy decided to tell this man about what happened to her son. When she finished, the cab driver turned to her, with tears in his eyes, and he said, "My name is Ebrahim. I know all about what happened to your son. We know that he and his friends were heroes; they did nothing wrong. And I'm so very sorry." Upon hearing this, however, Kathy's rage began once again to smolder. But then, in a moment of epiphany, she thought about Gandhi and knew that the only way that Somalia, or the world, could change would be to change herself first. She heard herself saying to this man, "I understand what the Somalis did. I hate what they did. But I forgive the Somalis." It was a turning point in her healing. "I don't know where the words came from," she told the audience, "but it was such a blessing to be able to utter them." At the end of the talk, she says, "Forgiveness is not about forgetting. Forgiveness is taking your power back. It's about you, not the offender, it's about becoming whole and healing."[54]

In our interview, Kathy then mentions that, as they walked

toward the UN building with all the flags fluttering in the wind, she remembered that among the many extraordinary things the medium Brenda Lawrence had told her was a vision of the United Nations flags around her and her daughter. One more thing that had come true.

All About Igniting

It is clear that Kathy has channeled the unthinkable tragedy of her son's death into a life of giving back and inspiring others. "I believe my whole purpose in life is to ignite other people, to help them achieve their potential, both for themselves and for others. I've spent a lot of time as a mentor, but I don't see my own wisdom as being the key to it. The key as to why people come back is that I open their eyes to their *own* power, which is what a mentor really does. It's like, 'Okay, you can do this. Go for it!' Because I've been around for a while, I can climb that mountain that's just up in front and maybe look a little bit further than the person who is slogging through that landscape of hardship. I can say, 'Hey, maybe you want to think about this and this.' Or, 'What do you really want to do? Well,

"I believe my whole purpose in life is to ignite other people, to help them achieve their potential, both for themselves and for others."

you can do it!' So it's a form of being a facilitator. It's igniting that spark. It's inspiring. That's what I do. I inspire. When people say I inspired them, it really touches me. It means I did something that lit their fire, and they breathed in. That's what 'inspire' actually means— to 'breathe in.'"

Living the Ren Life

"I think everybody would like to have the possibility of living

KATHY ELDON | 99

a fully activated, actualized life," Kathy says. "But often they haven't a clue how they can do it. People often feel, after they have chosen a path, that they are stuck in it. Now, because I've never been officially 'employed,' I've always had to create my own source of income, whatever it was. So I've gone from one thing to another. I think for me, actually, the excitement in life is the possibility that is inherent in every encounter, in every article that I read, in every image that I see. They can all lead somewhere. Nothing is the *destination* for me. I don't think you are ever trapped in something. There is always a way out; there's always more."

"I think everybody would like to have the possibility of living a fully activated, actualized life, but they haven't a clue how they can do it."

Her advice to those who want to live the "Ren" life? "Seize the moment! Be curious and adventurous and mischievous and go on journeys and have more fun. Also be willing to take risks. If you are going to actually accomplish something beyond the ordinary, you are going to need to stretch a little; you can't be afraid of disrupting things or upsetting people. You can do it tactfully sometimes, but, heck, nothing happens if you are not prepared to try something that other people haven't tried or that other people have tried but which may seem a little risky. I'm not talking about physical risks necessarily. I'm talking about taking yourself out of your comfort zone."

Kathy also feels that a Renaissance state of mind is crucial for life in the 21st century. "The age of labeling yourself as one thing is over," she says. "If you can't reinvent yourself every few years, you are probably redundant in society. So I think constant

"If you are going to actually accomplish something beyond the ordinary . . . you can't be afraid of disrupting things or upsetting people."

learning, however that comes in, is essential. We are exposed to information to the point of overload, but we also have the ability to take courses online for free or to learn another language for free. So what is it that you want to do? It's all available. Gather together a group or go to a Starbucks every Thursday with two other people you want to learn something with. Make a commitment to *you*. The book Amy and I did, *The Soul Catcher*, is exactly about this. It is a journal to help you become who you really are."

Kathy adds a final thought: "Looking back now at the sentence that has guided my life, 'Do more, be more, create more, experience more,' I think the thing that I would add is learn how to 'simply *be*.' I always felt that I had to *do*. And I love that I have done, but I'm learning now to stand still and take things in. If you want to be a real Renaissance person, I think you have to stand still long enough to *savor* who you are and how you are, and appreciate your relationships and just experience life fully. Turn off your electronic devices, and be fully alive in that moment."

And with this invaluable advice, our time is over, but it has been a true privilege to meet this vibrant, inspirational, and life-affirming woman.

Ren Gems

Kathy Eldon

"Everyone has a spark. There is a way you can take that spark and use it for good in the world."

"Don't be hampered by what other people tell you to do or think you should be doing."

"The definition of 'inspire' is to infuse into, as if by breathing, to affect as with a supernatural influence; to enliven."

"The most important thing in child-rearing is to have true respect for your child."

"Heroes have a sense of light about them. They make us feel that we can be bigger than we thought we ever could be."

6

Dale Franzen

"I'm one of those people who has to go my own way."

Opera and musical theatre singer and dancer, teacher, creator of
Academy for Entertainment and Technology at Santa
Monica College, founder and director of the Eli and
Edythe Broad Stage, producer

At 2:30 in the morning, fifteen-year-old Dale Franzen was awoken by her mother's frantic voice on the bedroom intercom: "Dale, come quickly, Daddy made a funny sound." When she arrived in her parents' bedroom, she took one look at her father and knew he was dead. In her work as a Candy Striper in the local hospital, she had seen her share of dead bodies. But her mother was clearly in denial, and it was the young Dale who called the ambulance, as well as a neighbor who was a doctor. This ability to take charge at such a young age was remarkable, and all the more so considering her father was the single most important person in her life, whom she adored and who had adored her. For Dale, losing her father was devastating, but his belief in her, as well as the example he had set, would have a positive influence on Dale throughout her life, in ways both expected and unexpected.

Dale Franzen is sitting in the living room of her light-filled Pacific Palisades home in California. A grand piano dominates the room and artwork abounds. Dale has a liveliness that is infectious. She has recently left her position as the director and founder of the Eli and Edye Broad Stage and the Edye Second Space at the Santa Monica College Performing Arts Center. The eclectic fare she curated for seven years, which included performances in dance, classical music, jazz, and much more, ranged from Baryshnikov to Alan Cumming, from Shakespeare's *Comedy of Errors* to the kooky *Celebrity Autobiography*, from the Diavolo Dance Company to Chris Lemmon's one-man show *Jack Lemmon Returns*. When Dale left this prestigious position, people thought she was crazy. "There was an event at UCLA recently," she says. "And they had this thing called 'What's the Boldest Thing You've Ever Done?' and the boldest thing I've ever done is to step down from what the world perceived as the perfect job, one that I had created. And I was thinking, everybody thinks I'm nuts!"

But then again, everyone thought she was nuts when she started the Broad. It was her brainchild and passion from its inception through its construction. It was also something she had never done before, and a huge leap into the unknown.

A Singer's Life for Her

If you had asked Dale when she was twenty, if she could imagine founding and running a multimillion-dollar performing arts center, she would have laughed. Her passion at that age was to be a professional singer, and that is just what she did. Her first serious voice teacher was the great Marni Nixon, who recognized Dale's talent for singing opera and encouraged her to study classically. Dale launched a very successful opera career, which lasted over twenty years. Like Marni, Dale was versatile, and performed in musical theatre, operetta, television, and radio. She also had dance training and thus was often given singing *and* dancing roles in both opera and musicals. Dale loved performing, but there was another aspect of the singer's life she enjoyed. "I liked the lifestyle of what it was to be a musician," she says. "You practiced 2-4 hours a day, so there was a lot of time in solitude and in focus and discipline. I liked the sanctity of that. Which I realize now is almost like what it is to meditate. There's the big public side of performing, but there's a big private side to it too, which is something a lot of people don't realize."

> *"There was a lot of time in solitude and in focus and discipline. I liked the sanctity of that."*

A Father and a Daughter

Dale's father was the first to encourage her gifts. Selig J. Seligman was the biggest influence in her life. He was also a bigger-than-life individual. A film and television producer and executive, Seligman ran ABC in the 50s and 60s and executive produced such television shows as *Combat, Name That Tune*, and *General Hospital*, as well as such films as *Candy, Hell in the Pacific*, and *Charley*. Beyond being a Hollywood powerhouse, he was also a true Renaissance man. As Dale explains: "My father was an army lawyer who served as a prosecutor in the Nuremberg war crimes trials. During WWII, he was in Intelligence. He loved opera; he loved all the arts; he had perfect pitch. He could come home after a symphony and play the whole thing on the piano perfectly. He started taking me to opera and to the symphony when I was five." Little wonder that once it was clear that Dale had singing, as well as dancing, talent, her father was completely onboard. "My father totally encouraged me. He always thought I'd be a performer and a musician; that was kind of a given." Interestingly, Seligman was also very much a man of the 50s with all the male chauvinism that entailed. "My father died before the feminist movement really happened. He married a very, well, *not* feminist woman. I found out later that he could have married a woman who was a lawyer who went on to become a judge. And he didn't. It was a big love affair, but he didn't marry her. I think it's because he didn't want a wife who would challenge

"My father totally encouraged me. He always thought I'd be a performer and a musician."

him. I often wonder how he might have responded to the feminist movement." She laughs. "He might have had some trouble with it! But yet, he definitely expected *me* to excel. And he was tough on me. But he was always much tougher on my brothers. I was his princess, put on a pedestal, completely spoiled."

The night that fifteen-year-old Dale was called into her parents' bedroom to find her father dead of a heart attack altered her life overnight. Not only did she have to take control that terrible night, but she also continued to care for her mother afterwards, as things fell apart. "We sold our house within three months, and my mother went into a very bad period. She was a 50s housewife; she'd never worked; she didn't even have a bank account. And then, a year after my father died, my youngest brother was diagnosed with quite severe Tourette's Syndrome. So my mother had to deal with that as well." Dale felt a responsibility for her mother, not just because of her father's death but because of the way that he had brought her and her older siblings up. "All three of us felt we had to be very strong people, that we were people who *fixed* things and were responsible for other people. That was definitely the message my father gave us." So she made sacrifices to be there for her mother, one of which was canceling a plan to attend college on the east coast and enrolling in Cal Arts instead.

Things changed again when she was 18. "This man who was like our family psychiatrist, he actually told me that the best thing I could do was to get out. When I was 18 and-a-half, I fell in love with a Canadian and took that psychiatrist's advice; at 19 I moved to Canada with him. I think, probably, that *was* the best thing I could have done. In the end, I had to save myself."

Although the relationship with the Canadian man didn't last, Dale spent eight years in Canada where she performed in musicals and operettas. She then returned to Los Angeles where she studied opera at USC and launched her professional opera career. In 1983, she married

> *"He actually told me that the best thing I could do was to get out."*

attorney Don Franzen, with whom she had three children. She continued to have an active career in opera, spending eight years with the Los Angeles Opera, as well as performing throughout the world.

Sprinkling a Little Magic

In her early forties, Dale felt it was time to leave the opera world. "It was after my third child was born. I just suddenly didn't need to be in the limelight anymore. It was like I had been a sailor on the ship, and I had a sense now I wanted to be the captain. I knew I couldn't do that as a singer. It was shocking for me because that's all I had ever done. I was so defined that way, and I didn't know what I wanted to do. Still, I felt something else was calling me. I just had no idea what it was. It was a different time in my life because I had three kids at home. So I thought I'd be a stay-at-home mom for a while. Well, that lasted six months before I was bored to tears. Then, knowing I still wanted to do something within the arts, I met with a lot of people, and all I said to them was, 'I'm done singing, I feel like I can do a lot of things in the arts and if you have any ideas call me.' Within three months, I started getting called to do a lot of different things, all of which I did. Two examples were a CD-Rom about Ragtime music, which I sang on, and a Showtime movie for which I was a technical advisor, and in which I performed."

Then, unexpectedly, she and another woman were hired by Santa Monica College to put together a school for entertainment and digital technology. This surprised Dale. Most of the people at the college knew her as a singer. "When I met with the Vice-President and said I might be interested in something else in the arts, he came up with this idea. I asked him, 'Why are you asking *me*?' I didn't have a computer, and at this point, I didn't even have an email account!" Well, clearly he knew Dale well, perhaps better than she knew herself at this point. He told her, "You'll figure it out" and that's exactly what she did. She and her partner successfully instituted and developed the Academy of Entertainment and Technology,

"I asked him, 'Why are you asking me?' . . . And he said, 'You'll figure it out.'"

which offered (and continues to offer) classes and specialty degrees in such things as animation, digital audio and video media, game design, and digital effects.

After the Academy was successfully launched, she asked the president of SMC for a new project. Dale explains: "She said to me, 'Meet me at 11th and Santa Monica Boulevard. We have this city block; what would you do with it?'" After some thought, Dale realized, although Los Angeles had major performing arts venues for theatre, opera, music and dance downtown, there was no all-encompassing performing arts center on the west side. After polling a number of her friends and colleagues about the idea and getting enthusiastic responses, she decided to go for it. For her, the thrill was in making something that wasn't there. "I was kind of swept away with the romance of being hired to build a theatre. It's kind of the ultimate Judy Garland, Mickey Rooney scenario. I was full of passion and adrenaline." Then she adds: "By the way, I had no staff, and this was all done seat-of-the-pants! Yet, it was very elegant, very exciting. That's why Dustin Hoffman came on. We were having a good time. It was just fun."

"I was kind of swept away with the romance of being hired to build a theatre. It's kind of the ultimate Judy Garland, Mickey Rooney scenario."

Having never spearheaded the founding and building of a major arts project, Dale was unaware of how truly monumental a task she was taking on. "I don't think I thought it was daunting. That's what is great about ignorance. I didn't know what it would take so I actually, in some ways, didn't think it was going to be that hard. This was a really good idea, there were plenty of wealthy people on the west side who loved and would support the arts, so *of course* this should be built. And, you know," she adds with a smile, "we didn't do any of the traditional fundraising. We did everything backwards. We raised major money before we raised minor money. I said to the first person who gave me $100,000, 'Can you throw a party for a hundred of your friends?' and then Dustin was involved at that point, so I would sing at the parties because we didn't have money to hire anybody else. I would sing a funny song about raising money to something like "I Could've Danced All Night," and Dustin would do a theatrical reading, and we'd show the model, and we'd ask for money and that's how we raised the first nine million. So it didn't cost me a thing, and that's unheard of!

"People like me envision things," Dale adds. "We are like alchemists. We see things that aren't there, and we want to get them done. But if everybody was that way there would be nobody to run these things. You need everyone, the team is extremely important, and also the donors who come on at the beginning and the ones who come on later. Even now I see, because I'm so used to leading now—it's been sixteen years of doing this—I see that there are different styles of leadership. But for me . . . I would say I'm most interested in magic. Which really goes back to being a performer. I liked creating a role; I liked making magic on stage. So, everything has this feeling like it should be magical; it should be surprising; it should be fun. My daughter just sent me a quote, a Ben and Jerry's quote, that I love: "If it's not fun, why do it?" I definitely think my strength is I am basically an optimistic, upbeat person. That is not to say I didn't have moments of tremendous doubt and moments of: 'Oh my god, this is too much, I need a break!' I mean, I probably tried to quit five times at least! You know, the first time you are in a neighborhood meeting, and they attack you and they say, 'You're going to destroy our neighborhood!' it's hard."

"People like me . . . are like alchemists. We see things that aren't there, and we want to get them done."

"It should be magical; it should be surprising; it should be fun."

But she persevered. And an important realization came to her, years into running the Broad and curating programming there. "When I started producing and running the Broad, people would interview me, and say, 'Oh, it's so strange you're doing this.' And it wasn't until recently that I thought, actually it wasn't strange at all.

Growing up, I always heard my father talking on the phone about budgets and working with difficult artists and deadlines and all kinds of things like that. But I didn't make that connection until later."

A Strong Home Life

Another key to Dale's success and to dealing with the pressures involved was having a very solid home life. "Malcolm Gladwell, in his book *Outliers*, talks about 'hidden advantages'," she says. "And I think the hidden advantage of having a secure home and a strong domestic partnership is huge. People don't realize, for example, how important that has been for men. Well, it's equally important for women. It's just much harder for women to find because a lot of men are threatened by strong, accomplished women. I happen to be married to a very extraordinary person who adores me and thinks I can do anything. I don't know that I could've done this without him. Honestly there were so many times when he picked me up and came up with brilliant ideas and was a total partner to me on this project. But also he never doubted that I could do it, he never once said to me 'Are you sure this is a good idea?' He got onboard immediately. He was very instrumental in starting L.A. Opera, so he had also started a very big idea that had tremendous resistance at the beginning (which is hard to believe now). He was the perfect partner to help me through this."

> *"I happen to be married to a very extraordinary person who adores me and thinks I can do anything. I don't know that I could've done this without him."*

Marching to Her Own Score

One reason Dale stepped down from her director's position at the Broad is that, for her, as she has said, the excitement is in the creation of something new and getting it up and running. Once it is on firm footing, she is not as interested in the daily running of it.

"My basic nature is to forge new ground. I kind of feel like that's why I was put here, in a way. I wasn't put here to be mainstream. Still, it's interesting how threatening and how upsetting that is to others. After I stepped down from the Broad, people pulled me aside and asked, 'OK, what's really going on?' and I would laugh and say, 'Nothing; I don't have cancer.' They thought I was either fired or had cancer! They couldn't believe that I voluntarily stepped down from something that I had created because most people wouldn't. I mean, we know that most men would hold a position until they dropped dead or were thrown out. Even a lot of women would.

"But here's the thing," Dale continues, "I don't mind creating the box, but I don't want to get into the box. I'm not a nine-to-five person; I kind of get a stomach ache when I go into offices, that's so not my personality. It's too confining."

For Dale, it's also about defining her own iconoclastic path. "Every single step that I've taken has been against the grain. But I would have this overwhelming gut feeling that it was the right thing for me. Even in the face of people saying 'You're crazy; this is wrong.'

"I don't mind creating the box, but I don't want to get into the box."

When I was entering a marriage and starting my career as an opera singer, in those days the thing to do was go to New York, and I chose to marry my husband and stay in Los Angeles. Everybody, including my agent, said, 'You're crazy; you're never going to work,' blah blah

blah. Then within nine months, three opera companies started in L.A., and all three hired me, so I ended up working way more than my friends in New York. Even the ones who got in at The Met, they were only at The Met for three months, then the rest of the year they were working as computer people in an office or in a law firm.

"So I'm one of those people who has to go my own way, I just don't fit into somebody else's vision. But also, I'm a person who, if I set a goal, I meet my goal. I don't give up. Like with The Broad, most people would have told you it was impossible, and now, looking back on it, *I* would tell you it was impossible.

"I just don't fit into somebody else's vision."

But my attitude is, it may be impossible, but if it's the right thing to do, the right time to do it, and in the right location, let's just get it done!"

Women in the Workplace and in the Home

Another way, earlier in her life, that Dale went her own way was to marry young and have a child in her early twenties when most other women of her generation were delaying marriage and children. "I came up during the feminist movement," she explains. "I very much felt, when I had my first child at 23, that people looked down on that, especially my feminist sisters, who were, like, 'You should do your career first!' There were these changing roles of what it was to be feminine. Luckily, I was pretty strong, so I didn't really care what they thought. In truth, I was more of a feminist than any of them. I was working. I was raising kids. I was married. Most of them were just working. And

"I very much felt, when I had my first child at 23, that people looked down on that, especially my feminist sisters."

a lot of them went on to not have children and then deeply regret it."

Even in her career as an opera singer, having a child was seen as a stigma: "It was very rare at that time for women to have children and be an opera singer. My agent would say to me, 'Don't tell people you have a child because you won't be cast to play the ingénue.' So there was a lot of hiding. Often people wouldn't take you seriously if you had a kid, so you had to work twice as hard to prove yourself. But all of that is gone now. Most of the opera singers that are coming up now will marry and have children. Even in the ballet world, this has changed. Dancers are now having kids and, guess what, they are fine. They can still dance, and they are great; in fact, they probably bring more to the table. All of this has been in the last forty years.

"For me, I always wanted all of it and it didn't occur to me that I wouldn't have it. Of course, I didn't know it was going to be so hard. Looking back at it now I honestly don't know how I did it! I was remodeling a house, doing a degree, performing, raising a kid, being married. But I had this incredible energy, so somehow I just pushed through. I also remember it was all very compartmentalized. How I was at work and what I talked about at work were very different from how I was at home. It was exhausting having to wear different hats like that."

Young Women Today

Dale is seeing very different trends in the women of her daughter's generation. "I talk to young females now, and the whole value thing is really different. They don't want to juggle fifty things at once. For instance, my daughter is a 29-year-old entrepreneur. She has an unbelievably successful online business, and so, of course, we are always saying to her, and everyone else is saying to her, 'Why don't you expand?' She just wrote this blog: 'The ten reasons why I won't expand.' In it she explains that she is not interested in more work, she is not interested in more money, she's interested in a certain quality of life. Maybe the twenty-somethings have watched us; they've watched their mothers work unbelievably hard and they think, you know what, I don't want to juggle. This daughter is also saying that she's not going to have kids. Now maybe that's true, maybe it isn't, but she's certainly not going to do it until she's older. I had my first kid young; she watched me and what I had to do. And maybe this generation of post-feminist young women are saying, 'I don't want that stress.'

"Maybe the twenty-somethings have watched . . . their mothers work unbelievably hard and they think, you know what, I don't want to juggle."

"What worries me is that many women are putting off childbearing until 40, then they're taking fertility drugs, which is not a good thing. It's understandable, but it's going to be a struggle to see how this will all work and how women can keep having children.

"The problem with books like *Lean In* is it still puts all the pressure on women. We all, we *were* the lean in generation, and we know what that cost us. Look at Arianna Huffington. She has done amazing work; no one can say anyone has leaned in more than she. But, as she describes in her recent book, *Thrive*, she completely crashed and burned. There are so many people now, men and women, who are burnt out and exhausted, but they're afraid. They're afraid to say anything because they'll be seen as weak."

Being successful, she explains, is not the same as having a successful *life*. "Even in the Renaissance," she says, "Did Galileo have a successful life? Did Michelangelo? Galileo had to falsify what he believed or be killed. Michelangelo was a closet gay. I don't think they had successful lives, but they were Renaissance people; they did many different things. So maybe the new definition of a Renaissance person is someone who also has a successful life."

> *"Maybe the new definition of a Renaissance person is someone who also has a successful life."*

Technology and Choices in the 21st Century

Dale sees a reason to be optimistic for the younger generation of women. Technology and the internet are creating more choices and more ways in which women can design their own paradigm-shifting versions of success.

"I think a lot of women, in my daughter's generation certainly, are redefining success for themselves, and a large part of it is because of the Internet. The thing about technology is that women can have careers and not have to go to a building or an office, so they can raise children and have a life. They can redefine their power structure because they have this freedom. My daughter, and a lot of her friends, they're not leaning in; they're taking a *side* route. They've almost gone side-bar. And in many ways, they're going to have a much better life." Technology, Dale explains, allows women to

> *"My daughter, and a lot of her friends, they're not leaning in; they're taking a side route."*

not only work from home, but to not have any overhead, to have flexible hours, and to start their own businesses. "The biggest growth factor in America right now," she says, "is small business owners, who are predominantly women. Frankly, I think that's the future, in many ways."

However, Dale explains, there are also downsides. "The problem with technology is that there's no time when you *stop* working. I've gotten emails from women who work for me, at 11 o'clock at night, and I'll write back, why are you emailing me at 11 o'clock at night, and why are you still working? And it's partially because they want time to be with their kids, and then at 11 o'clock when the kids are asleep, they go and work. So that's not good. The feminist movement didn't cut down the amount of work we have; we just have *more* work. So it's a double-edged sword. The *workplace* has to change. It has to change so both men and women can be involved, in work *and* in raising the children. We have to change our policies on how businesses are run."

She remarks how different it is now from 30 years ago, and how society hasn't quite figured out how to catch up: "Things moved

> *"The workplace has to change. It has to change so both men and women can be involved in work and in raising the children."*

at a certain pace before the 80s, when computers came in, and then they completely changed. The pace is so different now. And also, 60% of college graduates are women, so men are graduating at a lower rate. That in itself really changes the game. Yet the upper echelon, the upper 1%, is still predominantly white men. So there's still a lot of work to be done, and there are still a lot of breakthroughs waiting to happen."

A Renaissance Approach

Dale feels, in the 21st century, we have entered a time when being multi-skilled and having numerous careers is becoming the norm. "I think we're living in a more Renaissance time now. I've read that we've entered an era of *generalists*, not *specialists*. It used to be that you were looked down on for that. But now . . . take Jonathan

Miller, for instance. He's a neuroscientist; he's a director; he's a writer. I remember him talking about how, at one time, no one took him seriously as a director because he was 'actually' a neuroscientist. But he has been successful in both careers. He's written some of the leading material in neuroscience, and he's also a brilliant director. There's a new attitude now."

As Dale told Sara Ring in an interview for *Groundswell: The magazine of Antioch University Los Angeles*, "Life is long. If you stay healthy, you could live to 100 and you may end up having four careers. So the skills that you learn along the way are everything . . . As you enter a career, be open to the many different paths and skills that you might use someday. I think having some diversity in what you do is very important now. A lot of people are much narrower. They go, 'I'm going to be a singer, and that's all I'm going to be,' but I had other skills that I was open to exploring. I think the world is moving more and more toward hybrid careers, so accept the idea that you probably won't stay in the same career for your whole life."

"As you enter a career, be open to the many different paths and skills that you might use someday."

And now?

Well, the offers have already started coming in, but Dale is not rushing into anything. "You know, like recently, I spent an hour on the phone helping an organization that I love," she says. "They wanted to hire me to do something. I said, 'Look, let me just help you.' I knew exactly what they should do, so I told them and said I'd be happy to meet with them, but I wasn't looking for a job right now. It made me realize that I enjoyed that––I enjoyed sharing my knowledge with them. It's easy to do when you already know something, when you've already been there, but I can't see myself fitting into another thing like that. I suspect that if I end up doing something else, which I probably will, it will be something that I create myself, just maybe in a different arena.

"As I've already mentioned, I like starting new things. Even though I ran a six-million-dollar company and built this fifty-million-dollar theatre, it was non-profit. I've never done something like that in the for-profit realm. So, there's a part of me that is intrigued by that, but I suspect it would be something where there's a better good. I'm not interested in money for money's sake, but if there was a way to make money and do good at the same time, that might appeal to me. I don't know what that is yet. It's like when I decided to stop singing. I felt that was over and something else was calling me, but I had no idea what it was. It's very much where I am right now.

"I find I'm asking myself a lot, right now, how I should be spending my talent? I'm clear that I have very specific strengths, and it would be foolish to waste them in ways that don't honor them. Because when I'm on my beam, I'm pretty powerful. I feel there's nothing I can't do, and I can jump without a net and be fearless. That is a strength, and it's not something everybody has. So if I'm going to do something else again, and I probably will, it will be something that ignites that in me and makes me feel like it *must* happen."

(As of this writing, Dale is currently producing the folk opera *Hadestown* in New York City.)

With that, our interview with Dale Franzen is over. We have been privileged to spend time with this remarkable woman who has an unquenchable joie de vivre and an unerring enthusiasm for allowing life to reveal itself to her.

Alexandra Franzen

"A lot of Renaissance souls are looking for an overarching mission."

Online entrepreneur, freelance writer, ghostwriter, book author, workshop leader, communication facilitator, motivational blogger, licensed as helicopter pilot and massage therapist

Alexandra knew her parents were seriously worried about her. She was 19 years old and untethered. She had quit college after only 18 months, and thrown herself haphazardly into adulthood. For almost two years, with no real plan in mind, she worked a variety of random jobs. She completed training in two unrelated fields—getting her helicopter pilot's license and completing work for a massage therapy license—but she practiced neither professionally. Then, when she finally decided to go back to college, it was nowhere local. In fact, it was nowhere in the United States. She applied (and was accepted) to the University of Otago in New Zealand! There, she majored in English—not because it was necessarily her passion (although she already loved to write), but because it was the major for which she had the most credits going in. She was, in other words, a young woman who appeared to be at loose ends. And yet, now, at only 29 years old, she has built up a thriving online business and has coached countless people on how to live their dreams and how to communicate more powerfully in their careers and in their lives. Her professional calendar is booked until 2017. So how did she get from there to here?

The first thing you notice about Alexandra Franzen are her eyes. Large, almond-shaped and a piercing green, they mesmerize. Her dark sweep of hair and infectious smile only add to her striking looks. But talking with her, you soon realize that her outer beauty is complemented by an inner dimensionality of intelligence, warmth, and curiosity.

Alexandra Franzen was a late bloomer. But when she bloomed, it was as a multi-petaled flower! Her success clearly reflects the times we live in, as she has found her calling in the quite recent field of online entrepreneurship. She has also found a way to be a full-on RenWoman. She had been, all along, a nascent RenWoman, looking for a way to coalesce all her interests into an effective multifaceted package. By establishing her own business, which she calls a "communication agency" and defining the parameters of that business, she has been able to do all the things she's good at (which are many). She writes inspirational books; she conducts motivational workshops; she ghostwrites everything from blog posts to guidebooks and from speeches to website content; she acts as a life coach to other women entrepreneurs and to those struggling with their own multiple interests; she writes articles for platforms like *Time.com*, *Forbes.com*, and *Newsweek.com*; and she even contributes poems for art posters. In the process, she has collaborated with and guided a profusion of people from all walks of life, all ages, and all kinds of businesses. She also has an instinctive ability to gauge the times we live in, and as a natural consequence, she astutely markets herself and her business.

A Stimulating Upbringing

If creativity seems to be the driving force behind all of Alexandra's endeavors, this is no surprise, considering her upbringing.

Daughter of RenWoman mother, Dale Franzen, who has been a singer, teacher, innovator, and performing arts center founder and director, Alexandra grew up in a home that was filled with artists and intellectuals. As she says: "It was an extremely creative household. There were always fabulous parties and interesting people flowing in and out of our house: performing artists, visual artists, all kinds of people. And there was very much an attitude of: if there's something you love, there's absolutely nothing stopping you. It was a do-whatever-you-want kind of message. I never felt

> *"There were always fabulous parties and interesting people flowing in and out of our house."*

any pressure from my parents to choose a 'sensible' career." Alexandra feels her personality is a reflection of both her mother and her father, Don Franzen, an entertainment and business attorney. She explains, "I feel like I'm almost a perfect 50/50 split between my parents in terms of personality and just the way in which they move through the world. My dad is very stoic, very thoughtful, very even. He thinks deeply about what he's going to say before he says it. And my mom is this beautiful firecracker, she lights up the room, she's a performer! She connects things in interesting ways, and she's very playful." One of the traits Alexandra shares with her father is introversion. During her elementary school years, this tended to create problems for her. "At two different elementary schools, teachers noticed me not playing with the other kids and instead always reading, and that worried them. I remember they would tell me I couldn't go to the library; I had to go out to the playground. So then of course, I just took books out to the playground and sat in the

> *"I remember they would tell me I couldn't go to the library; I had to go out to the playground. So then, of course, I just took books out to the playground."*

corner. At that age, I didn't know what an introvert or extrovert was, I just knew that reading was awesome, and throwing balls around with loud people was, well, not. And I'm still that way. In big groups, for example, when there's a lot of chattering, I literally feel a ringing in my ears. So in my life, particularly these past couple of years, I've created, almost unconsciously, a career that really suits an introvert."

A Rocky Road

Getting to that place has not been a smooth trajectory for Alexandra. Instead, for a number of years, starting in her mid-teens, it was filled with turmoil and angst. Her mother described those years as "a nightmare," full of various "derailments." When Alexandra left home at eighteen for college, she had no desire to be there: "I wanted to do other things. I didn't have a major declared. I had phenomenal grades, my professors loved me, and I was miserable. So I dropped out."

That began a tumultuous search for herself. "I spent maybe a year and a half to two years having all kinds of wild adventures, living in Hollywood, working weird jobs, traveling for the first time alone as a grownup. I got my helicopter pilot's license, and then a massage therapy license. I did all kinds of random things, really trying to find myself and figure out who I was separate from my family, which created extreme tension for them. I probably didn't handle it as gracefully as I could." She smiles. "I think my parents had a few slip ups as well. It was a time for me of accelerated growth, kind of like catapulting into adulthood."

At 21, she decided it was time to go back to college. But

"I did all kinds of random things, really trying to find myself and figure out who I was separate from my family."

even here, she made a radical decision. "I wanted to go somewhere totally different, and I ended up applying to to the University of Otago in New Zealand. It all happened in the span of two weeks. I googled it, found the program, applied, and they let me in—just under the wire. Literally two weeks after that, I packed my one suitcase and flew to this country where I didn't know a single soul! The university, which is the oldest in New Zealand, looked like Hogwarts from the *Harry Potter* books. Initially, I planned to stay for just a semester, and kind of see what I wanted to do from there. But I wound up finishing my degree there, with a major in English. I only settled on English because I happened to have the most credits in that department, and I was like, well, I can graduate on time if I choose this, whereas if I choose something else I might have to take another semester."

Despite her ostensible pragmatism, her choice made sense on a deeper level. She had always loved not only reading, but also writing. As a young girl, she had written stories, and in high school, she wrote short plays and did a column for the school paper. She was also in the advanced English classes. "Writing was clearly a strength for me," she says. "And I have always been a speed reader. I could digest information really quickly. So actually, English turned out to be a great choice because it forced me to read all the classics, and it gave me great opportunities to write and think and put together interesting essays."

> *"Writing was clearly a strength for me. And I have always been a speed reader. I could digest information really quickly."*

Radio Beckons

Once she graduated, her student visa expired and she returned to the United States. After one week at home, she embarked on a road trip to try and determine where she'd like to live. She settled on Minneapolis. "It was summertime, it was beautiful, and it was really cheap to live there. I got an apartment for something like 500 bucks!" Using her skill at writing, she began to cobble together enough to live on: "I started doing random writing gigs. I was doing a little bit of freelance journalism, I was doing technical writing, I was doing transcription work, anything I could possibly find." And then, a great opportunity came her way. She landed an internship at Minnesota Public Radio/American Public Media. "This was huge for me; it was really competitive," she says. Ironically, she was hired for a rather unexpected reason. "They later told me," she explains, "that they only offered it to me because they thought it was cool that I was a helicopter pilot. The woman who hired me, who would end up becoming a really good friend, said I was not the most qualified, I didn't really have any radio experience, but when she saw I had trained to be a helicopter pilot, and had been the only woman at the helicopter school, she thought, here's someone who can do anything." (This is an example of Ren-ness in action. It

> *"They later told me that they only offered it to me because they thought it was cool that I was a helicopter pilot."*

demonstrates the importance of following your interests because they may end up serving you in unpredictable ways.)

Due to her natural intelligence, adaptability and writing ability, Alexandra flourished there. The paid internship quickly became a part- time job, then a full-time one, then she was given two promotions. Her duties became increasingly more complex and with more responsibility. "When I was an intern," she says, "it was very bare bones; I was doing fact-checking, proof-reading, things like that. Then the next job I got was in the area of audience/listener services. So that entailed anything from picking up the phone when furious

callers would call in (that was always fun) to answering emails from
people writing in—be it listeners or journalists looking for links in
our archives. After that position, I worked in the membership drive
department. So I was basically writing/producing the on-air drives,
which was not really as exciting as it sounds, a lot of it was just
sitting in the studio with the hosts and feeding them their scripts,
telling them when it was time to go, and generally being part of
the fundraising drives. The last job I had there was actually in the
technology department. I was writing and/or editing little on-air
spots, which were mostly promotional spots. So, it would be like:
"This Sunday, come see Garrison Keillor at the Fitzgerald Theater." I
would write those 15 to 30-second spots, distribute them to the hosts,
make sure they recorded them, give the files to the audio producer
to add the underlying music, etc. We were producing anywhere
from 50 to 100 of these little spots every month, and they had to
be perfect because we had to convey a lot of information in a short
period of time. But doing that was only half of my job. The other
half, honestly, was a grab bag of whatever my boss, the director of the
broadcast technology department, needed. So it was everything from
drafting emails for him to managing his calendar to being present
during meetings to take notes and consolidate information." Her
boss was also very supportive of ideas that Alexandra would bring to
the table. One such idea was an initiative she proposed: "I noticed,
being in the technology department which was primarily technicians,
audio engineers, and people running the control center, that in a
department of 48 people, there were only two women, of which I
was one. And I thought, there's something wrong here. Why aren't
they attracting more women in these technology fields? So I started a
little thing where we brought in, like, 20 or 30 girls from local middle
schools and high schools to give them a tour of the audio department

and basically expose them to careers that they maybe didn't even know existed. I had them go into the studios, I had them see audio engineers mixing, I had them go up into the control center, which is

"I noticed, being in the technology department . . . that in a department of 48 people, there were only two women, of which I was one. And I thought, there's something wrong here."

super cool because it looks like you're in a space ship. That was really exciting to me."

A Crisis of Self

Despite the excitement of working at such an interesting company in which she was able to expand and explore, she felt restless. "I was beginning to realize working in a 9-to-5 capacity in a cubicle, even at a really cool company, wasn't who I was." The real decision point came when an opportunity opened up for a promotion that would be a major step up from what she was currently doing. "It would have doubled my salary, it would have allowed me to work with legislators on public radio funding issues, it would have been

a communication position at the next level. In many ways, it was like this golden thing. And so, of course, I applied for it, and I got through a couple

"I was beginning to realize working in a 9-to-5 capacity, in a cubicle, even at a really cool company, wasn't who I was."

rounds of interviews, and then the man who would have been my boss took me out to lunch, and he told me they weren't going to give me the job. They decided to choose someone who had connections in local government, because they were really trying to do a lot of legislative work. And when he told me this, I started to cry. I realized, as I was weeping in front of my colleague, that I wasn't crying because I was sad I didn't get the job, but because I was *relieved*. I knew if he had offered it to me, I would have taken it. This man, who was a real sweetheart, then said to me that it was clear I didn't really want to be there. But it was hard. That company, I can't say enough good things about them. I loved working in radio. I got to meet so many of my heroes. Just knowing that they were producing great content that changed people's lives, there was so much to love."

Taking the Leap

But Alexandra couldn't hide from herself any longer the fact that, to discover her true calling, she needed to leave. "After that meeting," she says, "I think literally the next day, I went to my boss and told him I was leaving, and I asked him if he would give me a four-month window during which I could slowly transition out of my job while training my replacement. And he agreed. As soon as he said yes to that plan, the fire was ignited, because I had a date on the calendar. April 1st, 2010 would be my last paycheck. It scared me, but it also really got me hustling. Energized. I think this is something a lot of people struggle with when they're juggling a side-project or a heart-project with a full-time job, and they're sort of golden-handcuffed. There's never really an intense incentive to get things going. But for me, I knew that date was coming, and I needed to figure out my next move." This moment for Alexandra was an opening not only into a new life but also into one of the ways she would end up serving others. By recognizing that the traditional path was not for her, she gave herself and others permission

"April 1st, 2010 would be my last paycheck. It scared me, but it also really got me hustling."

to follow their own iconoclastic paths.

She launched into action. "I went into super-practical hyper-drive. I got a roommate to save money. I made sure I was saving as much as I possibly could to create a bit of a cushion. I hired a career coach, who really helped me to not only clarify what I was going to do and how to make money but also suggested very practical things like putting a website together. So I did a lot to get things in motion. I had already been doing a bit of freelance work here and there in addition to the radio work, but I started to really dial it up. I also began going out to lunch with people, telling them what I was doing, sending out my resumé, emailing past clients and letting them know I was available again. Just all of the stuff that you do. When the last day of my job came, I certainly had no idea that I would wind up building the business that I have today. I just thought: I'm going to give this a year, I'm going to do everything I can to be self-employed as a writer, and if it totally crashes and burns and I blow through my savings and I lose my house, or whatever, then at least I tried, and I can always get another job. I always had that as my plan Z. So off I went, and through a mixture of working hard, working my network, a couple of great lucky strokes and synchronicity, I managed to build something. I think in my first year of being self-employed, I made something like $500 more than my salary had been at the company. So I thought, I'm surviving. From there it just continued to grow. It worked, and for me it was the right choice."

"I'm going to give this a year … and if it totally crashes and burns … at least I tried."

There are both practical and idealistic lessons to draw from what Alexandra did. She did not just wish and hope her new business into existence. She worked it, hard, from every possible angle. As she said, she hired a coach, created a website, networked, and created a financial nest egg. But she also took a leap of faith. She let her passions guide her and took a chance on living the life she wanted. She also allowed her business to organically evolve, cultivating a willingness to expand and grow her abilities: "I started as a freelance writer and that quickly segued into primarily doing copywriting for marketing agencies and individuals. That, in turn, segued into a kind of ghost writing. Because people would come to me and say, I don't need you to write a tagline for me, but I'm working on a book, or I'm working on a digital program, or I'm putting a seminar together, could you help me with my curriculum, could you help me with my talk? It was often clients I had worked with in the past, who were then circling back to me and saying 'Can you do this?' And usually my response was, 'Well I never have, but let's see!' So then that kind of led into more consulting/coaching, and then that unfolded into people saying 'Have you ever taught workshops?' Then I started getting invited to do that, which positioned me more as a teacher/ coach. So today . . . the work I do is very much a hybrid of all of this. Sometimes people hire me to write for them, and other times they hire me to help them with their own writing projects, or to be in more of a teacher capacity. I think one thing leads to another. That's how it rolls. So this April will be my sixth year in business."

Keys to Success

Alexandra also had people who helped her along the way. "There were significant moments along the journey," she says, "where pretty high-profile business owners, motivational speakers, best selling authors, took note of me, hired me, and then spread the word about me after I did a great job for them." One woman in particular became a mentor to Alexandra during her first year on her own, and guided her into being all that she could. "Danielle LaPorte is a wonderful writer and motivational speaker, and in the circle of women entrepreneurs, she's, like, the high priestess. She was one of the first people who basically told me I needed to stop being people's 'assistant.' Because then, even though I was on my own, I was still kind of positioning myself as 'I can be your right-hand gal' kind of thing. And she told me it was time to have my own body of work. 'Where are your essays?' she asked. 'Where are your stories?' She encouraged me to position myself as someone who, yes, could be hired to be part of a creative team, but she didn't want me to only be that. And to have her see that kind of potential in me was transformative."

Alexandra continues to surround herself with supportive women. "Perhaps I'm living in some kind of magical bubble, but I only associate with women who support other women." She talks about how different things are in her generation from her mother's, where with less women in the workplace, the competition between women was fiercer, and thus not always as friendly. "Now, the fear factor's gone," she says.

"[Danielle LaPorte] told me it was time to have my own body of work. 'Where are your essays?' she asked. 'Where are your stories?'"

The Internet, of course, has also played an essential part in the development of Alexandra's career. "I would not be able to do the work I do without the Internet," she says. "My website and blog are like the entry point for people to find me." She makes the essential point that the best way to build an Internet business is by figuring out how best to help others. "The way that I've always approached self-promotion," she explains, "is that it is about being of service. I think for a lot of women, when you flip that switch from 'I'm out here sleazily promoting myself' to 'There are people that need what I've got, whom I can help,' it really changes the energy of it. So my approach in any networking event is how can I be of service, whether or not it leads to them hiring me or not." And two other factors come into play in her success. As she explains: "I try to write from the heart. I think if you do that consistently, and you're striking a resonant chord, people start talking about you. And the other thing that I think is at the

> *"The way that I've always approached self-promotion is that it is about being of service."*

core of the way that I promote my work is that I do really *work*. I'm not saying that to be self-aggrandizing, I'm just saying I take my work seriously. I'm very professional. I do what I say I'm going to do, and that's not common, unfortunately. A lot of people are very flaky, or they're not present. The biggest single way that I get new students, new readers, new clients is through referrals and word of mouth, in other words, people talking. And to me, when someone complains that marketing is so hard, what I always say to them is, start by taking an honest look at the quality of your work. Are there ways that you could dial it up? I think, if you start doing that, inevitably the referrals start coming in. It's not all you need to do, but that's where people ought to begin, in my opinion."

A World of Possibilities

The other thing that technology and the Internet allow people to develop is a more Renaissance approach to life. When information is available at the touch of a keystroke, when resources are so readily available, whole worlds of learning and exploring open up. "I have a friend, Kelly Rae Roberts, a wonderful visual artist," Alexandra says, "who calls herself a *possibilitarian*. Meaning, she moves through the world with a spirit of everything is possible, everything is figure-out-able. That's what I would say I am, a possibilitarian. And interestingly, my clients have run the gamut from every industry and career you can imagine, from physicians writing *New York Times* best-selling novels to women going through menopause and hormone care to burlesque dancers to Tarot card readers. I have gotten to interface with so many different types of people who all needed help telling their stories, and in doing so, I've learned a lot about these people and their lives. It's one of my favorite things about

"I have a friend ... who calls herself a possibilitarian. Meaning, she moves through the world with a spirit of everything is possible, everything is figure-out-able. That's what I would say I am, a possibilitarian."

what I do because I'm not just writing about, or for, one person or one topic or one thing. There's this cornucopia of people that I get to play with, which is really cool. Even within the context of my own work and business, although I make the majority of my income as a ghost writer and a writing coach (primarily for women entrepreneurs who are running different kinds of businesses), I always have a little collection of side-projects going on. I just wrote my first romance novel, for example, which I'm self-publishing. I've written a couple of other books that were published through traditional outlets. One of them was a journal for couples, and one of them was a book about gratitude and the art of writing a thank-you note. I'm also working on a children's book, a film script, and some fine arts collaborations where I've written poetry that was then put on paintings. So all of that feeds me as a Renaissance woman. Because if I was doing just one thing with the same company or the same people day in and day out, I'd go a little crazy. In fact, that's part of the reason I chose to leave the public radio world and start my own business, so I could have more freedom."

She also talks about the essential difference between a Renaissance-type person and a specialist. "The terms I hear are *scanners* and *divers*. A diver tends to be a person who goes deep, deep, deep into one topic. They are often drawn to the sciences or law. Doctors tend to be divers. Divers can be almost obsessive about their one thing. It's their world. I know this man, for example, who is a meteorologist, and weather and storm chasing is his obsession. That's all he cares about, pretty much. Scanners are more like Renaissance souls. They like to play in different fields, they find connections, they rarely choose one thing and just do that." Alexandra talks about the stigma of "dilettantism" that many of her Ren-style clients feel. "I hear from a lot of them that they identify as a Renaissance soul, but there's also almost a kind of sadness around that, a confusion or identity crisis. It's like they have "diver envy." They look at people who do one thing so well, and there's this longing. And these are people of all ages. I've had clients in their twenties, and

> *"A diver tends to be a person who goes deep, deep, deep into one topic ... Scanners ... like to play in different fields, they find connections, they rarely choose one thing and just do that."*

on the other end, in their sixties and even early seventies. What I find a lot of Renaissance souls are looking for is a sort of overarching mission or cause that serves as an umbrella for all the things they do. That's actually why a lot of people hire me, to help them see that, because they can't see it themselves. And it's usually very simple. One example that I use a lot, when I'm telling stories in workshops, is this woman I met who is a Yoga teacher, an interfaith minister, a wedding officiator, and also a writer. When I interviewed her and grilled her a little bit, she said 'I just want to add to the love in the world.' That was it. That was what she was trying to create through all of these different channels. And once she said that out loud, she felt such confidence, knowing that she had this cause driving all of her work. I feel like, if there's one thing Renaissance men or women are aching for, it's that overarching mission. Once you have that, there's a sense of integrity in your body of work, and it all makes sense. You're no longer just a dilettante."

"I feel like, if there's one thing Renaissance men or women are aching for, it's that overarching mission."

At this point in our conversation, Dale Franzen has joined us, and she offers a very relevant observation: "I discovered that the origin of the word *dilettante* is Latin," she says, "from the verb *delectare*, which means 'to delight,' which then became the verb in Italian, *dilettare*, also meaning 'to delight.' And the Italian noun *dilettante* originally meant 'a person loving the arts.' So that first meaning had nothing to do with dabbling or superficiality but instead reflected joy and love."

And joy and love are two things that are clearly reflected in the person and work of the young RenWoman Alexandra Franzen.

Ren Gems

Dale Franzen

"If you can imagine it, you can make it happen."

"Choose your spouse wisely. It can make all the difference."

"Renaissance people synthesize ideas, they connect dots."

"I'm pretty fearless. I always ask myself, What's the worst
that can happen? It's all about perspective."

"With the Broad Stage I wanted to create an artists' sandbox.
A place for trying new things. Where it was okay to fail."

Ren Gems

Alexandra Franzen

"Fear is the root of all stagnation."

"Pretending to be less happy, less smart, or less ambitious than you really are does not help you, your community, or the planet."

"What are you aching to make with your own fingers, your mind, your muscle and heart, your bare hands?"

"When you lead with curiosity—rather than convention— you'll be stunned by the gems you unearth."

"As an entrepreneur you will wonder if you're delusional, if anybody cares about what you're doing, and if your work really matters. The answers are no, yes and very much so."

7

MARINELA GOMBOSEV

"I always knew that I wanted to be a generalist; I wanted to work at the level of the bigger, broader picture."

Electrical engineer, market developer, MBA, technology and business executive, patent holder, fluent in several languages

Marinela Gombosev was nine years old when rumblings of war spread through her town of Tuzla in Bosnia and Herzegovina. Her mother, worried, packed up some things and told her two girls, "Let's get out of town for the weekend and go visit some relatives." Those relatives lived outside of Bosnia and Herzegovina, and it turned out that her mother had made a very wise decision. Their bus was the last bus to leave the region before war broke out. The borders were shut down, and everyone else was locked in—including Marinela's father, who didn't make it out until three months later. The family escaped to Germany, leaving everything behind. For them, it was a strange new country where they had few opportunities and, as immigrants among many fleeing Bosnians, were treated as second-class citizens. But her parents never lost their positive attitude and willingness to make sacrifices for a greater good, and Marinela learned from them lessons in resilience that would serve her for the rest of her life.

In 2015, Marinela Gombosev was inducted into the alumni Hall of Fame for the Henry Samueli School of Engineering at the University of California, Irvine. In 2013, she was featured in *OC Metro Magazine* as one of the "Hottest 25." This annual article, which has been a yearly tradition since the inception of the magazine in 1990, seeks to highlight Orange County, California, individuals who, as the magazine describes it: "are making headlines, shattering expectations, and building and leading in never before seen ways."

Marinela certainly fits this bill. Raised in Bosnia and Herzegovina, in Germany, and in the U.S., she has shown herself to be a resourceful, intelligent, driven, and highly ambitious woman who has developed multiple skill sets and has held positions of prestige and responsibility. And she's only 32!

It all started with her remarkable parents. In their native land of Bosnia and Herzegovina, they were both professionals. Her father was an electrical engineer, and her mother was an economist. Both were also multi-talented in their own right. They had, for example, designed and built their own home. That home was in Tuzla, a city to the north of Sarajevo (where the winter Olympics were held in 1984).

"They built our home, and then three years later, we had to leave it all behind!" Marinela says. "But my mother's attitude was: 'What choice do we have? We need to keep going forward, keep looking ahead and be positive, go with the changes.'"

And those changes were not easy. When they moved to Germany, her accomplished parents became grocery baggers. "We were second-class citizens," Marinela explains. "Because there were a lot of immigrants from Bosnia and there was no path to

"We were second-class citizens because there were a lot of immigrants from Bosnia, and there was no path to citizenship in Germany."

citizenship in Germany." For her, it was a challenge as well. "I had to not only learn a new language and make new friends, but I had to get used to a whole new cultural environment. So, I had to adapt very quickly."

Moving to the U.S.

The family spent five years in Germany. With so few options there, her parents considered returning to Bosnia, but soon ruled that out. "They didn't feel it was a good environment for my sister and me to grow up in," Marinela explains. "There were no real economic prospects and no stability in the country." So, they decided to try and move to the U.S.—more specifically to Orange County, California, where they had relatives.

"We ended up coming here as a family on a refugee program. We were at risk for returning to our home country because my mom's side is Muslim, and Muslims were being persecuted. So we were accepted under the U.S. refugee program. We were on a welfare program for six months; we were in low-income housing, and we had food stamps. But when all of that was happening, I wasn't quite aware of the stigma attached. I always knew my parents were hard-working.

"What I remember from that period is this very difficult adjustment, more so even than going from Bosnia to Germany. There were so many cultural differences! And even though I had learned a semester or two of English in a classroom setting, it was very hard. Still, I would say that within six months I spoke English pretty well, and within a year, both my sister and I had lost our accents."

Meanwhile, any ties with their homeland were hard to maintain. "We had family there," Marinela explains, "but I lost touch with friends. It was difficult to communicate back and forth. Even with family, there was rare communication." It would be many years, in fact, before they visited Bosnia and Herzegovina. "My grandparents on both sides are still there to this day," Marinela says, "but when we go and visit them and go back into that culture, it's a little bit odd because I've been so Americanized, and I don't belong to that world anymore." She calls herself, in fact, a "third culture kid." She explains: "That means you have grown up in multiple cultures. It's not just the one you were born into or inherited but multiple different ones. President Obama, for example, is a third culture kid. TCK's acquire certain traits as a result of that, which include resilience, adaptability, and the ability to seek out ways to connect to people."

> *"TCK's acquire certain traits as a result of that, which include resilience, adaptability, and the ability to seek out ways to connect to people."*

The First Glimmers of Leadership

Because of these cultural disconnects, Marinela often felt like she didn't belong. "My first years here, I felt like an outsider. Always. I never had a set group of friends; I was not often invited to parties."

But then, in high school, something changed. "In high school, when I joined sports, that's when I started developing strong relationships. I was in water polo and swimming and eventually became team captain of the water polo team. So it was really there that my leadership started to come out, and through that I acquired a network and group of friends. I think people gravitated towards me more when I was in a leadership role."

It was in college that her leadership skills really took off. "I joined the Society of Women Engineers, and I started really seeing the deficiencies in the clubs on campus. So when I became president of the society, I woke up one day and thought: I don't want to just run an organization. I don't just want to put this on my resumé. I want it to have a purpose. I thought, we have an incredible industry; I want to be the one that connects the student body with the industry. So I organized panels of women engineers to come and speak and inspire students about their experiences. And we had a big event called the Industry Networking Event, where we had a couple of people from Boeing come in, along with a number of others. I would cold call different companies, and say 'Hello, would you be interested in coming?'"

"I thought, we have an incredible industry; I want to be the one that connects the student body with the industry."

Her Job in Aerospace

Once Marinela got her electrical engineering degree she went directly into the aerospace industry. "This was an exciting field, and I jumped right in," she says. "I was responsible in part for designing circuits with components called 'transient voltage suppressors'— essentially circuits that protect the aircraft from a lightning strike. So I designed electronics that were inside the aircraft or on the wings. These little devices inside electronics boxes would absorb the energy from the lightning and ensure that nothing would get damaged and take the aircraft down.

"Eventually, I became

"I was responsible in part for designing circuits with components called 'transcient voltage suppressors' —essentially circuits that protect the aircraft from a lightning strike."

responsible not just for the circuit or the circuit board, but for an electronic box that had five or six different circuit boards on it, and I became the project engineer, which means I had a team of engineers under me who were responsible for different things, and I had to lead their efforts as well as the schedule and the budget. Even though it was challenging because I was the only woman on the project—and I was also the youngest—I loved that it was a leadership role. I had the chance, for example, to travel to Brazil and present to the customer!"

A Drive to Do More

Still, Marinela was brimming with ideas and the urge to expand. "I always wanted to do more and more and more but I was literally told by the general manager, 'If you move too fast, you'll crash and burn.' At the time, I didn't understand enough about my own ambition, and frankly I didn't accept it. I sensed

> "*I always wanted to do more and more and I was literally told by the general manager, 'If you move too fast, you'll crash and burn.'*"

that I was ambitious and driven, but I never would have used those words to describe myself. It wasn't until I went through some personal growth and did some seminars and classes to understand why I had this burning drive and why I got so frustrated when I couldn't get to that next stage that I began to accept it."

One thing she knew she needed was more outlets for her energy. "I wanted not only to do more," she explains, "but to explore other avenues. I felt like I was in a box and even when I got to do more in the world I was in, I wanted to experience *another* world." Motivated by her innate interests in leadership and management, she decided to get an MBA.

She enrolled in the Master of Business Administration program at Pepperdine University. There, she took off with a vengeance. The program allowed her to not only develop her leadership and business skills but also to do so in a multifaceted and extensive way. "I didn't just go to the classes. Pepperdine has these E to B projects—'Education to Business'—where they pair student groups with businesses and give them a challenge or a project. I wanted to learn as much about every industry and every company as I could. So I ended up taking on five projects during the two years. Normally, you might do two, but I took electives just so I could get that experience. On every single one of them I was the team leader."

C200 Scholar

Then came for Marinela a career-and-life-enhancing opportunity. "I applied for the Scholarship for Women in Business," she says. The scholarship program was run by the prestigious group for women in business called The Committee of 200, or C200. "This group of women consists of some of the world's most influential and powerful women," Marinela explains, "So you have the President of Google and the President of Intel and just a lot of exceptional entrepreneurs. They set up this foundation for young women—the 'C200 Scholars.' I found myself identifying a lot with the criteria of the scholarship. It was a leadership type of award for successful entrepreneurship or for advancement as a female within corporate environments. I interviewed with these incredible women, and I ended up getting in! It has literally changed my life being a part of

"I just felt so at home in that female-oriented environment and hearing people finally say, 'Look, it's okay to be ambitious in this world. Go for it!'"

this group. I just felt so at home in that female-oriented environment and hearing people finally say, 'Look, it's okay to be ambitious in this world. Go for it! Think even bigger.' This light switch flipped, and I was like, Okay, that is what I'm going to do!"

She started with the scholars group itself. When one of the C200 members and mentors said to her and two fellow scholars, "Look at all these scholars all over the country and abroad, they don't talk to each other. It would be great if they all had their own group," a fire was lit under Marinela. "Over the next three years," she says, "I led the team, and we formed this network called the C200 Scholars Network. Members are all over the country and all over the world. There are people in England, South Africa, Dubai, and Israel. We also started putting together these sub-group councils where we could speak with each other about personal issues, business issues and kind of mentor each other. It was peer mentoring. We would also bring in speakers from the Committee. They absolutely supported us. We now have a leadership group, as well. I'm the Chair of the Scholars Network with over 100 scholars worldwide and growing! It was like building an organization within this incredible group of women. Our visionary team seized an opportunity to create something significant for the next generation of women business leaders. It's such a beautiful and supportive environment and everyone's so positive and encouraging. I think, as a woman, that's another thing I thrive on: encouragement, rather than an environment of pervasive criticism."

A Chance to Fly

During her studies, she had continued working at her job in aerospace. A couple of years after graduation, however, she knew it was time for a change. With more confidence and with both technical and business skills in her toolbox, she applied to and was hired by a company called Source Scientific—later bought out by the BIT Group—which developed and sold advanced medical devices. Her responsibilities included forming client relationships, dealing with the product line, and managing the engineers. Unlike her previous job, at BIT she was encouraged to fly. "The CTO (Chief Technology Officer), who was also the founder of the company, trusted me with the biggest project that they had in their thirty-year history. It was a multi-million-dollar project, and he gave me a chance! I'll never forget that. We are friends to this day."

Her project was the development of a robotic allergy analyzer to test serum for a number of patients for a large quantity of allergens. "It was a multi-year project. I started it with a team of six, and I ended up growing that to a team of twenty. So I had twenty engineers, and all of them,

"It was a multi-million-dollar project, and he gave me a chance!"

with the exception of one, were older than me, with the majority being men. Source Scientific was a very dynamic, very entrepreneurial company. I really had a chance to go from a big corporate environment where I was in this little box to a smaller entrepreneurial company where I could say to the CTO, 'I want to do this and that … ' and he'd say, "Well, what are you doing in my office talking about it? Go and do it.' Now I had that freedom."

In this environment, Marinela also had the opportunity to really hone her style of leadership. A lot of what she did involved team dynamics. "It's not just about the work; it's also about the people. I always made it a point to communicate to the

"I could say to the CTO, 'I want to do this and that . . .' and he'd say, 'Well, what are you doing in my office talking about it? Go and do it.'"

team: 'This is where we are going. This is the bigger picture. This is why we are doing this. I know it's hard now, but there's going to be an accomplishment at the end, and we'll celebrate.' In fact, three years into the project, our team was awarded a patent for our work! But it's difficult when you have a multi-year mission. I'm very driven, but not everybody else is, so it's also about finding ways to motivate people." To her, being a good communicator is key. "I always think of communication as an art form," she says. "I can't say that I've completely mastered it, but it's something that I think a lot about. I'm very careful in the words that I choose when leading a team."

When asked if being a woman factors into her leadership style, she acknowledges the role of empathy in her style, a trait which she considers to be generally more feminine. "If I find a disruptive personality, I intervene with him or her. I don't let negativity drag down my team. However, first I have a specific conversation with the person and try to understand where they are coming from. Because their attitude is coming from somewhere, right? And if I can turn it around, isn't that so much better? I've done that on a number of occasions. But if you're one of those negative people, and you're letting that infect the rest of my team, then I will see if there is a better fit for you on a different project."

Marinela made another career move when she was recruited to Evoke Neuroscience, a company that specializes in cutting edge health technologies. "It was like another leap into the generalist mold," she remarks. "It took advantage of all of the skill sets I acquired during my MBA, as well as my past work experiences. I had an opportunity to use

> *"It was like another leap into the generalist mold. It took advantage of all of the skill sets I acquired during my MBA, as well as my past work experiences."*

my engineering background, my project management capabilities, my marketing strategy abilities, and my experience in the industry because Evoke deals with medical devices, which I had done at BIT." When recommended for the job by a colleague, she was intrigued by the company for a number of reasons: "It's a very entrepreneurial company. It's fourteen people, very small. The founders, both of them PhD's and scientists, needed somebody with a business focus, somebody who could understand the technology and the product, but then also figure out the marketing and sales." They hired her as Executive VP of Operations & Marketing, which threw her into a brand new deep end.

"Talk about the discomfort level of that learning curve!" she says. "Of course, I had the education, and I had done some projects, but there are people who spend their entire career in marketing and sales! I hired an international sales team of thirty, and they all said, 'OK, Marinela, you've never done sales, and you are female!' They are all men and very experienced, that's why I hired them. So I'm really learning very quickly (and sometimes painfully) how

"They all said, 'OK, Marinela, you've never done sales, and you are female!'"

to manage this group of cult cowboys all over the country, and we are succeeding as a team. At the same time, I'm developing the marketing strategy and collateral and branding. I'm also bringing on all the operational tools like salesforce.com—which provides Cloud computing technology and is a tool we need in order to be able to service our customers and communicate with our leads. That's a whole other learning curve, which is wonderful, and I love it!"

What's interesting about Marinela, and emblematic of all the RenWomen we've interviewed, is that daunting learning curves stimulate and excite her, rather than intimidate her.

When asked about marriage or children, whether she sees these things in her life, she answers, "Having a family is important to me. I am looking to have kids. I always think of the term 'having it all' and I haven't quite figured that out yet. But I am looking for the right kind of partner ,and I'm sure that time will come. I see family as life-enhancing, and I want to have that experience, even if my career has to take a backseat for a while. But I do have a lot of tools and support available to me that I plan to use, like, for example, my mom. I mean, I was raised in part by my grandparents."

> *"I see family as life-enhancing, and I want to have that experience."*

And certainly Marinela was no worse for it. In fact, in so many ways, her mother was her model and her inspiration. As she says: "I have so much respect for my mom. She is the reason we are here in the U.S., and anywhere, for that matter. She just has so much energy and life, and she is feminine and tough at the same time. She is just . . . wow! She sews and knits, she's into interior design, and she is an incredibly savvy business woman and all-around navigator of life. She negotiates like a pro, too, and is just amazing."

From one powerhouse RenWoman, it seems, came another. And it is clear that Marinela is just going to continue to grow, expand, and soar!

Ren Gems

Marinela Gombosev

"If you view life as an adventure, you are more likely to enjoy its successes, be open to its opportunities, and be more resilient to its challenges."

"I never want to stop learning."

"It is my life mission to continue to improve the ways in which I can make a positive impact on the world and people around me."

"New and challenging experiences don't scare me, they energize me."

"Recognizing and embracing my own ambition has unlocked my desire to leave a mark."

8

EVA HALLER

"I am not a leader; I am a mentor."

Mentor, philanthropist, psychologist, social/political activist,
arts patron, chairman and board member of multiple non-profit
organizations, Magnusson Fellow, recipient of multiple awards for
humanitarian achievement and mentorship

*In 1944, Hungary was occupied by Nazi Germany, and Jews were
being deported to concentration camps. Eva Haller was fourteen years old
when she stood in a line of fellow Jewish children who had found refuge
in the Scottish Mission of Budapest. It had been a safe haven for while,
but now Hungarian soldiers had raided it. She stood in this line, holding
the hand of a ten-year-old boy for whom she had been given responsibility
when her parents and his mother had gone into hiding. As a young soldier
approached, Eva knew it was death if she didn't think of something fast.
So she pulled herself up to her full adolescent height, stared the soldier in
the eye, and told him she was much too young and beautiful to die. With
this, the astounded soldier let her go, as well as the ten-year-old whom she
grabbed as she escaped. Of course, with no money, with no clothes except
the ones on her back, and in the dead of winter, this was only the start of
her troubles.*

Eva Haller's life story is so astounding you would think it came straight from the pages of an epic novel. From her upbringing in upper- class Budapest, Hungary, to her escape from the Nazis, to a life of poverty and an abusive spouse in Ecuador, to cleaning houses as an illegal alien in the United States, and even to a suicide attempt, Eva has survived ordeals that would make most people crumble in despair. But the fire of resourcefulness and strength that glow so clearly in the woman we are privileged to feature in our book must have also existed, even if only as a spark, as she faced all these challenges. Because Eva fought her way out of misfortune after misfortune and created not only a life of success, but one of kindness, philanthropy, and mentorship.

The War Years

Eva was born in Budapest in 1930 to wealthy Jewish parents who had converted to Catholicism. Although she never felt close to her parents, Eva adored her brother, John, who was seven years older than she. Like a Pied Piper, where he went, she followed. This included, in 1942 and 1943, helping John, who was involved in the Hungarian resistance, print anti-Nazi leaflets and distribute them by cover of darkness. But in 1944, the Germans marched into Hungary, and John was put into forced labor.

Eva's family mistakenly felt they were safe because they had been a Christian family since Eva's father had converted in 1919. As she says, "My father felt that nobody would touch us, because, after all, we were not Jewish; he served in the Hungarian army, and we had documents indicating that we were good upright, citizens. But mostly because we weren't Jewish. By all the laws those days, anybody who was converted before 1930 was not considered a Jew. But that was before Hitler."

To paint a picture of what their lives then became, Eva gives the analogy of a frog in a pot of water. "If you put a frog in hot water, it dies quickly, but if you put the frog in cold water and heat it up, it can live longer. It's a slow death." That was the way of the Nazi occupation. "At first they restricted us to going out only three times a week," she says. "Then they demanded that we hand in all of our radios, cameras, and tools of communication. Then they removed us from our home, and we had to move into the Jewish quarter, which was a place where there were apartments from which they had already removed Jews into concentration camps. So we moved into those people's homes. Finally, we all had to wear a five-inch Jewish star on our clothes, and we were not allowed to go out into the street without the star. Although," she adds, illustrating signs of her early defiance, "I never wore mine."

It was then that Eva's parents knew they had to go into hiding. Meanwhile, they decided the safest

"We all had to wear a five-inch Jewish star on our clothes, and we were not allowed to go out into the street without the star."

place for Eva would be the Scottish Mission in Budapest, which was a boarding school for well-to-do girls, both Christian and Jewish, but had more recently also become a refuge for Jews. Eva was accompanied by a ten-year-old boy whose mother had gone into hiding with her parents (his father had been captured). The Mission was run by a compassionate Scots woman named Jane Haining, who is said to have wept when she saw the yellow stars on the Jewish girls' clothes. The Church of Scotland, concerned, sent repeated letters urging Jane Haining to come home. Her response was: "If these children needed me in days of sunshine, how much more do they need me in these days of darkness?"

"She was an amazing woman," Eva says. "And she saved my life. Those couple of months that I was able to be in that place during which time they rounded up all the last possible Jews left in the city, I was safe because of Jane. I just feel so grateful to her. She didn't have a Jewish bone in her body, and she knew that she was putting her life in danger." And in fact, Eva never met the woman who saved her because shortly before Eva arrived at the Mission, Jane was arrested on suspicion of "espionage on behalf of England and working among Jews" and was sent to Auschwitz, where she died at the age of 47.

After two months of safety, Hungarian soldiers—under German command—raided the school, and this is when Eva came up with the words that saved her and the ten-year-old in her care. As she describes it, "At that point, it was like, I don't care, to hell with it. Out of a feeling of sheer 'I-don't-give-a-damn,' I said, 'I'm not going with you. I'm much too young and much too beautiful to die. I'm leaving!' And the poor young soldier was taken aback. He said, 'Then hurry up, go.' And I left and I was gone maybe 100 feet, when I realized, 'Oh shit, I can't go without the kid!' So I went back and I said, 'Oops, I forgot something,' and grabbed the boy and started running with

"I said, 'I'm not going with you. I'm much too young and much too beautiful to die.'"

him." (This was an early indication of a characteristic that Eva would carry throughout her life—that of a brazen resourcefulness.)

Now in many accounts of Eva's life, the story stops here—at the soldier letting her go. But, as Eva puts it, "That wasn't the big deal. The big deal was, 'Now what?' It was December, it was snowing, the streets were full of snow banks. I had no clothes and no money, and I had a kid. A scared ten-year-old holding onto me for dear life. I got frost bite in my knee, which still to this day has a scar."

With no idea of where to go, Eva decided to walk the long

distance back to her home. The beautiful modern apartment building where she had grown up was now empty of Jews—those apartments having been given to non Jews. She could only think of one thing to do: "We went to the floor above our old apartment, which was owned by my mother's best friend, who was a countess and who couldn't have been more Christian. But she had a Jewish husband, whom she was hiding. So in some way, I can understand the fact that our arrival was not taken with glee. I asked if we could stay the night until I figured out what to do next. But mainly I came to her because she would know where my parents and the boy's mother were. I didn't know, because they had felt it would be safer for me not to know. In some way, I was hoping that the countess would keep us. We could hear the bombing. We knew from Radio Free Europe the end of the war was near. So I just figured if we could live another couple of months, we would be safe." Instead, the countess told them where to find their parents, gave them two sandwiches, and asked them to leave.

Her parents were living in a blue-collar, industrial suburb. Although Eva now knew where, she did not know the name under which they were hiding or who was hiding them. When she arrived in the suburb and starting asking around, this alone could *"I just figured if we could live another couple of months, we would be safe."* have given them away. "Luckily, the woman who was hiding my parents came out and invited us in, and then we all made up this story that we were not our parents' children but we were their niece and nephew, to explain why we hadn't been with them before."

It was a difficult time. Because of the constant air raids, 150 people often spent up to twenty-four hours a day in a one-room air-raid shelter. There were also posters appearing everywhere saying that if you hid a Jew or you knew of anyone who was hiding a Jew, then you would be shot. With that many people in a room together, it was not always easy to avoid giving themselves away. For example, even the games she and the ten-year-old played were suspicious. "We played chess. And chess just wasn't a working class pastime. And then, every once in a while, I didn't remember that my mother wasn't my mother and what to call her, 'Aunty,' or whatever. So we were incredibly fortunate not to have gotten caught."

In early 1945, Soviet forces liberated Budapest. Or, as Eva puts it, "They 'liberated' us by taking whatever we had, which was almost nothing, and by raping all the women." She tells one harrowing story of her own near-rape: "Our little room where we were hiding was taken over by a Soviet corporal who was very kind to me and brought me food, real food. Then at some moment he decided to rape me, and it was

> *"[The Soviets] 'liberated' us by taking whatever we had, which was almost nothing, and by raping all the women."*

an evening in January. It was horrendous weather. My father ran out to find the Soviet headquarters and convince the head of it to come back and save me. It took such courage for my father to do that! To get that man to come back with him, to remove the corporal from my body. Because my best friend and her mom were raped twenty-four times! And when the mom tried to protect her daughter, they shot her to death and kept on raping my friend. The Soviet occupation of Hungary was a very shameful moment."

When the war officially ended, Eva and her parents returned to their home. "There were people living in our apartment," Eva explains, "but they kindly shared with us. There was no school at that point, as there were no windows in any building in Budapest because of the bombing. So we lived without windows, and we didn't go back to school for a few months, and we didn't have money, and we didn't have food. It felt funny to be so poor, but it was okay because we were still living in the apartment from when we were rich. And Mother was selling whatever we still had."

Meanwhile, her father decided he was the chief of the building and of everyone who lived there. His family wealth had come from owning the largest bakery chain in Hungary, and the main store was a few blocks away. "So," Eva explains, "my father would go everyday with a big rucksack on his back and bring back bread for the entire community. But the bread wasn't made out of flour, since there was no flour. It was made out of dried bean or dried peas. You can't imagine the weight of a loaf of bread when it's made out of beans or peas. He was carrying something like sixty or eighty pounds on his shoulders because he wanted to feed the building. This after all that time in the shelter, lying down or sitting in a corner."

Then news came about Eva's brother John. During the war, he had escaped with four comrades from the labor camp. Their intention was to

"He was carrying something like sixty or eighty pounds on his shoulders because he wanted to feed the building."

go to Yugoslavia to join up with Tito and the Partisans, but, while hiding in an abandoned cottage, they heard the noise of a German military unit approaching. "My brother told his four friends to go out the back door," Eva explains. "And he would stay and cover for them." While his comrades escaped, this act of sacrifice got him shot.

When her father heard the news about his son, this, combined with the physical stress of carrying the heavy rucksack, caused him to have a heart attack. He became bedridden, and in and out of the hospital until he died several years later, in 1951. This, of course, made life even more difficult for Eva and her mother. "Father had a very small pension that helped a little and by that time our housemates had disappeared and mother rented out what used to be my room, which helped to pay the rent."

Of course, the effect on Eva of her beloved brother's death was devastating and long-lasting. "For years," she says, "I was so fearful of loving because I just felt that I would lose that person. I wanted so much to love, and I was so afraid of the pain of loss. That stayed with me a long time."

> *"For years I was so fearful of loving because I just felt that I would lose that person."*

Life in Ecuador

In 1948, Eva's mother decided there was no life for her daughter in Budapest, and encouraged her to get out of the country. Since there was no clothing for Eva, her mother took John's suit to the tailor, where they made a skirt out of his pants and shortened the jacket. "So I wore my brother John's suit, which was his one and only good suit, for years," Eva says. "It was the only thing I owned. That was okay because I felt he was with me all the time."

Getting out of now Soviet-occupied Hungary was no easy task. But, once again, Eva's resourcefulness came into play. She was seeing a young man at the time, with whom, although she was only eighteen, she had gotten engaged. "I think we both realized, soon after, that it was a bad idea," she says. But fortunately this young man worked in a passport office, so Eva made him a deal. "I told him, 'I'll give you back the ring if you can get me a passport. Wouldn't you like to get rid of me?' And he said he'd love to get rid of me." So, passport in hand, and with only twenty dollars and a couple of pieces of jewelry,

> *"I told him, 'I'll give you back the ring if you can get me a passport.'"*

she nervously made the train trip through the four occupied zones of Europe, finally boarding a ship out of Genoa, Italy, heading to South America. The only place she could go was a small village in Ecuador where an aunt and uncle lived. When she arrived there, it was quite a shock. "They lived in a small town with no electricity and no sewer system. I came from the fanciest building in Budapest - even if it wasn't fancy anymore. I grew up with electric appliances, with a subscription to the opera and concerts every night at the music academy. Now here I was in a village where the *Indios* would crouch on the ground to pee and then pick lice out of each other's hair. It was a very basic life for my eighteen-year-old self!" Later they moved to the city of Quito, but their lives were still substandard given that her aunt and uncle were quite poor.

Eva soon met and married a military man, who was quite handsome, but as it turned out, very poor marriage material. At the time, she felt she had no choice.

"I had nothing else I could do," she says. "I couldn't get a job; I didn't speak good enough Spanish. Even if I did, there were no jobs for women and I had no training. I couldn't get to the United States because I couldn't get a visa. I couldn't go back to Hungary as I was stateless— they had revoked my passport. So there was nothing more I could do at that point. Nothing."

> *"I couldn't get to the United States because I couldn't get a visa. I couldn't go back to Hungary as I was stateless— they had revoked my passport. So there was nothing more I could do."*

It didn't take long before she realized she had traded one sort of hell for another. "The first night we were married he was so drunk that he left the house to go to the whore-house where he had a favorite whore. I tried to explain to him that *I* was his new favorite whore.

But what happened next felt like a rape. The next day the sheets were full of blood and I was in so much pain! About three or four months after the marriage, I got pregnant because I was told I had to and also I didn't know how not to. By this time, my husband was out every evening and when he came home at night all jacked up, he would beat me mercilessly."

One night, she just couldn't take it any longer. "I was miserable, and there was no hope for anything. I took out his gun, and I stood at the window trying to figure out to hold the gun to my head, so I wouldn't botch the job. We lived on the main floor and the light was on. I suddenly saw a little Indio woman looking in at me, with her

"I took out his gun, and I stood at the window trying to figure out how to hold the gun to my head, so I wouldn't botch the job."

Indio hat and a baby on her back. She had her nose pressed against the window, and I became so embarrassed that I dropped the gun. I thought: *This woman has her baby on her back, and I'm pregnant with a baby, and I'm killing a baby. And even though I am not fit to have a baby right now, it's a human life, and I'm responsible for it.* So I dropped the gun."

She realized she had to leave this man. Luckily, her aunt and uncle were willing to take her and her baby in. She worked in a bookstore to help out and spent every available hour trying to get a visa to go to the United States, where she felt there might be hope for a good life. She had other relatives living there, her father's sister and two children. She finally obtained a visa to visit them. She traveled there alone and, once there, tried to get a student visa, but it was impossible. Nonetheless, she remained as an illegal alien, attending college and taking jobs cleaning houses—sending whatever money she could back to her child and to her aunt and uncle.

Turning Point

Then something happened that would change her life forever. Friends told her about a place called International House, a residence founded in 1924 and originally funded by John D. Rockefeller. International House was a place where foreign students from all different countries, working on graduate degrees, could live together and and learn about each others' countries and customs. Her friends encouraged Eva to apply. She did, although she thought her chances were slim. "I went there, and I met Miriam McDonald, the Dean of Admission," she says. "Here I was, twenty-three, I hadn't finished my bachelor's degree, and I was a divorced mother with a child. Plus, I was working. At the International House you had to be a graduate student and you couldn't work because they want you to have time to interact with the other students. But I didn't have enough money to go to college and *not* work. So I was totally unqualified, and there was no precedent for anyone like me to be allowed in. Why Miriam McDonald decided that I was the kid for whom she was going to break every rule, I will never know. But she changed my life."

It is interesting to contemplate why indeed Miriam McDonald allowed Eva in. Clearly she saw something in this young woman that perhaps Eva didn't yet see in herself. Embers of intelligence, commitment and strength that just needed the right spark to ignite into flame.

In fact, within months after Eva was accepted into the International House, she was the chair of the student council. And she was taking twenty-one credits at night and working all day in a jewelry store for fifty cents an hour. "It was as if . . . after all those years of drifting from one horror to another, I needed to validate myself. And always, in the back of my mind, was my brother. It was an offering to him." Since the moment her beloved brother John had died, Eva knew, if given the opportunity, she would live

> *"It was as if . . . after all those years of drifting from one horror to another, I needed to validate myself. And always, in the back of my mind, was my brother. It was an offering to him."*

her life as a testament to him. His courage and integrity, as well as his deep concern for others had imprinted themselves on her heart, and she wanted to live in a way that would make him proud. The International House provided her the first opportunity to do so.

"The International House gave me the basis for everything I am today," Eva says. As a student leader, she attended board meetings with the likes of David Rockefeller, and she attended a student council dinner where Eleanor Roosevelt sat on one side of her, Dag Hammarskjold on the other, and David Rockefeller across from her. "I felt so honored to be there, and once I realized I was going to be seated next to Mrs. Roosevelt, I planned to ask questions and to absorb and learn from her. But," she laughs, "the truth is, she was more interested in talking to Dag Hammarskjold. Although . . . when I worked in the United Nations gift shop, she would come in and buy Christmas presents. So, I had the pleasure of serving Eleanor Roosevelt there for a couple of years."

Many of the friends Eva made at the International House have remained her friends to this day. "They became my family," she explains. "And they still are my family." In a full-circle moment, Eva was recently honored at the International House.

Interestingly, Eva also recently attended a celebration for David Rockefeller's 100th birthday. She went up to him and said, "I'm Eva Haller. I'm old and you're old, but I want to take this opportunity to thank you." And she told him how important the International House had been to her, especially being able to attend events like that student council dinner. "And he said to me, 'You know, I remember that evening. It was the only time we had Dag Hammarskjold with us.'"

Another International House connection that helped launch Eva in the right direction, was Dr. Ruth Westheimer (Yes, *that* Dr. Ruth). Long before Westheimer became a famous sexologist, she and Eva were friends who met through International House's Jewish group. Eva was working on her bachelor's degree in psychology when Ruth recommended her for a summer job working with the autistic child of William Shawn, the editor of the *New Yorker*. "I worked with Mary Shawn for many, many months until the doctors felt that there was nothing more that could be gained. I was asked to institutionalize Mary. The parents didn't have the strength to take her up to Massachusetts, to the institution where she has lived ever since."

Because of this position with the Shawns, Eva was able to get a job as a kindergarten teacher at a school for the mentally handicapped, called the Berman School. Here, she discovered she had another innate skill.

The four students in Eva's classroom were autistic. "None of them spoke," she says, "and they all hit their heads, and they hit me. But by the end of the year, they all spoke, and they never hit anything, and I was declared the greatest miracle worker ever. But I was very lucky. There was a sink in the room, and I got a lot of soap powder, and we played a lot of water games, and there was a kitchen, too. So we would make Jello, and we would make

> *"None of them spoke, and they all hit their heads, and they hit me. But by the end of the year, they all spoke, and they never hit anything."*

scrambled eggs, and I had a recording of 'Mickey Mouse' playing every morning, and we would march around our little room. Everything I did with them was instant gratification. I felt the secret to autism was instant gratification. They never had to be intolerant; they never had to be in pain. There was always something to do, in the instant.

"By the end of the year my students did so well that the school decided that I would never have a classroom again, that I was basically a born therapist, and I became a therapist for the entire school. All the kids in school became my patients. I loved it." She was a therapist for six years and got a big name in the field. At that time, in 1956, there was little literature on autism or schizophrenia. But one of the few prevailing theories was that both were caused by a lack of parental connection at birth. "But that was a problem for me," says Eva, "because if that were true, why did a mother have three other kids, and none of them had autism or schizophrenia?" So she took guilt off the table, which of course made the mothers feel better and, in turn, they related to their children better. In this way, Eva was well ahead of her time.

Home and Hearth?

During this period, Eva met the man who would become her second husband. It had been important for her to find an American husband who was secure financially because this was the only way she could bring her son from Ecuador. "I couldn't go back to Ecuador to bring my son out because I wouldn't have gotten back in, and there was no reason that they would've

> "I couldn't go back to Ecuador to bring my son out because I wouldn't have gotten back in, and there was no reason that they would've allowed him in."

allowed him in. I needed to find a nice American man who wanted to marry me and have my son around, but also who earned a living because what I earned as a teacher or therapist was not enough to support me and a kid." The man that she met appeared to qualify. "He seemed like a nice guy. He was never married, he was twenty-nine years old, and he had his parents still living with him at his home in Queens. It was not a big home, not a fancy home, but it was a home. And he had a profession, he was an engineer."

They married a year later. And Eva was able to get her visa and working permit and to finally bring her son from Ecuador. He was now eight years old. It was not a smooth transition for him. "He hated me. He kept on threatening to leave and go back, and I said, 'I don't blame you. I'm not sure I want to be a mother either, and I can understand that you are having a hard time being my son when you had such good parents back there.'" Instinctively, Eva knew what might help. Since her son only spoke Spanish, which made him feel more out of place in the U.S., she enrolled him in a United Nations school. As she puts it, "Everyone was a foreigner there. That made it so much easier on him."

The family moved at one point from Queens to New Jersey, and the drive to her job on Long Island became impossible. But to get other jobs in her field, she knew she had to complete a graduate degree, so she went for her master's in social work at Hunters College. Around that time, her marriage fell apart. Her husband was having an affair with his secretary and he took off with all their money, leaving her only their house, with a large portion of its mortgage unpaid. So now, very isolated out in New Jersey, and with little money, Eva had to sell the house.

Not long after that, in 1964, her life completely changed again. She met Murray Roman—and it was love at first sight. But true love frightened Eva, and she tried everything to push him away. She still struggled with the fear of loss that had plagued her since losing her brother. "Murray loved me so much, and he said to me, 'Why are you running away from me? Where are you going?' I answered, 'I don't know, I feel so insecure, I feel so hurt about being hurt.' And he said, 'But I haven't hurt you.' 'But you will,' I said. He responded, 'Then why don't you wait to feel hurt until I hurt you.'"

> *"He said to me, 'Why are you running away from me? Where are you going?'"*

She couldn't argue with this logic. "Murray's ability to deal with my neurosis after losing John has been, really, one of the single most important facts in my life. I realized I was running away from the one relationship that could give me joy and pleasure and security." And so, finally, Eva allowed herself to love again. And, as she puts it, "Life for the next twenty years became pure magic."

Murray was in public relations at the time, and consulted for a number of charities. Then he was asked to look at a political campaign, and he subsequently had the innovative idea of putting together a catalog for candidates that contained everything from bumper stickers to buttons to speeches. Eva became his partner in the business, a testament to Murray's recognition and respect for Eva's business skills. "We provided anything that any candidate could possibly need in order to run," she says. "So it became the bible of our candidates. We also offered to make films, arrange car rentals from Hertz Rent-A-Car, get them American Express credit cards, and deal with Western Union. So there was absolutely nothing else that any human being could possibly need in a candidacy."

They called their company Campaign Communications Institute of America, and it took off like gangbusters. It was a game changer for the business of politics. "No one had ever done this before," Eva remarks. "*The New York Times* wrote an article about us, and then *Newsweek* came out, and they did an article. Then on and on and on, and by

"The New York Times wrote an article about us, and then Newsweek came out, and they did an article."

the end of that year we had every country that ever had an election, from Australia to Fiji, sending their reporters out to interview us." At its height, Murray and Eva had 1,200 people working for them. One of the most revolutionary aspects of their company was their very effective form of political telemarketing. Targeted telemarketing was not something, at that point, that had ever been used. What was usually done were just random cold calls, using the telephone book. "50% of what we did was taping a message from the candidate and getting it out to interested voters," Eva explains. "Murray invented a device, shaped like a donut, that attached to a phone and transmitted a taped message. And using a list provided by the Democratic party," Eva explains, "we would call people and say, 'Mrs. Thomas, we have a message here, a recorded message from Vice President Humphrey. Would you be interested in listening to it? It will only take two minutes.' And if they said yes, we would press 'play.' Then afterwards we would say, 'We hope you will vote for him,' or ask if they had any questions. This was the first time ever to have a true political telephone marketing campaign." And of course, politicians have used this form of marketing in their campaigns, in some form or another, ever since.

Eva and Murray were intensely involved in the 1968 elections, working eighteen hours a day, seven days a week. After the elections were over, and with a profit of one million dollars, they felt set for life and decided to close shop. They donated much of their equipment to UNICEF, and decided to follow up on invitations they had received from countries all over the world who wanted to learn from them about the democratic election process. They presented their itinerary to UNICEF and offered to use their expertise to also aid children's education around the globe. UNICEF was happy to accept. "So we bought plane tickets for $50,000 for around the world," Eva says. They traveled to Hong Kong, Singapore, Malaysia, Burma, Thailand, and Australia, along with other countries.

Australia was a particularly surprising experience because of the degree of male machismo. As Eva explains it, "Whenever we arrived in countries, we would always be welcomed at the airport because we were famous, and we would be photographed and interviewed. In Australia, they didn't want to photograph me; they only wanted my husband. But he refused to be photographed without me, so they took my picture. But the next day, the headline in *The Australian* only had his picture. So then they asked him to go on TV, and he said

> *"In Australia they didn't want to photograph me; they only wanted my husband. But he refused to be photographed without me."*

he didn't do that, only his wife did, so they had to accept me." In that interview, Eva called out the Australians. "I pointed out that this was the most macho country so far we had been to. The next day in the newspapers, there was an opinion poll about this American psychologist, which asked if the Australian population agreed that they were macho. It was quite the experience."

Their visit to the Philippines turned out to be particularly harrowing. Although Eva and Murray were personally opposed to the Marcos regime, their policy was to not speak about or interfere in a country's politics. Their job was to promote a UNICEF program for children, along with another program that dealt with medical equipment. However, when Aquino, who was running against the

Marcoses, invited them to a sugar plantation, things got tense. "We had jeeps, provided to us by the Aquinos," Eva says, "several of them in front of us and behind us, with machine guns! Once I realized we were not on friendly territory at all times, I never had one good night's sleep in the Philippines."

"We had jeeps, provided to us by the Aquinos, several of them in front of us and behind us, with machine guns!"

At some point during their travels, Eva and Murray realized their money was running out. It looked like a million dollars wasn't going to take them as far as they thought it would. Luckily, they had received a call while in Bangkok from *Readers Digest*, who wanted them to start a telemarketing campaign for them. So, once home, they revived their company and started what would become a four-year commitment to *Readers Digest*. Soon other publishers became interested in working with them as well. Murray also invented a program for compiling a library of all the university presses. He also wrote and published a textbook on telemarketing that is still used today.

But running a business was not the only thing that interested Murray and Eva. They were both passionate about social causes. Even before she met Murray, Eva had chosen to take her 13-year-old son and go to Selma to join the Martin Luther King march. "To be more specific," she says, "we flew into Montgomery and started going backwards to join the marchers that started in Selma." That day, Eva came face to face, once again, with a frightening situation. How she responded was

"We flew into Montgomery and started going backwards to join the marchers that started in Selma."

indicative of her strength of character. "We did the grand finale and that was scary! There were sheriffs with big German Shepherds and sticks. There was nothing glorious about Montgomery that day. I couldn't wait to get out. I was scared for my kid, and I was scared for me. But I wanted to see it through, witness as much as I could. After all, I hadn't flown all that way just to run away."

She is grateful to have had the experience, and also feels it was deeply valuable for her son. As she tells Xenia Shin, who interviewed her for The MY HERO video blog *Women Transforming Media*, "I think that if I could ever encourage people about what to do when they become parents is expose your kids to experiences that they can feel enrich their lives. That they can then transmit. Because we become history."[55]

Interestingly, when it was over and she was flagging down a car to catch a ride to the airport, she only trusted getting into a car with a black driver. And when she arrived in New York, she had an overwhelming urge to embrace the first black person she saw on the street. "I had so much respect and love for that man at that moment. I needed to hug someone who was black."

Charitable work and support for the arts were also key parts of Eva's life with Murray Roman. "Together we made millions of phone calls for charities," Eva says. "And also for arts institutions like The Metropolitan Museum. It was part of our life." They also both fought for women's rights. "Whenever something like the women's movement or the National Organization of Women happened," Eva proudly asserts, "Murray was often the only man marching there! He'd be right up front with Bella Abzug in her big hat."

Sadly, in 1975, Murray was diagnosed with advanced prostate cancer. Many years of fighting the

"Whenever something like the women's movement or the National Organization of Women happened, Murray was often the only man marching there!"

cancer followed, with surgeries and treatments and hospital visits. "He really had terrible struggles," Eva says. "But every time we could, when he felt better between treatments, we would get on a plane and travel. We'd go to China, for example, and climb the great wall." Still, in 1984, Murray lost his battle and died four days before his birthday. He was only 64 years old. Eva was inconsolable. "I can't even imagine how I survived from one day to another. I was desperately missing him! Also, I love being married. I don't do well alone." Still, she had a company to run, one that had grown to international proportions. Over time, she gradually gave it over to the staff. "I didn't want it any more," she says.

At the age of 57, three years after losing Murray, Eva met Dr. Yoel Haller, an OB/GYN, who shared her passion for social causes and activism. He was the medical director of Planned Parenthood, San Francisco, and was also a professor of Obstetrics and Gynecology. Though their connection was immediate, it was difficult for Eva to care for someone new. As she says, "It took a couple of months of not being ready for him. He would drive down from San Francisco over the weekends to visit me, and," she smiles, "my home had a guest wing, which is where I put him. He was not allowed into my wing."

After a few months, Yoel asked her if she would come visit him in San Francisco. She agreed. He met her at the airport and took her to his house on the water in Marin County. "It was an adorable little home, with a deck and a dock where we could watch the boats go by." She was introduced to his family and to his friends. And she became more aware of the character of this man who was wooing her. "On one level, he was a society doctor, for wealthy or famous A-listers. But he was also a doctor to teachers and rabbis and ministers and to some who didn't pay. He was a good man and a kind man and a caring man, and by wanting me in his home and introducing me to his family and friends, he was making a commitment to me and asking nothing in return." It was actually a small thing that made the final difference for her. "He took out some stainless steel flatware to serve me something, and it was the same set that I had! It was a mid-century modern style which they had at the Museum of Modern Art. I was struck by the fact we both loved the same modern design. I started to laugh and I said to him, 'Would you please put my luggage . . .' (because he was taking my luggage to his guest wing), 'Would you please put my luggage in your bedroom.'"

That was the beginning of a happy marriage of, now, over 25 years. And as Eva says, "We still love the same things, and we support each other. Yoel especially supports me in all my charitable work and is infinitely patient with me. I often think about what will happen if he dies, and I'm still around." Then she smiles. "I told him if he did, I would probably look for another husband. So if he doesn't want me to have another husband, then he has to stay around."

"So if he doesn't want me to have another husband, then he has to stay around."

Together, Yoel and Eva have continued their involvement in social, educational, and environmental activism, as well as philanthropy. Eva also expanded her activities to serving on boards for countless non-profits, as either a board member or chairman. An incomplete list of these boards include: Sing for Hope, The Rubin Museum of Asian Art, Creative Visions Foundation, The Foundation for the University of California at Santa Barbara (UCSB), Free the Children USA, A Blade of Grass, Video Volunteers, and Asia Initiatives. As someone who often comes in at the beginning of such organizations, Eva has been remarkably effective in shepherding these worthy non-profits into visibility and vitality.

The Art of Mentoring

Through this, Eva has developed what she considers her most important role in life, that of a mentor. As she tells Xenia Shin in the *Women Transforming Media* blog, "I love to get involved in projects that are not yet formed. I love to incubate. I love to envision what an organization can be when it gets started or when it grows. And how we can together cooperate with other human beings to make things happen."

As an example, in 1997, she was approached by 15-year-old Canadian Craig Kielburger about his organization Free the Children, which he had started at the age of 12. At that young age, he had been shocked to learn about a boy his same age, Iqbal Masih, who was born in Pakistan and sold into slavery at the age of four. This child, who lived across the globe, had spent six years chained to a carpet-weaving loom. Once freed, Iqbal spoke out about children's rights, and was subsequently murdered. Moved and inspired, Craig began his grass roots organization, based on children helping children, and focused on issues of child slavery and child prostitution. His older brother, Marc, whom Eva knew, was aware Eva had been doing a number of fundraisers. "So," she says, "he had his little brother knock on our door one day in New York and say, 'I have a charity, and I'm going to have a fundraiser, and I have the Royal Ballet and the Royal Philharmonic, what do I do next?' I told him, 'You have to have a board, and you have to have a committee for the fundraiser, and you need to figure out a location. . . .' I

"He asked, 'Would you help me?' So I said, "Yes, I'll come up to Toronto and figure it out with you.' And that is how I got started with Free the Children."

told him all sorts of other things, and he asked, 'Would you help me?' So I said, 'Yes, I'll come up to Toronto and figure it out with you.' And that is how I got started with Free the Children." She also joined their board and served in that capacity for 17 years.

Free the Children has continued its advocacy of children, as well as helped build schools and school rooms around the world. They have also brought the innovative "Adopt a Village" model of community development (which encourages self-empowerment and sustainability) to eight countries. As Eva explains to Xenia Shin in the *Women Transforming Media* interview, "We have about 1,000 schools, clinics, hospitals, and villages that we have built with our grandchildren, who go every year with the local children in a number of countries in Africa and Asia. And it's another one of those things it's lovely to look at and to know that it happened."

Another example of Eva's mentorship started with an encounter in an elevator with a young woman named Jessica Mayberry. "We began talking, and it turned out we were going to the same place, namely her parents' apartment, where I had been invited to have dinner." During the evening, Jessica talked about wanting to go to India to start a project training media-deprived communities to produce socially relevant videos. It was to be called Video Volunteers. Eva encouraged her to pursue her dream. And, in fact, by the end of the evening, Eva had gotten her a three-month documentary internship. Later, she also was able to help obtain an initial investor, who started the company off with a $40,000 grant. Video Volunteers is going strong and describes its mission as empowering "marginalized communities to produce stories, take action, and devise solutions."[56]

"I don't know if you've noticed by now," Eva laughs, "but I have very few planned activities in my life. These things just happen. There are another dozen charities that I am actively involved in because they came to me with a question or with something that I might be able to help them find the answer to.

"I always look at people's potential and I try to open a door for them to figure out what that real potential is," she says. "So I guess I'd say I'm a door opener. I watch them go through the door, and I relish the doors that they open for themselves afterwards. Which is how I now have twelve young people in my life whom I call my children. I was lucky enough to be there, at whatever moment in their lives when I could give some inspiration or some encouragement or some love or some warmth that allowed them to take a step that they didn't even know they wanted to take."

> *"I guess I'd say I'm a door opener. I watch them go through the door, and I relish the doors that they open for themselves afterwards."*

In 2013, Eva was given the inaugural *Award for Excellence in Mentoring* at the Forbes Power Redefined Women's Summit in New York. As she took the stage, she was given a standing ovation. This was one of many awards and recognitions she has received over the years. These include, just to name a few, an Honorary Doctorate and the Magnusson Fellowship from Glasgow Caledonian University in 2014, a *Lifetime Achievement Award* from the United Nations Population Fund in 2013, the *Mandala Award for Humanitarian Achievement* from the Rubin Museum of Art in 2011, and selection as one of the "21 Leaders of the 21st Century" by *womensenews* in 2006. And most recently, in May of 2015, she was given a *Daily Point of Light* award by The Points of Light organization. Interestingly, when asked about "giving back," she says she doesn't like the term. "I'm giving to myself actually. I'm being entirely selfish. Because to give makes me feel good!"

Reluctantly we've reached the end of this fascinating interview with a woman who has risen from terrible hardships to a life rich with purpose, and rich with inspiring and helping others. And even though the conversation has been about her, Eva has a way of wrapping you in the warmth and intensity of her complete attention, so that you too feel you have your own true calling in life.

Ren Gems

Eva Haller

"I think that we have a core that gets established early in life, and it's about remaining true to your core."

"None of us is creating an ocean. But we are dropping little drops of water. And it does create ripples."

"So many of the best and brightest ideas come from young people. They have hope and energy and refuse to believe that something is impossible."

"Kindness, empathy, giving, and sharing abundance—they create endorphins. So, if for no other reason than to make yourself feel good, be generous!"

"I am for human rights, civil rights, women's rights, and children's rights."

9

FRANCES HESSELBEIN

"Leadership is a matter of how to be, not how to do."

Former CEO of Girl Scouts of the USA, journal and book editor, author, founder and director of the Frances Hesselbein Leadership Institute, recipient of Presidential Medal of Freedom, holds 21 honorary degrees, board member of multiple organizations

It was 1976. The world was reeling from the upheaval of the 60s and 70s. The worldwide Girl Scouts organization was not exempt. It had suffered eight straight years of declining membership. Frances Hesselbein, who headed up a Pennsylvania Girl Scouts council, had been invited to New York City to be interviewed for the position of CEO of Girl Scouts of the USA. As she stepped into the large headquarters on 3rd Avenue, she figured there was no chance she would get the job. She knew it hadn't been filled by someone within the organization for 64 years. As far as she was concerned, they were just casting the widest net. So, as she sat before the six-woman search committee, she felt completely relaxed. And when they asked her if she were to get the job, what she would do, she unreservedly described a complete transformation of the organization. The world had changed, she asserted, and the Girl Scouts needed to as well. To start with, they should get rid of their outdated handbooks filled with recipes and sewing merit badges, and fill them instead with math, science, and technology. Next, they needed to increase the diversity of the Girl Scouts, and reach out to all ethnicities. They also needed to question the hierarchical structures that divided the national offices from the local councils. Girl Scouts of the USA needed an over-arching mission statement. It needed to be "One United Movement." Frances continued on in this fashion, speaking to the ways Girl Scouts of the USA could become relevant again. When she left, she felt good about the meeting but figured "that was that." So, it was to her great surprise when she got a call soon after offering her the job! Within a month, she and her filmmaker husband, John, had moved into an apartment in New York City. And life for Frances Hesselbein would never be the same again.

We called the offices of the Frances Hesselbein Leadership Institute at the allotted time to interview the former Girl Scouts CEO, renowned leadership expert, and Presidential Medal of Freedom winner. This impressive woman soon put us at our ease. Even across the phone lines, her warmth, enthusiasm and zest for life were evident.

She began by telling us that the mission of her beloved Girl Scouts became, under her guidance, "To help each girl reach her own highest potential." It is evident that Frances has helped and continues to help many people and organizations to reach their highest potential.

Frances has reached a venerable age, but she shows no signs of slowing down. The institute that carries her name is an influential organization which promotes effective and ethical leadership that is mission and values-driven. Through their award-winning journal, *Leader to Leader* (the #1 journal or magazine for eight years of the 2,100 published in the United States), and through online interviews, virtual roundtables, podcasts, and webinars, the institute discusses today's most relevant leadership challenges and opportunities, and have a global reach.

Frances's life story is, itself, a primer in leadership. It illustrates how leadership qualities are nurtured and developed, and how humble beginnings can lead to expansive and unexpected horizons.

The Early Years

Frances grew up in Johnstown, in the mountains of western Pennsylvania. "It was a big coal, big steel company town," Frances explains. "A small town, but with warm energy." Her family was very close-knit. She was particularly close to her maternal grandmother, Sadie Pringle Wicks. "Mama Wicks," as Frances called her, had both a personal and professional impact on her. As Frances explains in her memoir, *My Life in Leadership: The Journey and Lessons Learned Along the Way*, "Her wisdom, her depth, and her love began to shape me from my earliest years. When she talked to me, I still remember, she would look into my eyes intently. For that moment she made me feel like the most important person in the world."[57] Mama Wicks was also Frances's link to family history. She regaled her granddaughter with stories, for example, about the seven Pringle brothers (which included Sadie's father) who volunteered to fight for the

> *"For that moment she made me feel like the most important person in the world."*

Union during the Civil War. As a little girl, Frances would often go with Mama Wicks to the Pringle Hill cemetery, and pause over each of the seven headstones of her great-grandfather and his six brothers.

Another relative who was a great influence on Frances was her aunt Carrie (Mama Wicks's daughter). An elegant and charming woman, Carrie recognized Frances's potential early on. As Carrie expressed in a letter she wrote to her niece in 1985, "I knew, from the time you were five years old (in kindergarten) that you were destined to do great things."[58]

Then there was Frances's father, who instilled in her, among other values, the importance of being kind and considerate to others. Her father had been in the army, as well as the Pennsylvanian State Police cavalry. "He was the most inspiring, energetic, and wonderful person," Frances says. And like her grandmother, he made their family history come alive with wonderful storytelling. She describes one such story in her memoir. "My father . . . told me about the certificate, now framed and hanging on my wall in Easton, that says 'William Richards, 1853, $150 contribution to the Western Reserve Eclectic Institute' (later to become Hiram College). He was one of the founders and then a trustee of the Institute. I think about this giving man, William Richards, a farmer dedicated to education. In 1853, $150 was a huge amount of money. 'How much better is wisdom than gold,' he would inscribe in his books."[59] Frances's most illustrious ancestors, on her father's side, were John and Abigail Adams. "Only recently," Frances remarks, "did I learn that John Adams was the only founding father who did not own a slave." Frances made a

"'How much better is wisdom than gold,' he would inscribe in his books."

point to keep the family stories alive, telling them to her own son as he grew up. For Frances, where you came from was as important as where you were headed.

When she was only 17 years old, Frances's father became very ill. "Somewhere in his army experience," she explains, "he had been exposed to some kind of gas or chemical, and it destroyed the aorta leading from his brain to his heart. There wasn't anything anyone could do." She remembers his last moments: "I was in the hospital room with him, all alone, and my father was dying. Mother was in the hall crying because she couldn't bear to be there. I was stroking his face, and I said, 'Daddy, I don't want you to worry about mother and Trudy and John. I will take care of them,' and a tear went down his cheek. I patted his face, and he was gone." Already, her commitment to serving others had begun. As the oldest in the family, she went to work, only able to attend the University of Pittsburgh part time.

"I said, 'Daddy, I don't want you to worry about mother and Trudy and John. I will take care of them.'"

Turning Points

During this period, Frances met and married John Hesselbein who was working as a journalist and night editor for the *Johnstown Democrat.* When World War II broke out, John volunteered for the Navy and was sent to Pensacola to train as a combat aircrew photographer, leaving behind his young wife and eighteen-month-old son, Johnny. Despite her mother's objections (but with Mama Wicks's encouragement), Frances chose to travel with her baby to Pensacola (and later to a base in San Diego) to be with her husband. "Those few years in naval towns, with very little money," she writes in her memoir, "were some of the best years of our lives . . . I'd say prayers and sometimes smile while thinking that a guy who had never even shot a BB gun was in a clear bubble under the plane with a camera and a big gun."[60]

After the war, they returned to Johnstown, where John set up his own photography studio and production company and began making a number of award-winning documentaries. Frances helped her husband in his business, lending a hand in every way possible. "Little did I know," she writes, "that everything I learned by 'helping John,' would provide me with indispensable tools and a background

I would need in the future I never envisioned, one I never thought I wanted when it came."[61] That future began with a small enough incident. When her son was eight years old, Frances was approached by a Girl Scout chairman about being a Girl Scout Leader. She felt it was not for her and made no bones about it. "I said to this woman, 'I'm sorry, I don't know anything about little girls. I am the mother of a little boy.'" But the woman kept persisting, and, as Frances describes it, "One day she caught me at a weak moment. I was walking up the street, and she stopped me and said, 'I have thirty little girls, 10 years old, in the basement of the second Presbyterian church. They are a Girl Scouts troop, and their leader has gone to Australia to be a missionary. If we don't find a new leader, we are going to have to disband them.' I said, 'Alright, I'll take them for a few weeks until you find a real leader.'"

"I said to this woman, 'I'm sorry, I don't know anything about little girls. I am the mother of a little boy.'"

In preparation, Frances read about the founder of the Girl Scouts, Juliette Low, who in 1912 told girls: "You can be anything you want to be—a doctor, a lawyer, an aviatrix, or hot-air balloonist."[62] This visionary thinking, at a time before women even had the vote, inspired Frances. And once she began to lead the troop, she was impressed with the enthusiasm and energy of the girls. Suffice it to say, she didn't leave after six weeks. "We ended up staying together until they all graduated from high school," Frances says, with a little laugh. During that time, Troop 17, to whom Frances gave much responsibility in planning out their projects, sold so many Girl Scout cookies and managed their assets so well, they used the profits to do things like travel to Mystic, Connecticut for a week on the *Joseph Conrad*, a four-masted sailing ship, and to New York City to visit museums. Later, one of the girls from that troop would write, "When we met Leader Frances, we were 30 girls unsure of ourselves with little ambition to do more than get married and stay in Johnstown. When we graduated from high school, we all had high ambition and confidence."[63] For Frances, who had only reluctantly taken on this small troop of girls, a life in leadership had begun.

Soon after, she became the Chairman of the Board of the local Talus Rock Girl Scout council. Subsequently, she joined the National Program Committee, worked as a national trainer of board members, and served on an international committee, traveling to Girl Scout gatherings in the U.S. and abroad.

United Way

Then along came what seemed an unlikely offer. In 1970, Frances was recruited to chair the local United Way campaign. "I was the first woman ever to chair a United Way campaign," she remarks. "We're talking about long, long ago, and there were people who were saying, 'What!? A woman? Can women raise money?'"

One of her first responsibilities was to choose her vice-chairman, who the following year would automatically become the chairman. "I chose Ernie Wadsworth, president of the United Steelworkers of America in Johnstown," she says. "He had never been involved in a United Way campaign, and it was shocking to the committee when I suggested my choice. They said they would have to ask Bethlehem

"There were people who were saying, 'What!? A woman? Can women raise money?'"

Steel about this, and I said, fine. The answer came back. Bethlehem Steel would meet Mr. Wadsworth's plane and bring him to the meeting, and they would host a kickoff luncheon for the campaign at the Bethlehem Steel plant. And that night, the United Steel Workers held a dinner. There were two hundred men and women, some part of the union, and some community leaders. It was the most incredible coming together. That year, in our little town in Pennsylvania, we had the highest per-capita giving of any United Way in the country! That campaign was a wonderful example of opening doors."

The Great Adventure

Just before taking the United Way chairmanship, another key opportunity arose. Frances was asked to be the new executive director for the local Girl Scouts council. She had been serving as the chairman of the board of that same council, but that was a volunteer position. This would be her first professional job with the Girl Scouts. Just as when she was first approached about being a Girl Scout leader, she demurred. She could not see herself in a professional management role. But they persisted and she (again) said she would take the job on a temporary basis until they could find a "real" executive. What she didn't realize was that what awaited her was a job she was born to do. "I realized," she writes in her memoir, "that, for me, management was the great adventure."[64] She found, in this executive position, a rich opportunity to lead and inspire others.

Frances had been reading and was deeply influenced by the work of Peter F. Drucker. He was an author, professor and management consultant whom Business Week has since called "the man who invented management." He wrote such influential books as *The Effective Executive, Managing for Results,* and *The Practice of Management.* When Frances first read *The Effective Executive,* she was struck by how perfectly his philosophies and vision aligned with her own. "I thought he had written this book just for us," she remarks.

So, as she dove into the new job, Frances brought the theories of Peter Drucker with her. As Frances explained in a November 2011 article in *Fortune Online*, "I had read everything Peter Drucker ever wrote. On my first day with the Talus Rock Council, I showed up with six copies of Drucker's *The Effective Executive* under my arm—one for each staff member."[65]

A key element of Drucker's innovative approach was circular rather than hierarchal management, banning such concepts as top and bottom, superior and subordinate—thus allowing all members of a team to feel valued. Drucker's system was inclusive and allowed for diversity and appreciation of differing perspectives.

> *"On my first day with the Talus Rock Council, I showed up with six copies of Drucker's The Effective Executive under my arm."*

It was also ethical and mission-based. In her position as executive director, Frances launched what she called a "quiet revolution," which embodied these philosophies. She held the position there until 1975, and then went on to be executive director of the Penn Laurel council in Eastern Pennsylvania, during which time she presented a groundbreaking speech on "What It Means to Belong" at a conference for Girl Scout executive directors in their six-state region.

Still, when the call came from New York that they would like to interview her for the position of the new CEO for the national organization, Frances almost did not go. "I knew they couldn't be serious," she says, "because in 64 years they'd never had anyone from within the organization. So they weren't going to start then. I was going to just write a nice note. But my husband said, 'It's the perfect job for you! I'm taking you to New York.' So we drove there. And the six women who were interviewing me could tell, I think, that I loved the

> *"My husband said, 'It's the perfect job for you! I'm taking you to New York.'"*

organization. But since I was sure I wouldn't be offered the job, when they asked me what I would do if I were CEO, I described the total transformation of Girl Scouts of the USA. I had a wonderful time describing what I really believed the organization's future could be. Two days later, they called and said, 'We want you to come.' And what was so marvelous was because I had been so open about the transformation, they had bought it. There was no push-back; it was everybody's baby. It was the most exhilarating experience!"

While staying true to the original mission of serving girls, Frances instigated a complete overhaul of the structure of the organization in ways that would respond to the turbulent times in which they lived, and that would embrace inclusion and diversity. As she writes in her memoir, "We poured our energy into developing a highly contemporary program . . . designed to meet the very special needs of girls growing up today, reaching out to all girls, of all races and ethnic groups."[66] Frances also implemented the groundbreaking management theories of Peter Drucker. In 1978, a three-day conference of meetings was called of all the executive directors of the Girl Scout councils, as well as one hundred national staff members, to present the new Corporate Management

> *"We poured our energy into developing a highly contemporary program . . . designed to meet the very special needs of girls growing up today, reaching out to all girls, of all races and ethnic groups."*

Plan. Those present at the meeting would need to buy into and make the plan their own because they were the ones who would be putting into place and managing this massive transformation.

Frances, however, was not present at this important conference. Instead, she was at the bedside of her husband. As she writes in her memoir, "I was in a hospital in Manhattan, beside the bed of my husband, John, who was dying of a massive malignant brain tumor. He had been in a coma for weeks and was now brain dead."[67] In the middle of this ordeal, she recorded a short message to be played to those who would be at the conference. In it, she explained that her husband was dying and that she trusted that all those present would make the decisions that would be best for girls and

"I was in a hospital in Manhattan, beside the bed of my husband, John, who was dying of a massive malignant brain tumor."

for their "One Great Movement." Frances then writes in her memoir, "It seemed that the tragic death of a good man, one very much part of our Girl Scout family, added a sobering dimension to the deliberations of those three days. Some who came to the conference perhaps with the intentions of challenging parts of this massive change shared with me later that John's death gave them a broader perspective, and somehow the tragedy of death and separation brought the participants closer together."[68] On Wednesday, the last day of the conference, John died. And the new management plan had passed. For Frances, it was a sad ending of a cherished life. But it was also a hopeful new beginning of a cherished organization. Frances would end up heading Girl Scouts of the USA for thirteen years.

Enter Peter Drucker

In 1981, five years into her tenure as CEO of Girl Scouts of the USA, Frances had the opportunity to meet her inspiration. She describes this encounter in the *Fortune Online* article: "I went to the University Club in New York City to hear Peter speak, knowing I would never get to talk to him in that mob. Growing up in Johnstown, PA., 5:30 means 5:30. I was alone with two bartenders, and I turned around, and there was a man standing behind me. And he said, 'I am Peter Drucker.' And I was just stunned—I forgot my manners. Instead of saying, 'How do you do?' I said, 'Do you realize how important you are to the Girl Scouts? If you go to any one of our 335 Girl Scout councils around this country, you will see all of your books—you will see your philosophy alive.' And he said, 'Tell me, does it work?'"[69]

Drucker was legitimately curious, since, at the time, his books had been aimed at the for-profit sector, and here was a woman at the head of an international

> "Instead of saying, 'How do you do?' I said, 'Do you realize how important you are to the Girl Scouts?'"

nonprofit using his management techniques. Frances explained to him that it worked very well, and asked if she might sit down with him for an hour to pick his brain regarding further ways to use his methodology to move the Girl Scouts into the future. He agreed, and this encounter blossomed into a longstanding mentorship and friendship that would continue until Drucker's death in 2005. In subsequent years, in fact, Drucker would expand his work to include nonprofits. In a key article that he wrote, "What Business Can Learn from Nonprofits," published in 1989 by *Harvard Business Review*, he states, "The Girl Scouts, the Red Cross . . . —our nonprofit organizations—are becoming America's management leaders. In two areas, strategy and the effectiveness of the board, they are practicing what most American businesses only preach. And in the most crucial area—the motivation and productivity of knowledge workers—they are truly pioneers, working out the policies and practices that business will have to learn tomorrow."[70]

A significant moment for the Girl Scouts was when Drucker emphasized to them the importance of their work, thus taking them to a new level. As Frances explains in *Fortune*, "When Drucker came to speak at our board meeting, I brought the entire national board and 100 national staff members. He told them, 'You do not see yourselves life-size. You do not appreciate the significance of the work you do, for we live in a society that pretends to care about its children, and it does not. And for a little while you give a little girl a chance to be a girl in a society that forces her to grow up all too soon.' What we all realized at that moment was that the work we did in the social sector was as important as business or government; we were not simply junior members of a society."[71]

> *"What we all realized at that moment was that the work we did in the social sector was as important as business or government."*

No Rest for the Leaders

In 1990, Frances, now in her seventies, said goodbye to Girl Scouts of the USA. When she left, Girl Scouts had its highest membership, greatest diversity, and most cohesive structure. Her plans at this point? To serve on a couple of boards and start on a memoir.

But semi-retirement was not in the cards for Frances Hesselbein. The morning after she left, she received a call from William Flynn, the then chairman of Mutual of America. He asked her when she was coming to see her office. Confused she told him she had just left her office. He then invited her to visit their headquarters on 5th Avenue where he showed her an office with her name on it, and a shared secretary sitting outside. As she writes in her memoir, "He said, 'This company does not know what you are going to do in the future, but whatever you do will help our clients. So you have to have an office.' I was grateful and overwhelmed."[72]

What she did with that office was to create, with Peter Drucker's permission and guidance, the Peter F. Drucker Foundation for Nonprofit Management. The foundation would spread the Drucker philosophy across the nonprofit world,

"He said, 'This company does not know what you are going to do in the future, but whatever you do will help our clients. So you have to have an office.'"

and would do so through connecting with various cutting-edge leaders in the management field. It would also focus on providing management resources and education to struggling public service organizations. Although Peter gave the go-ahead, he did so with one important proviso––that Frances be at the helm of the foundation as its CEO. "So, six weeks after leaving the world's largest organization for girls and women," Frances writes in her memoir, "I was now CEO of probably the smallest foundation in the world."[73]

Frances's leadership was invaluable. Over the years, the foundation grew into a much respected and influential organization through corporate and nonprofit executives that served on its board, exceptional thought leaders eager to speak and write for the foundation, generous gifts, and remarkable individuals from many fields who volunteered their time and expertise. Frances began publishing and served as editor-in-chief of the groundbreaking journal *Leader to Leader*; she authored, edited or co-edited 28 books (translated into 29 languages); and she represented the foundation through speaking engagements and conferences worldwide. She was the recipient of 21 honorary degrees, as well as countless awards and recognitions. The one she is proudest of is the Presidential Medal of Freedom, awarded to her by President Bill Clinton in 1998.

The foundation eventually became the Frances Hesselbein Leadership Institute, and Frances and the Institute continue to work as potent forces in the field of forward-thinking management.

World Travels

"To live is to serve," Frances often says. And she has been of service not just in her native country but around the world. To date she has traveled to 68 countries. She feels every experience was valuable, even when in the midst of turmoil. A case in point was her visit to Iran in 1979. "I was speaking in Iran as the government fell under martial law," she remarks, "and I got out the same day the Shah and his wife left. I was on the last American flight that ever left Iran. But those people, the people I spoke to, the women who had this big dinner for me, you've never met more wonderful people."

A joyous travel memory was the time she flew to New Zealand to accept the Fulbright New Zealand John F. Kennedy Memorial Fellowship. She was the first woman and the 15th

"I was speaking in Iran as the government fell under martial law, and I got out the same day the Shah and his wife left."

American leader to receive the honor. The fellowship recipient's role was to speak on leadership and voluntarism to groups across the country. Interestingly, there were Maori leaders at every gathering. At one such gathering, after her presentation, a small group of Maori women wanted to meet Frances. As she describes in her memoir, "I walked over to where the five Maori women were standing in a half circle. Nothing prepared me for the ceremony that followed, but instinctively I knew what to do. The first woman took my hands in hers and lightly touched her nose to mine; we looked into each other's eyes and held that position until the spirit within had connected. (This is my interpretation.) Then I moved to the next Maori leader and clasped her hands; we pressed our noses together, and our eyes communicated.

This continued until all five women had greeted me . . . Then the six of us clasped hands, and in a circle, they sang a beloved Maori song . . . Then the

"The first woman took my hands in hers and lightly touched her nose to mine; we looked into each other's eyes and held that position until the spirit within had connected."

Maori women hung a cord around my neck with a sacred green stone . . . It was one-half dark green, one-half lighter green. One woman pointed to the lighter half and said, 'This is you,' and then to the darker half, saying, 'This is us.' Jade is considered a treasure by Maoris. This ceremony has deep meaning . . . I will always remember it." [74]

Leaders Who Happen to Be Women

When asked about what women bring to the workplace, Frances answers, "I would say that women bring some unique qualities to the workplace. I think one of those—and this has been my experience working across all the sectors (private, public, social)—is an openness to the work. There is a respect for the ideas, the philosophy, the work of other people. I think there is also an eagerness to learn. And successful leaders who are women know why they do what they do. They have a mission, and they are very

"I would say that women bring some unique qualities to the workforce . . . There is a respect for the ideas, the philosophy, the work of other people."

conscious of it; they articulate it, and it's in focus. They are also very open about what they value, and the values of their organization, their company, their group. I think what's exciting is where women are today and how they have moved this society forward."

She makes a point of using the phrase "leaders who are women," rather than "women leaders," since, as she explains, "We're not a category." She also emphasizes the difference in language that a leader who is a woman tends to use. "A leader who is a woman is more likely to talk about influence, not power. Their language is also not 'up and down,' 'top and bottom,' but circular. These women, I believe, are changing the language of leadership for society."

Onward into the Future

Frances took a fall in 2013, but that hasn't stopped her. Although her doctor forbade her to travel (the year before she had gone to Russia, New Zealand, China, and taken twice-monthly trips within the United States), she has adapted. She takes advantage of the wonderful world of technology by holding Skype meetings and webinars, which allow her to continue to fully communicate with her global community. "Global Webinars are so effective," she says. "I now travel all over the world that way, and if you go to our website, you'll find examples of these. The other day, 40 countries, 400 leaders, and I just sat in front of big computer screens, and it's as though we're in the same room."

She tells us of one wonderful Skype exchange that turned into a personal encounter. Eight years ago, she had co-founded,

"Global Webinars are so effective . . . The other day, 40 countries, 400 leaders, and I just sat in front of big computer screens, and it's as though we're in the same room."

with The University of Pittsburgh, the Hesselbein Global Academy for Student Leadership and Civic Engagement, whose mission is to inspire and develop accomplished student leaders from the U.S. and abroad, through a yearly Student Leadership Summit. Frances explains, "They have twelve students who are from universities all over the United States and twelve from universities all over the world, and they bring them to the University of Pittsburgh for five days. And we have someone famous and wonderful like Jim Collins or Rosabeth Moss Kanter open the summit with a speech. Then they work in groups, each of which has a distinguished mentor guiding it. In the beginning I wondered how long it would take them to come together, when you have, for example, Albania and Alabama sitting next to each other. But they walk into the room, and in ten minutes, you don't know who is from where. It's amazing how they come together. During their five days, they live at the university, they work there, they meet the most remarkable people, and then they go out into the community and do a service project." She goes on to tell us, "Recently, since I could not make the trip, I went in by Skype and spoke to them, and we had a dialogue. The next day when I woke up, there, at my door, were these three handsome young men, in suits and ties, beautifully dressed. And they said 'We are your Hesselbein Fellows. We came from Pittsburgh this morning, and we made another return flight home tonight, so we could visit with you.' One was from Albania, one was from Algeria, and the third was from somewhere in the Middle East. And we had the best, most marvelous half-day together, before they had to go. They were just so charming. They couldn't wait to tell me what had

> *"There, at my door, were these three handsome young men . . . and they said, 'We are your Hesselbein Fellows.'"*

happened at Pittsburgh, and to thank me for founding the Academy. And as we were standing there talking, the one young man from Albania went down on his knees, and reached over and touched my big toe—I was wearing open-toed sandals—and he looked up and said, 'I hope you were not offended. In my country, this denotes the highest level of respect.' I said, 'I am so honored.' These students every year are just amazing, and they stay in touch. They're all over the world, and yet they're still the 'Hesselbein Fellows.'"

These are not the only young lives Frances has recently touched. In 2009, she was named Class of 1951 Leadership Chair for the Study of Leadership at the U.S. Military Academy (the first woman and non-West Point graduate to do so). Frances has always had intense pride in her family's military service, and her connection with West Point gives her enormous joy. Colonel Bernard Banks, head of the Academy's department of behavioral sciences and leadership, was quoted in *strategy + business* magazine as saying, "Her relationship with West Point runs very deep. I still hear cadets who met her years ago comment on the influence she had on them [and] how she exemplifies the leadership qualities we value here, like passion, intellect, character, and vision. When she's here, you'll see her surrounded by cadets. This very small woman speaks so softly that you have to lean in to hear. But she exudes this huge emotional presence that the cadets find fascinating. . . . The cadets are inspired by her because, despite their great difference in age and experience, they recognize that she respects them. She has a genuine appreciation of anyone called to service—her own life exemplifies it."[75]

And that, in the end, is what it is all about for Frances Hesselbein. Serving and leading others through respect, appreciation and collaboration. As she says, "Leadership is a matter of how to be, not how to do." And the woman Frances is can inspire us all to place character at the heart of action, and integrity at the core of success.

"Leadership is a matter of how to be, not how to do."

Ren Gems

Frances Hesselbein

"It is the quality and character of the leader that determines results."

"When you see a roadblock or challenge as an opportunity, it is amazing how you are already halfway there."

"Language is the greatest motivating force. You can phrase something positively and inspire people to do their best, or negatively and make them feel worried, uncertain, and self-conscious."

"It's not hard work that wears you out, but the repression of your true personality."

"Communication is not saying something; communication is being heard."

10

L O R I E   K A R N A T H

"Explore. Discover. Share. Preserve. Sustain."

Explorer, author, former international investment banker, organizer
of leading edge symposia, education advocate, painter, arts patron,
former president of The Explorers Club

*Lorie Karnath wondered what in the world she was doing there.
Yes, Antarctica had thrilled her with its stark and pristine beauty when
she first stepped off the plane into that endless expanse of white. Yes,
she had found the adventure of reaching the South Pole bracing and
exhilarating, but now, the magic had seriously begun to dim. A storm was
raging and she was imprisoned in the confines of her tent while, outside,
violent winds hurled ice chunks at the tent's thin shell, which swelled and
collapsed with a deafening roar as the frame writhed convulsively. And
even worse, if the weather prevented the team from leaving when they
planned, they could be stuck there for a long grueling winter. Lorie found
herself praying to every god in the universe to get her out of there!*

*Well, luckily, she did get out. Once home, the memory of that night
in the tent faded, and, instead, Lorie remembered the magnificence of the
place, and the awe with which it filled her. And she knew she would keep
pursuing adventures like this. How could she not? This was who she was.*

If you don't equate women with exploring, with going out into wild and remote regions of the world, with pushing past both physical and personal boundaries to make new discoveries and face daunting challenges, then you haven't met Lorie Karnath. But beyond this extraordinary specialty, Lorie also pursues or has pursued a number of other fields, contributing not only to the world of exploration, but to the worlds of science, education, the arts, and even, for a while, to international banking! Talking with Lorie on the phone was both enlightening and inspiring. Her even-timbered voice was calm and focused as she spoke of her remarkable and often daunting accomplishments as if they were the most natural things in the world.

Not Just Because "It's There"

Lorie Karnath is only the second woman to have held the post of president of the formidable Explorers Club in New York City. Members of this club have included Sir Edmund Hillary, Theodore Roosevelt, Neil Armstrong, Dian Fossey, and Chuck Yeager, just to name a few. During her three-year tenure (from 2009 to 2012), she did much in terms of fundraising, increasing membership, and refurbishing the venerable, old building in which the Club is housed. She also broadened the definition of exploring to ensure that it included scientific discovery.

Lorie has been to the North and South Poles, to remote regions in Burma and China, to Borneo rainforests, to much of the Silk Road, and to many other far-flung parts of the world. For Lorie, exploring is much more than just "climbing the mountain because it's there." It is instead about making a difference. She has been on expeditions to examine the effects of global changes in Antarctica, to conduct field research on flora and fauna in Malaysia, to bring school supplies to isolated regions of Burma, and to do paleontological digs in Alberta, Canada. "Exploration with a purpose builds bridges around the world," she explains.

Five words guide Lorie's exploration philosophy. Explore. Discover. Share. Preserve. Sustain. These describe, in her view, how explorers can contribute to the world we live in. She explains, "*Explore* means going out there and asking the questions. *Discover* is uncovering the answers and sometimes finding that the answers are completely divergent

"Exploration with a purpose builds bridges around the world."

from the questions we asked. *Sharing* is one of the most important: We share what we've seen with people who can't explore in the way we can, but we also share with people who might use what we bring them to gain answers to new questions, whether it's someone in a laboratory, or creating policy, or in business. Those answers then help to *preserve* what it is we've discovered, and then we can work on ways to *sustain* that for future generations."

When asked to give an example of how these last two work, Lorie says, "Take something like a rain forest. It's not as simple as saying, this rain forest shouldn't be cut down because a certain species is there. That may work in some regions, but may not in others. But if you understand how villages that depend on those forests need to survive by alternate means, and if policies are written that respect this, then this particular rain forest is preserved and sustained for future generations. So it's not just to preserve what is, but how do you sustain it going forward? How do you incorporate elements so that people are benefited in the best way? How do you symbiotically protect the planet?"

"It's not as simple as saying, this rain forest shouldn't be cut down because a certain species is there."

Bringing Education to Remote Regions

One passion that has particularly driven Lorie's expeditions is education. "Education has been a big motivator of mine from early on," she explains. "So I started getting involved in helping to fund schools in places that didn't have any, or had very few. I've done a lot of work in China, as well as Burma—which has been a big passion of mine for the last 20 years or so. Whenever I go there I bring supplies. I've been doing this for a long time because they haven't had books, they haven't had paper, they haven't had anything. We would bring supplies up rivers and to school building, books, pens, papers, whatever we could, to places you couldn't easily access. That has been a good way to combine my ability as an explorer with my desire to help further education, because not everyone can just drop off books, as they are not necessarily easy journeys."

"We would bring supplies up rivers and to school buildings . . . to places you couldn't easily access."

In terms of funding and constructing new schools, logistics in these countries have not always been simple. But because of Lorie's many trips to both Burma and China, she has developed many contacts and come to understand how each country works. "For example," she explains, "you can't fund directly into Burma, although it may have changed now with the opening up of the country, but generally you have to do it through an established group. Also a lot of schooling in Burma for many centuries has been through the monastery. That has been at times the only formal education children could get. So what we've done on each trip is sponsor different monks through their initiation process, and when you do that, you take them on for life!"

China is a different process. "China is transitioning very quickly from a rural economy to a more urbanized economy," Lorie says. "They understand that in the rural areas they need more education quickly. So the Chinese government actually set up a program where you can co-sponsor schools with them. They even sometimes build roads to a school, often going through mountainous areas. In many of these places, if there was any school at all, the children had to walk for hours to get there and then sleep on a floor or trudge back in the dark, again for hours. It made no sense and they got very little education. So now there are not only buildings where they can learn, but dormitories and other facilities as well."

Like most of the RenWomen we have spoken to, Lorie is deeply motivated to give back. Education, for her, is an empowering way to do so. "I think in my particular case," she says, "you go around the world and you see so much that needs to happen, and you see so much despair, and when you're just one person, even if you form a group, the challenges are daunting. I think education is something an individual can achieve, whether you're just one person without a support group or if you're able to build support, whether you're able to provide your own funding or raise money from other people; it's something that at every level you can have an impact on someone."

"Education is something an individual can achieve . . . it's something that at every level you can have an impact on someone."

Gifts from Walden Pond and Beyond

Lorie's urge to explore, as well as her passion for learning and education was rooted in her childhood and early adulthood. "I grew up mostly in Concord, Massachusetts," she explains. "So I had some very good mentors. Although," she gives a small laugh, "they were not alive. But their spirits were. They were Henry David Thoreau and Ralph Waldo Emerson. I lived not far from Walden Pond, so it was a great area to go explore. Back then it was very untouched, and very much the way Thoreau had seen it. Concord was a small town, a safe town, with lots of wildlife. And so I spent every second I could exploring the forest, the ponds, the streams, following the footsteps of these mentors, and going farther and farther afield."

When Lorie was ten, the family moved to Europe for her father's work (he was an international business consultant). They lived first in Belgium, and later Lorie also went to school in France and Switzerland. Attending European schools wasn't easy for Lorie and her siblings. "It was intimidating to be in a place where nobody spoke any English, and we were completely immersed from day one. Also the system was a lot tougher than what we were used to. Much more disciplinarian, with much more homework. So in the beginning we sort of rebelled. But I ended up sticking it out, and that was really the best thing I ever did for myself. It taught me how to really pursue something and surmount a challenge." Lorie's father was also instrumental in teaching her the importance of taking on hard things and overcoming them. During summers, while her friends were off having vacations in various fun locations, Lorie, who was interested in art and painted a lot, would attend programs like the Académie Julien in Paris. "And they were great," she says, "but they were very hard schools where you worked all day and often into the night. At one point I asked my father, 'All the things you do for us are wonderful, but why is it always so hard? Why can't I relax and do what my friends do and just run around?' And he

"And he said, 'Well, the one thing I don't want to take away from you is the challenge in life.'"

said, 'Well, the one thing I don't want to take away from you is the challenge in life.' Even at that second, I understood completely. That was probably the greatest gift he ever gave me. Challenge is really what inspires people to do the type of travel I do and take on the types of projects I take on."

Her mother deeply influenced Lorie as well. "My mother is a very artistic person, very creative," she says. "She worked in the social sciences. And then she mostly did a lot of photography, and different creative projects. I think she inspired our creativity. And she was the one who was mostly behind making sure we balanced our rigorous educational side with other things in life. For example, while we were in Europe, my parents rented a farm in Normandy. And my siblings and I were taken out of school for a while, and we were just allowed to run wild and experience nature and learn about how a farm works, and it was one of the best experiences of my childhood." Lorie stresses the importance of this balance. "I think my father could see that his children had intellectual potential, and we should learn this, and this, and this. But my mother could see it was also important to understand the full experience of being a human being and to keep open to all things."

Both parents also encouraged an acceptance of diversity in their children from an early age. "Considering I spent much of my childhood in a place as

"My mother could see it was also important to understand the full experience of being a human being."

mono-cultural, at the time, as Concord, Massachusetts, they did everything to make us see that the world was made up of many kinds of people. They would, for example, bring inner city kids to our house and have big picnics for them, along with music and things, not just so those kids could have different experiences, but so we could too.

We could learn that the world was a little broader than our own backyard. A lot of children didn't get that lesson in towns like that."

A Kid in a Candy Shop

When the family returned to America, Lorie's tough educational training in Europe made high school in the U.S. easy to the point of boring. As she points out, "I'd come back from very rigorous training, and what we were learning in high school in the U.S. were things I already knew or had gone beyond. But one of the things in high school you have to balance is you don't want to be seen as the 'nerdy kid.' So I didn't want to seem like I knew too much."

But everything changed when she got to college. It was here she could allow her Renaissance personality to fully flourish and to give her avid curiosity full rein. "It was like a huge door had opened! All of a sudden, it was okay to know more than someone else, and it was okay to learn! I was like a kid in a candy shop; I wanted to try everything. Anything I could learn, I wanted. And that was what propelled me into different educational programs abroad and into studying science, and everything new that was coming out in science, like molecular biology, and also into studying economics." Art classes were also a key part of her curriculum. As mentioned above, Lorie had been painting since an early age. Her major ended up being art history, which

"I wanted to try everything. Anything I could learn, I wanted."

combined many of the things she wanted to learn about. "It had the literature, the history, the art," she explains, "It had the travel, and it had the languages." But she also added a concentration in economics and science.

The resourcefulness that has been a hallmark of Lorie's

personality showed itself in these early college years. "One of my very significant moments in college was when, as a freshman, I had to give a presentation on DNA to my molecular biology class, and I realized a few days before that I really needed to learn a lot more in a hurry! So I saw these papers authored by James Watson (of Watson and Crick, two of the discovers of DNA), and I noticed he lived close by at Harvard, and I called him and he actually answered his phone! He *spoke* to me, someone he didn't know! I'm sure he doesn't remember this, but I remember every second. I was calling from a payphone at my university, and I couldn't believe he would just talk with me. When I did my presentation to the class a few days later, my professor was, like, 'How did you know all that?' I didn't want him to think that maybe I hadn't read all the material I was supposed to read, but I finally confessed that I had been speaking with Jim Watson. Instead of him reacting negatively, he was impressed and I got an A, which perhaps was deserved because of the information I had. I didn't understand at the time that I was being resourceful, and I was very lucky and fortunate that Watson was willing to speak to me. That access and the ability to interface with someone like that at a young age changed my world."

Where did her varied university studies lead? Well, at first, and somewhat surprisingly, into the world of finance. "I'd been doing some volunteer work," she says. "It was part of the university science

"I was very lucky and fortunate that Watson was willing to speak to me. That access and the ability to interface with someone like that at a young age changed my world."

program where we would go to different places like Sloan Kettering and do work in the lab. And I loved it, except for one thing. I met these scientists who had been there for 14 years working on a PhD.

And I was thinking, 'I'm not going to sit in a little six-by-eight laboratory office for 14 years, I want to go out and see the world!' Now, at the same time, I was learning about Wall Street and stocks and bonds. I had been put in charge of the portfolio that my parents had for me, and I found it so interesting that I insisted with my stock broker that I go to every annual meeting. I wanted to be part of everything and learn what was going on. So I ended up getting some job offers in finance, and, at the time, investment banking was the most entrepreneurial place you could be. It was that aspect of it, the creating of new projects, strategizing, and putting things together, that excited me. And that's very similar to science, where you're putting puzzles together. The difference is, in finance you're doing it a lot faster. And what I did also was try to go in the direction of my passions. So a lot of my clients were in the art world or in the science world, and all international. It was a good way to quickly put together multiple passions." She went on to get an MBA degree and, as an international banker, help launch a number of start-up companies, particularly in innovative scientific areas like biotech, and other new technologies.

> *"A lot of my clients were in the art world or in the science world, and all international. It was a good way to quickly put together multiple passions."*

She explains, in typical RenWoman fashion, how that first career helped enormously in the career paths she pursued later: "My background in finance helped provide a very important tool I would use to help companies, individuals, and ideas along the way."

Spreading the Word

One way in which Lorie Karnath combined her experiences

in finance and entrepreneurship with her various passions was by conceiving and organizing worldwide symposia on creativity, discovery and the sciences. As she puts it, "When there is something I'm particularly interested in, I've found that one of the best ways to learn about it is to put together a conference or a symposium. So I would link up with a university or other organizations to put these programs on around the world. This led me to connecting with a number of Swedish Academy Nobel committee members, as well as with some Nobel Prize winners themselves." In 2001, she helped found the Molecular Frontiers Foundation, which brings high- level scientists together for symposia on various cutting edge scientific topics. The Foundation's goal is to spread science education around the world, with a particular focus on young people. Symposia titles have included: "Exploring the Boundaries—the Science of the Extremes," "The Brain, Achievements and Challenges," and "Emerging Technologies in Biomedicine." To Lorie, educating the world about science is no longer a luxury, but a necessity. "I firmly believe that you can't survive in this world without scientific knowledge," she says. "You need an understanding for your day-to-day life in terms of medical decisions, technical decisions, and lifestyle decisions."

These symposia are generated both from Lorie's "extreme desire to learn," and her equally strong desire to share that learning with others. "I also feel there's no age limit to learning," she asserts. "One of the things I dislike the most is when people say, 'Oh, I'm too old.' I totally disagree with that. We should all be learning everything we can at every age."

"One of the things I dislike the most is when people say, 'Oh, I'm too old.' . . . We should all be learning everything we can at every age."

Having had early opportunities like her conversation with James

Watson, Lorie also seeks to bring that experience to young people. "I'm trying to recreate that for them," she says. "At our last symposium on the brain, we got a very generous donation from a group that has supported me in the past, and we used all of that money just to bring top-level high school science students to Stockholm from all around Sweden. It was the largest high school gathering that had ever occurred at the Swedish Royal Academy, and the largest science high school gathering ever in Sweden."

The thing that pleases Lorie the most about these symposia, as well as her other work, is not so much getting praise or recognition, although she acknowledges of course that this is nice, but seeing the results of her work in the lives of others. "That's a complete high for me," she explains. "I see how people who perhaps should have been interacting a long time ago meet each other for the first time and share expertise, and that is exciting! With programs like the symposia, you see it resonate. Amongst the speakers, amongst the audience, amongst everyone. You just see that you're taking everyone to a higher plane or to a different place than they expected."

"You just see that you're taking everyone to a higher plane or to a different place than they expected."

Writing as Exploration

Among her many skills, Lorie is a prolific writer of books, articles and blogs. These, for her, are another way both to explore and to educate. Her latest book, *Architecture in Burma: Moments in Time* shows how Burmese architecture represents (as the first lines of her prelude states), "a mixture of the country's unique history, politics, natural assets, religious beliefs, and superstitions."[76] She felt

LORIE KARNATH | 213

the timing was particularly right to write this book. "In the last two years, Burma has opened up significantly, and now these buildings that have been there for centuries are in jeopardy, so I wanted to write about them while they were still there. That's why I subtitled the book, *Moments in Time.*"

An earlier publication of Lorie's was about the photojournalist, still photographer, and film producer Sam Shaw, who shot the iconic image of Marilyn Monroe standing on a subway grate, her dress blowing above her knees. Shaw photographed practically every major Hollywood star of his day, including Marlon Brando (remember the photograph of Brando in a ripped t-shirt for *A Streetcar Named Desire?*), Paul Newman, Audrey Hepburn, and Sidney Poitier. He later produced such Hollywood films as Elia Kazan's *Panic in the Streets* and John Cassavetes's *Woman Under the Influence.* Earlier in his career, he worked for *Collier's* magazine and traveled the states taking photos that documented American life in the mid-twentieth century.

As a young woman, Lorie met Sam Shaw when she was doing a little modeling. They became fast friends and for twenty years often traveled the world together. As she tells it, "Over many trips, he and I had ongoing discussions about photography, art, the way individuals see things, and I had all these notes I had recorded from these talks. So my book, *Sam Shaw* (2010), was sort of *our* story. It is a book I'm really proud of. There are many books of Sam Shaw's photos, but nothing about Sam. And I believe that I knew him as well as anybody."

A children's book she co-wrote in German (Lorie and her American/Swiss husband

> *"So my book . . . was sort of our story. It is a book I'm really proud of. There are many books of Sam Shaw's photos, but nothing about Sam."*

live part time in Germany and part time in the States) entitled *Where Does the Sun Go When I'm Sleeping? (Wohin geht die Sonne, wenn ich schlafe?)* has a fascinating story behind it. Gustav Born, with whom she wrote the book, is the son of renowned quantum physicist and Nobel Laureate Max Born, who helped to define the realm of quantum physics. "Gustav and I," Lorie explains, "produced a lot of symposia and conferences together on originality and discovery. We decided to write a children's book on science to answer questions children might ask. We actually used the questions that his granddaughter, Amalie, would ask, and we answered those questions in simple scientific terms, because we felt strongly that science is a language, and language is much easier if taught young. Even if you forget that language later on, if you're re-exposed to it, it's a lot easier to re-learn. Many people don't seek out more than a cursory science education or don't keep up with science because they become fearful of it. This book is a way to help kids feel comfortable with this language of science. And it's also to help parents. So often kids will ask things like, 'Why is the sky blue?' and this provides parents with simple answers that have their basis in science. I've heard from many parents who appreciate it."

> *"[Gustav Born and I] felt strongly that science is a language, and language is much easier if taught young."*

Another of her books, also written and published in German, under the title *Verwegene Frauen (Daring Women),* describes the history of women explorers. The book disabuses the reader of the idea that exploration is only a man's field, and also pays tribute to the women whose achievements have helped foster many of Lorie's own accomplishments.

The Story of the Storks

One children's book Lorie wrote in German was inspired by a unique experience. "I prepared an expedition that followed the migration of storks," Lorie explains. "In Germany, there's a lot of these European storks, which are white storks. They are facing many challenges as a result of pollution and other man-made things, so they're dwindling significantly in numbers. I spent time up in this little village in Germany where many of the storks go to breed and, from there, organized an expedition where I followed the migration of the storks down to South Africa and back, to highlight these challenges, like hunting, and plastics, and high-tension wires. I realized there were very few things that one individual person could do about many of these logistical, structural, and cultural issues. But the way that I could make some difference was to start a nature sanctuary, to allocate lands that would just be used for the storks during breeding season. So I helped provide some money and worked with this organization and we did that. The nature sanctuary was very difficult to negotiate because it went through six German states, along a river. And the farmers used this land for their cattle, so the arrangement that ended up being worked out is the land was leased for two months, for when the storks need it for breeding, and the farmers use it the rest of the time. It's like an ecological lease structure. While I was there, I learned a lot about the German village as well as the storks. So I made up a children's story about these storks traveling to their nest. Almost everything in this story is true other than this fictional part involving a magic man—

> *"The way that I could make some difference was to start a nature sanctuary, to allocate lands that would just be used for the storks during breeding season."*

although he was actually based on a real person who lived in the village. They have these people there called healers, and this man was the healer for the village. It was just so interesting how these villagers have been living completely in balance with the natural world around them for a thousand years or more. They have always understood intuitively about environmental issues. They have always culled trees knowing you should cull some and not the rest, and that animals can live together amongst the farmers, and, without all this, it doesn't work. It's instinctual when you live on the land and you see this."

A Castle Looking for a Purpose

Lorie's newest project is also exploration-related. "I recently started something called the Explorer Museum. The organization's global expedition base will be housed in a castle in Ireland. The castle needed a purpose." And the purpose she gave it made inherent sense, since this castle was once owned by a remarkable explorer named Charles Howard-Bury. "If you read about Charles Howard-Bury," Lorie explains, "he was one of the first to consider cultural and philosophical implications of the regions that he visited. He did things like dying his skin with walnut juice so that he could blend more seamlessly with the people he was learning about. He would not only learn their languages (he spoke something like 27!) he would study their philosophies and culture before traveling to a their region. Few at the time did that." She is currently in the thick of planning activities for the museum. "We're putting together programs which will involve talks by many of the world's greatest explorers. Sir Ranulph Fiennes serves as the museum's patron. And then we have several discussions on museums and the importance of museums and why to start a museum, and had several big international gatherings in Ireland."

Her goal with this museum is not only to celebrate exploration and the ways that groundbreaking explorers have opened up boundaries but also to re-think the definition of exploration. "I want to broaden the definition to mean *discovery*," Lorie explains, "wherever it may happen. To me, a scientist in a laboratory is an explorer. I think that we have to understand and give credit to all who discover."

In fact, to Lorie, the process of discovery is layered. "Discovery is about creativity and observation and new ways of looking at things, ways that

> *"I want to to broaden the definition [of exploration] to mean discovery . . . A scientist in a laboratory is an explorer."*

maybe people have not seen yet. Whether it's in the field or in the laboratory or in front of your computer or at your desk, wherever, it's really about the discovery process fueled by originality and creativity."

Interdisciplinary Innovation

Another key factor in the discovery process, Lorie remarks, is allowing fertile interactions between various fields. This is a natural Renaissance way of thinking. "We really need to get people from all different realms looking at similar questions," she asserts. "I think if you go back to the Renaissance or even before, people combined the arts and the humanities and the sciences. But, over time, boundaries were created and people were segregated into specific fields. It became increasingly specific. So a lot of people didn't talk to each other. Imagine a case where two laboratories in the same building are pursuing the same question. If they just walked 10 minutes and knocked on each others' door, they might have a whole new way of looking at it, which would not only help avoid duplication but also help the idea go to the next level. You know the famed expression 'think outside the box' has been around for a long time, but for the past 70 years or so, universities or corporations have often served to *put* people into

"If they just walked 10 minutes and knocked on each others' door, they might have a whole new way of looking at it."

a box. Of course you need a certain number of people thinking in a similar way to avoid complete chaos. But over and over I've heard different thinkers say that the most important thing is to take bits of information from all over and try to approach a problem from a completely different angle." As a case in point, there was the discovery of DNA, which involved not only biologists Watson and Crick but two other key individuals from the field of x-ray crystallography, Rosalind Franklin and Maurice Wilkins. Lorie once interviewed Maurice Wilkins and got an interesting perspective on early attitudes toward DNA. "He told me when they took on DNA, no one wanted it. It was just the junk. So he kind of got saddled with something that, as he suggested, few serious scientists at the time were interested in. He said fortunately they took it on and were able to see it in a different way!"

Being a Woman Among Men

When asked what it has been like being a woman in fields like finance and exploration, which are traditionally dominated by men, Lorie responds, "A lot of my career choices have been more male-dominated, but I never thought about it that way. I just thought of myself as somebody who was willing to work hard, and hopefully could bring some new ways of seeing a problem and become known for being a creative thinker. That's how I always thought I was being evaluated. Although I got a little bit of a shock at the Explorers Club because exploration is a *particularly* male-dominated thing, and people pointed at me and said, 'You're a woman!' And I was, like, 'I know that.' And I'm thinking: as long as I'm doing a good job, doing what I'm supposed to do, what difference does it make?" But Lorie feels that the world is beginning to shift when it comes to women in the workplace. "I think that's the sign that things are much different because, by and large, I haven't had to think of myself as a woman in these different workplaces. I think of myself as someone taking on

"People pointed at me and said, 'You're a woman!' And I was, like, 'I know that.'"

whatever challenge develops. I do believe there's a new Renaissance afoot where we don't have to think of ourselves as a woman or a man. In certain contexts, obviously, but in terms of what we do, in terms of career, and in helping people, we don't enter it as a woman or a man, but as a compassionate person who wants to do something. I think that's huge."

When asked about what modern women bring to the Renaissance table, she responds, "If you look at today's women, it's their ability to be flexible, and receptive and creative. I think that those are definitely traits that women have had more ability, in recent years, to cultivate. One of the easiest things to do is to become rigid in your ways. And one of the hardest things is to be flexible and continually accept new things. I think if you have the toolset that allows you to learn and ask questions and be able to understand different answers, you are more able to take risks. And women are a lot more confident and strong in those things today, so that probably produces a great mixture for a Renaissance person. And it's not the Renaissance of the past. It is a new renaissance. It's a *different* renaissance. Because it's

"It's not the Renaissance of the past. It is a new renaissance. It's a different renaissance."

a different time and a different way of thinking. Our parameters are just so much larger now and so much more varied. My belief is that a change is truly happening. These programs I've put together, for example, at the beginning were all men, and now it's more and more women. And the women are doing unbelievable things!"

There is no doubt that Lorie Karnath is among the women doing unbelievable things. She has been and continues to be an explorer in every sense of the word.

Ren Gems

Lorie Karnath

"Never be afraid to ask the next question. Often the question is more important than the answer."

"Push beyond personal boundaries, to where discovery and beauty can be found."

"Even the briefest walk along nature's path can reinvigorate and inspire."

"Embrace challenge! That's what makes life interesting."

"Your imagination is the pathway to new thoughts and new directions."

11

LYDIA KENNARD

"Education is the great equalizer."

Degrees in urban planning (MIT) and law (Harvard), CEO/
Founder of KDG Construction Consulting, Executive Director of
Los Angeles World Airports, real estate developer, board member of
multiple companies

As Executive Director of Los Angeles World Airports, Lydia Kennard was responsible for managing 3,000 airport personnel and all airport operations, including a thousand-person police force, a massive busing operation, concessions, and all other aspects of airport life. At 6:30 AM on September 11, 2001 she was preparing breakfast for her six-year-old daughter. In the background, "Barney the Dinosaur" was playing on the TV. The telephone rang. It was her Director of Operations. "A plane flew into the World Trade Center," he cried. "We've got to ground-stop these aircraft, the FAA's closed the airspace!" Lydia found herself thinking, "The World Trade Center, New York? The World Trade Center, Chicago?" She had no idea, just that she had to go. She jumped into the car, and, by the time she had hit Downtown Los Angeles, she had made a number of calls to discover what had happened. She also found out that the mayor of Los Angeles, Richard Riordan, was in Washington, DC, and her LAX Commission president was in Germany. She was it! She had to evacuate the approximately 57,000 people who worked at the airport, along with the 350,000 other people there that day. The very real fear? That LAX would be next.

Interviewing Lydia Kennard over the phone, I was struck by the even timbre of her voice. This is probably no surprise given the level-headedness and calm she has had to display in high stress situations, the most striking of which was managing LAX during 9/11.

Lydia Kennard was born into a family of African-American high achievers and raised in the Hollywood Hills of Los Angeles. Her father, Robert Kennard, was a prominent architect whose firm's many projects included Carson City Hall, Carson Civic Center, the trauma center at Martin Luther King, Jr./Drew Medical Center, and three parking structures at Los Angeles International Airport. Her grandfather on her mother's side was college-educated (and this was in the early 1900s!) and very entrepreneurial. "He was a restaurateur; he had a ranch; he was a real-estate developer," Lydia explains. His wife, her grandmother, was remarkable as well. "My grandmother, who only had an eigth grade education, was one of the most phenomenal women I've ever met. She had seven children and was a real partner with my grandfather. It's just amazing when you think about the era in which they made their way. In addition, my grandfather's sister was the founder of the largest African-American-owned bank here in Southern California. Of course," she adds, "she never got any public credit, even though she had an ownership share, because she was a woman. But it was an incredible family. All the children went to college. My mother

"My grandfather's sister was the founder of the largest African-American-owned bank here in Southern California."

graduated from the University of California, Berkeley." Her father's mother was also an incredible woman. "My father always said," Lydia remarks, "that if she had been born in a different era, she would have been a great business person!"

Parents in Sync

It was not surprising that her parents, Robert and Helen, met and married. They were part of a small community of professional African-American families that socialized together, which included Paul Williams, the famous architect (designer of the homes of many celebrities, including Frank Sinatra and Barbara Stanwyck), who became a mentor to Robert. There were many inter-marriages within the community, so, as Lydia says, her parents' marriage was somewhat of an "arranged one." But, she explains, "They were a perfect match. My mother had come from this wealthy entrepreneurial family. My father had come from more limited means, but he was very, very ambitious. He went to USC on the GI bill, after WWII, and started his own business in the 50s."

The business that her father started was his own architecture firm, the Kennard Design Group. This was as much out of necessity as desire, Lydia explains. "He was with a major firm that's now known as AECOM, which is one of the largest in the world. One of his cohorts ended up getting to the top rung, as chairman and CEO, but my father knew he wasn't going to do that. There was no way, as talented as he was. So he charted out a new course by starting his own business, and he was extremely successful." This resourcefulness on the part of

"One of his cohorts ended up getting to the top rung, as chairman and CEO, but my father knew he wasn't going to do that."

her father, while facing institutional racism, was an important lesson for Lydia.

Lydia was like him in many ways. In a *Los Angeles Times* article from November of 2001, Stan Sanders, a lawyer who knew Robert Kennard, is quoted as saying, "Lydia is her father's child. She gets a lot of her toughness and certainly her competitive spirit in business from her dad."[77] When she was fourteen, Lydia started working every summer at her father's firm. He made sure not to coddle her, and in fact she was always responsible to someone else there. But she and her father were very close. Lydia makes an interesting observation about this: "If I think about the women I know with whom I went to law school or who were very successful in business, without exception—because our generation didn't have strong women role models—they had some male, typically their fathers, with whom they were close."

An Exceptional Education

Her father particularly stressed the importance of education. "He wanted my sister and I to have great educations," Lydia says. "He never wanted us to be financially dependent on a man. He was very progressive. He told us education is the great equalizer. So we didn't do much more. We didn't do sports; we didn't do a lot of extra-curricular activities. Our job was to get great educations. And that turned out to be exactly right. I must say that my career is founded on the fact that I got a prestigious education that gave me instant credibility."

"Our job was to get great educations."

Indeed, it *was* an impressive education. Lydia earned a bachelor's degree in urban planning and management from Stanford University, a master's in city planning from MIT, and a law degree from Harvard.

What is even more impressive is that she did her master's and law degrees at the same time. The story behind this is that Lydia was studying city planning with the ultimate goal of joining her father's business to launch with him a real estate development division. She was planning, once she completed her master's, to do a PhD in Urban Planning. But, as she puts it, that's when she had a "life changing" conversation with one of her professors. "He said, 'Don't do that. The better thing for you to do is to go to law school. If you want to be a real-estate developer, focus on real estate law. A law degree is a great set of skills.' I was already on my way to MIT, so I wanted to go to the closest law school to MIT which happened to be Harvard." She decided to do the two degrees at the same time. "I was on a mission, I was ambitious!" she says. "But it was quite a challenge. Harvard wanted me to do my dual degree at the Graduate School of Design at Harvard, and I said, 'No, I'm here because of MIT' and so I had to basically do my first year of law school, drop out, then do

"I was on a mission, I was ambitious!"

my first year of graduate school, then do courses concurrently at both places. MIT was very gracious and let me count some of my Harvard classes. Harvard was not so gracious, so I had to do a full load there. I'm forever grateful to MIT."

After completing the joint degrees, she passed the California Bar and spent one year working in a law firm that did real estate law. Then, in 1980, Lydia joined the family business, where she would remain for the next 14 years. As planned, she founded a development corporation, the Kennard Development Group, as an offshoot of her father's architectural firm. She not only headed up KDG's real estate development, she subsequently led the company into land-use planning and development services in both the public and private sectors. "We did a lot of public work and got to know many of the political people here in Los Angeles," she says. Which, as it turned out, for Lydia, would be good training for what the future held.

Entering the World of Aviation

In 1994, because of her background in planning and law, the Los Angeles airport agency offered Lydia the job of Deputy Executive Director. To a number of people in her life, this seemed like a strange move. "They would say, 'What are you doing in aviation?'" Lydia remarks. "But really, when you think about it . . . airports are really just big real estate operating companies. Planes happen to be flying in and out, but they're actually real estate holdings with the airlines as the tenants. I ran the construction, real estate, engineering, design, and facilities groups for Los Angeles World Airports (LAWA), which includes LAX, Ontario, and two other smaller airports." Of course, Lydia had to tap a number of other skills for this position, some that she hadn't known she possessed. One was an aptitude for bringing people together, for negotiating deals between disparate parties.

"I ran the construction, real estate, engineering, design, and facilities groups for Los Angeles World Airports."

Despite a nine-year impasse, for example, she was able to bring about an important deal between the airlines and the Ontario International Airport that led to a $250 million new terminal complex there.

As Deputy Executive Director, Lydia managed a number of large scale projects, including an annual capital-improvement budget of nearly $600 million, which financed construction and engineering projects, and an annual residential-soundproofing program of $250-million.

A Hard-to-Refuse Offer

In 1999, when her boss, John Driscoll, Executive Director of LAWA, decided to retire, Lydia was given a hint that she would be tapped by Mayor Riordan for the interim position, but would probably not be allowed to compete for the permanent position. "I was lukewarm about both of those things," she comments. "One day, sure enough, I got this call from Dick Riordan. And he said 'Lydia, where do you live?' And I was, like, 'Uh, I live in Pasadena, Mr. Mayor.' He said, 'Okay, meet me at my place, 8 o' clock in the morning,' and I said, 'Where would your place be?'" Lydia laughs at the memory. She didn't realize that Mayor Riordan was referring to the iconic, original Pantry restaurant which he owned in downtown L.A.

"I sat there at the Pantry the next day," Lydia recounts, "while Mayor Riordan smoked a cigar (in my face) and said 'I'm going to offer you the interim job.' I said, 'You know, Mr. Mayor, I don't think I want this job.' Well, apparently, no one told Dick Riordan 'No,' particularly when it was a big job like being at the helm of the second-largest aviation system in the country, and probably in the world. So, long story short, I said 'I'm mid forties, and I don't see running airports as my end game. This job is usually the last stop for an ex-military guy up from the ranks. I know nothing about aviation, and it's not what I want to do for the rest of my career.' And then Mayor Riordan proceeded to convince me that this was exactly what I needed to do. 'Let me tell you how great this offer is!' he said. 'I'll help you. You do this for five years, and you can leverage it into so many things. The airport system is a billion-dollar enterprise through which you will gain enormous operating experience that you can take anywhere you want to go!' So I said, 'Let me think about it and get back to you.'"

Lydia had another concern about the job. "My daughter was very young and I would have a long commute," she says. "So I went to my mother (my father had passed by this time), and I said, 'Mom, I just got this opportunity, what do you think?' Now, I was sure she was going to tell me not to do it, because of how hard it would be. But to my surprise she said, 'Oh no, you have to do this!' When I asked her why, she responded, 'Because they've never asked anybody like you before to do this job. You're a person of color and you're a female and, therefore, it's your responsibility to take it. And by the way, you better do a good job.' *(Ha*, I thought, *no pressure!)* So I took the job. And I didn't realize it at the time, but I became the highest ranking African-American woman ever in the city of Los Angeles, and the highest ranking woman in the national aviation system."

> **"[She said], 'They've never asked anybody like you before to do this job. You're a person of color and you're a female and, therefore, it's your responsibility to take it.'"**

It was, as expected, a demanding and intensive job. As Interim Executive Director of Los Angeles World Airports, Lydia managed nearly 3,000 people and a billion-dollar budget and capital program. She supervised an LAX Master Plan to deal with projected increases in passengers and cargo. She reported indirectly to the Mayor, but had a five-person commission, politically appointed.

Interestingly, after a national search, Lydia's temporary position became a permanent one when the mayor ended up offering her the job. As high-powered a position as this was, Lydia Kennard flew mostly under the radar (forgive the pun) until the fateful day in September of 2001.

High Alert

When Lydia received the call on the morning of September 11th, she went immediately into action. She knew that LAX was a possible terrorist target. "We always knew we were an iconic target. There had been, for example, the millennial threat in 2000." The FAA ground-stopped 178 aircraft at LAX alone, not to mention the impact on the other three airports owned and operated by LAWA. Lydia and her staff evacuated all the terminals, got people off the planes, and released any non-essential personnel. "I don't know if people were just in shock," she remarks, "but it was calm, people did what they had to do. And those that stayed there, including myself, we knew we were at risk. I remember the night of 9/11. I was sitting in my office, which overlooked the central terminal area, and for the first time in history it was quiet. And then, all of a sudden, there was this sound of sirens, and I called my director of operations, in kind of a panic, and said, 'What's going on?' and he said 'It's probably just the sheriff or the police making the rounds.'"

"We always knew we were an iconic target. There had been, for example, the millennial threat in 2000."

This was one of the times during the crisis when Lydia realized her reactions as a woman were different than those of many of the men that surrounded her. "Later that morning, I guess 2 or 3 o'clock, when I finally got back home and explained this one incident to my husband, he remarked, 'Lydia, think about it. This is their moment. These guys are going to get on their motorcycles and go get the terrorists.' And that was kind of the mindset. I had to deal with that very high-charged testosterone attitude that I had little understanding of."

There was another situation where Lydia's female perspective luckily held sway. "Shortly after the attack, within 48 hours, we were the first airport system of any size to reopen, and certainly we were very

"That was kind of the mindset. I had to deal with that very high-charged testosterone attitude."

proud of this. But one of the requirements from the FAA to be able to reopen was to secure the terminal areas differently than before 9/11. So terminals had to be a certain distance from parking structures—I remember it being 500 feet—as someone could use a car-bomb, park it in a structure, detonate it remotely, and cause catastrophic damage to the terminal in terms of both life and structure. Well, at LAX, the terminals are within 500 feet of parking. So we couldn't open the central terminal area immediately. Some of our guys went to the FAA and got a waiver, and I said 'No, we're not doing this, we're going to implement a remote, off-site-parking bus system, because I'm not comfortable that we can actually secure and patrol our on-site parking structures.' And the guys were like, 'Well, even if there's a car-bomb, it'll only kill about 200 people in one structure.' My response was, '200 people are 200 lives. I'm not taking that risk.' So in 24 hours we instituted off-site busing. We opened at 6 o'clock in the morning, and, by noon of that day, I was in a big meeting with

my director of operations who said, 'We've got it all figured out, we can open the central terminal area. We're going to do this; we're going to do that . . .'

"The guys were like, 'Well, even if there's a car-bomb, it'll only kill about 200 people in one structure.' My response was, '200 people are 200 lives. I'm not taking that risk.'"

But I was still not comfortable. So we were having this big debate, and law enforcement was also pounding me, telling me it was okay, the

FAA was going to allow us to do it, and I was just tortured, because I didn't want to take the responsibility of something bad happening on my watch. At that point, my chief of staff, who was male, said, 'Lydia, step out for a minute.' So we stepped out and he said, 'Look, you get to decide. You're in charge. Tell them what you're going to do.' As a female, you know, you always want to build a consensus, and you don't think you can tell them what to do. So that was very empowering to me. I just went back in and said, 'Look guys, this is what we're going to do.' And so we kept the central terminal closed for several weeks.

"Then, weeks after 9/11, when we were still busing people into LAX from remote parking lots, a number of people started pressuring us to 'get back to normal.' The airlines were really hurting, and they were laying off people by the tens of thousands each week. The hotels suffered too, and all the businesses that relied on the airport. Travel was really down, so they started blaming us. And passengers were getting cranky because of the inconvenience of busing in. So, the mayor was calling me, and the commission president as well, saying, 'You've got to open it back up!' However, I still wasn't comfortable that we could adequately secure and protect the airport with private vehicles being allowed free entry. Finally, I agreed to have a public meeting, with the press present, where the commission would *order* me to open up. This would force them to make the decision publicly, and I would simply be accepting their orders.

"But here's where it got surreal. We were having that public meeting, and there were all these news cameras there because it was a big deal that we were finally opening

"We were having that public meeting . . . when all of a sudden, in raced the CIA, the FBI, the chief of police, and they said, 'We have to go into closed session!'"

up the central terminal roadway to private vehicles. When all of a sudden, in raced the CIA, the FBI, the chief of police, and they said, 'We have to go into closed session!' The FBI and the CIA proceeded to tell us they had some new information from Afghanistan. They'd identified a full-scale replica of LAX as a training center for terrorism, and they didn't think we should open the central terminal area!" Lydia sighs, still struck by this memory. "So I was vindicated!"

In the middle of all this, there was another, more personal story happening in Lydia's life. "Two weeks after 9/11," she explains, "I was there 24/7, just trying to manage my way through it all. And I began not to feel well. I was tired, I felt like I had the flu, and I was thinking, *I have Anthrax*, because it was around the time of the Anthrax scare. So I went to my doctor, and I said, 'Look, I'm in the airport system, I have to work! I need drugs, I think I have Anthrax!' So the next day he called me . . . he was kind of laughing, and he said, 'What you have is more permanent than Anthrax, and you can't take drugs.' For a split second I thought, oh my God, I'm going to die and it's going to be painful and quick! But then he told me, 'You're pregnant.'"

> "*So I went to my doctor, and I said, 'Look, I'm in the airport system, I have to work! I need drugs, I think I have Anthrax!'*"

Lydia made the decision not to tell anyone (except her husband) until the end of the year. "I was so much older, and I didn't know if I could sustain a pregnancy. So I would go to these big meetings with law enforcement. And let me tell you, it was *big* law enforcement. It was CIA, FBI, NDA, everybody! And we'd go into these meetings, and I'd leave for a moment, go throw up and come back. I also never shared this with the guys because they had no clue how hard morning sickness is!"

It was, by the way, a successful pregnancy and her little boy was born eight months later.

Lydia in the News

The 9/11 crisis also put both LAX and Lydia Kennard in the news. She appeared in a number of newspaper articles, including in the *L.A. Times*, and was profiled by *CNN* and *People Magazine*. "A funny story about People Magazine," Lydia says. "My brother and his family were visiting for Thanksgiving. At the time, he was working in the Clinton administration as chairman of the Federal Communications Commission, which was a very public position. I told him that *People Magazine* had called to ask me to do an interview and I had told them 'No.' I didn't want to be in *People*. It was a gossip rag. And he said, 'Oh my God, Lydia, I've been trying to get into *People* all my career. Millions of people read *People Magazine*. I can't believe you're not going to do it!' So I called my press guy the next day and said, 'I guess I'm doing *People Magazine*.' Interestingly, years later, I got a call to be on a public board. And I asked, 'How did you find me?' And he said 'I saw the article in *People Magazine*.'" She chuckles. "So I guess it was helpful!"

> *"And he said, 'Oh my God, Lydia, I've been trying to get into People all my career. Millions of people read People Magazine. I can't believe you're not going to do it!'"*

Motherhood and Work

Along with all of this, Lydia was raising two children. She was a dedicated mother, and when it came to balancing her professional and family life, it was, as for so many working women, a challenge. As she puts it, "The women's revolution was fantastic. It got us into professional schools; we got opportunities in the workplace. But what it didn't do is help with domestic responsibilities." She tells a story to illustrate her point: "There was this young couple I knew; they're now in their forties. They were both getting out of UCLA business school, and they both got great entry level positions at Nestlé. She was running Friskies, or one of those PetCo brands. I don't know what he was doing. She had her first child, and she could still manage it. But with the second child, Nestlé just wasn't accommodating, and her husband wasn't stepping up, because he had his own career, so she had to step out and become a 'consultant.' 15 years later, when the kids were off to college there was no way she could get back on that track." She adds: "I do think more and more fathers are getting more engaged. But here's what I believe the quintessential problem is: Men pick and choose what they want to do with the childrearing. They don't embrace it as a full-on responsibility."

Clearly, Lydia didn't get off a track. So how did she manage? She explains, "I say to young women, 'Look, you can have it all and you can have it all at the same time, but you can't *do* it all.' So you have to find out how to shed some of the domestic responsibilities if you still want to have a career. And the unfortunate thing is that the heavy push years where you're really formulating your career is in your thirties. And those are the prime childbearing years."

But she believes a shift is coming. She explains, "Women are now sitting in more seats in universities, and more seats in some of the professional schools than men are. So society is going to have to figure it out. I have a daughter who's 20. I'm hopeful for her that she has a different world in terms of the domestic sharing than I did."

> "I say to young women, 'Look, you can have it all and you can have it all at the same time, but you can't do it all.'"

Moving On

Lydia continued as executive director of Los Angeles World Airports until 2003. During that time, along with her many other responsibilities, she implemented new security measures at LAX. But the costs of that, and the revenue lost during the 9/11 crisis, left the airport agency with a $100 million gap in its budget. So Lydia and her staff cut expenses and tapped into a reserve, and, by 2003, LAX received the highest bond rating available to airports at the time.

In 2003, for various reasons, she decided to move back into the private sector. She began serving on various boards, including the Rand Corporation and the California Air Resources Board. But in 2005, Lydia was asked by then Mayor Antonio Villaraigosa to return to her former position. In fact, as quoted in a *Los Angeles Times* article from November 2006, the mayor, repeating a favorite story, said, "My first call, my absolute first call, before I was even sworn in as Mayor of Los Angeles, was to Lydia. I said to her, 'I need you. This airport is an engine for Southern California's economy. I need your leadership, your communication skills. I need your ability to build consensus.'"[78] And Lydia did return, feeling there was still unfinished business, though she told him it would only be a short time. She stayed for a mere 15 months, but in that time she was able to push forward badly needed renovations, and prioritized making LAX's runways safer, along with other much-needed improvements.

After this newest stint at the airport, she co-founded an airport management company (Airport Property Ventures), which operates and develops general, non-commercial aviation facilities. And in 2011, she returned to the helm of KDG Construction Consulting, a position she still holds. She has also continued her active involvement on the boards of numerous nonprofits and publicly traded companies, including Prologis, an industrial REIT (Real Estate Investment Trust), and Freeport McMoRan, a natural resources company. She also serves as a trustee for the University of Southern California and a board director of the UniHealth Foundation.

A No-Victim Policy

How has Lydia Kennard, a woman of color, accomplished so much in so many areas that have largely been dominated by white males? Well, as for her father, it has been about both attitude and pragmatism. "I don't ever want to be the victim," she says. "I tell my children, who think of racism a little differently than I do, but who are not completely immune, I say, 'Look, it is what it is. You can't change that; you can't change people. But what you can do is find ways to deal with it.' It's kind of like a chess game, figuring out how to move the pieces around so you get what you want. So, as I said, I don't ever want to be the victim. I actually take the reverse position. I refuse to have people tell me no."

"I tell my children . . . 'Look, it is what it is. You can't change that; you can't change people. But what you can do is figure out how to deal with it.'"

A great example of Lydia's resourceful "moving of chess pieces" happened when she was in her twenties. "I've always been in a male-dominated industry," she says. "Even in law, at the time when I entered the field, it was still male-dominated. And certainly the construction industry was and still is. I did my first development deal when I was 26 years old. I had practiced law for only a year. I'd represented some developers, but I didn't really know how to do development yet. But I had this great opportunity because I could leverage my father's architectural practice and the resources there.

And my father was very close friends with the Southern California head of a very large construction-management company. So we cut a deal where we hired them to teach me how to do development. And then, when we wanted to do the financing, I knew we were facing another challenge. Nobody was going to give me seven million dollars to build this building. I was African-American, 26 years old, and a woman! So I hired a very prominent mortgage banking company, who packaged the deal, without identifying who I was. And we got the funding."

Through the years, Lydia has shown that same resourcefulness and stick-to-it-ness. She has also shown herself to be up to any challenge, to be the unwavering calm within a storm, and to bring her female sensibilities to building consensus and finding practical solutions to daunting problems that have eluded many others before her. She has been an excellent model for her daughter, who, like her mother before her, is currently attending MIT. "My daughter wants to be an aerospace engineer," Lydia remarks proudly. "She would like to do robotics for deep-space exploration. She's been very committed to that since she was probably in 9th grade. She's really very passionate about it."

"My daughter wants to be an aerospace engineer. She would like to do robotics for deep-space exploration."

With the mother she has, it is no wonder. Lydia Kennard is living proof of how far persistence, resilience, and not accepting society's limitations can take you.

Ren Gems

Lydia Kennard

"The path will not be a straight one, but embrace the twists and turns as each can provide important lessons for the journey."

"My experiences in 9/11 gave me renewed hope in the resiliency and compassion of the human spirit."

"Don't focus on not being able to do something. Focus on getting it done."

"Working mothers are important role models for their children, who learn the lessons of hard work and self-reliance, which promote responsibility and independence. These are lessons they will carry with them throughout their lives."

"There will always be prejudice and stereotyping. But my parents instilled in me the truth that if you're well prepared and work harder than everyone else, you can overcome anything."

12

BARBARA LAZAROFF

"No education is ever wasted."

Studied theatre, lighting design and bio-chemistry; ASID designer, co-founder with Chef Puck of the Wolfgang Puck Worldwide brand; author, speaker, product designer, philanthropist, producer

Eleven-year-old Barbara Lazaroff watched the girls at the more privileged school across the street strutting into school in the latest fashions. She looked down at her simple pleated wool skirt, one of only a few she owned. She had paired it with a white, starched blouse, which she alternated with her two other starched blouses. What choice was there? Her father, and her beautiful, resourceful mother were constantly working just to make ends meet. She thought of the words of her mother at this moment: "A mother does whatever she has to do for her child." And she realized that it didn't matter how many clothes she had. She was lucky. She had a mother who was her champion, her haven, her mentor. And she decided then and there that she would make her mother proud.

To walk into the home of Barbara Lazaroff is to walk into a wonderland. Vibrant colors abound. Modern works of art adorn every surface. Each object, from the individually created picture frames that elbow each other for room on the Yamaha baby grand, to the six-foot-high, aboriginal-inspired zebra sculpture that dominates part of the living room, has been chosen with the ultimate care. This proliferation of beauty and whimsy is a perfect metaphor for the woman herself. A compelling presence, she is long-limbed and graceful, her raven hair spilling over her shoulders and down her back, her large brown eyes arched by expressive eyebrows. Her voice, calm and authoritative, rumbles with just the slightest hint of the Eastern shore from which she originally hails.

Barbara Lazaroff is most famously known for her partnership with her former husband, Wolfgang Puck, for whom she designed many of their renowned restaurants. These include Spago in Beverly Hills, a tranquil and poetic space (there is even a poem that Barbara wrote etched into glass panels) in a palette of lush greens, amethysts and ambers; Chinois on Main, a sensual, undulating fantasy of Asian-infused décor in bamboos, custom ceramics, and riotous flower arrangements; Granita, a lyrical underwater-inspired fantasia of stone and ceramic, with biomorphic sea shapes dancing among deep-sea coral grottoes; Eureka, a "neo-industrial whimsy" of gleaming copper and pewter, decorative nuts and bolts, and light-infused glass blocks. The list of restaurants, past and present, goes on, each stamped with its own inimitable Lazaroff style. Included in that style are the innovations she was instrumental in introducing to the restaurant industry: the sparkling exhibition kitchen, the walls filled with work of contemporary artists, the organic flow between indoor and outdoor spaces, and, above all, the restaurant as a vibrant entity, as much about the aesthetic space as the food. These innovations are now so much a part of the restaurant zeitgeist as to be ubiquitous.

Although many people may not realize this, Barbara is not just about design. She was the initial motivating power behind the brand that is Wolfgang Puck. When, early on, her chef husband decided to open a pizza restaurant in the West Hollywood Hills, he pictured it as a simple space with red-and-white checkered tablecloths and wanted to call it "Trattoria Vesuvio." Barbara's response? "Over my dead body," and she launched into a design that became their first restaurant, Spago Hollywood. Her vision was of a dining experience that began well before the food was ever placed before the patron. As she puts it, "You dine with your eyes first." Her insights were inspired as much by psychology as by aesthetics. She knew that people have visceral reactions to colors, light, and textures, and that they love being swept away by welcoming spaces rich in fantasy and imagination.

"You dine with your eyes first."

Barbara also knew, early on, how to combine artistic inspiration with business savvy, co-owning and co-operating with her husband not only the fine-dining venues, but their expansions into such areas as catering, retail food lines, and "Wolfgang Puck Cafes," which dot countless shopping malls and airports throughout the country.

Disadvantage Into Advantage

Barbara's life began far from the star-studded Beverly Hills world she currently inhabits. "I grew up rather poor, really," she says. "Very working class. I was raised in small apartments in the Bronx and in Queens. My father worked hard but ended up losing his job multiple times due to changes in the workplace. My mother was constantly employed but was still always there for us when we were young. We lived in Flushing, Queens, and right across 73rd Avenue was Fresh Meadows, where the more affluent kids lived. As I watched those girls come to school, I never saw them in the same outfit twice for an entire year. Later, attending New York University, I could only afford t-shirts and jeans. When I had my first really substantial job, I swore I would never wear jeans again. Perhaps that is one of the reasons I'm now so consumed with fashion and have four closets full of designer clothes and shoes."

The Renaissance characteristics of exploration and growth were evident in Barbara's college experiences. "I started out studying theater, which included acting, set design, lighting, and script analysis. Actually, I went to NYU in 1970 to study theatre *and* dance. But then I broke my left ankle three days before classes. Really badly. So I could only study dance in a more theoretical way. Meanwhile, I was also taking my core requirements which included classes in biology and chemistry, which I found fascinating. I had taken a number of college-level classes in high school and I had placed out of college English, so I was able to pursue more challenging classes from the start."

Barbara had to support her way through college. "Since I was a working-class student, I had to work three jobs (along with receiving a government loan and an academic scholarship). One of the jobs was at the Roosevelt Hospital in the acid/base laboratory doing blood-gas analysis. I also worked in a retail store at the same time, selling clothes. Some people would come into the shop and be nice, while other people would be quite rude, so I had that revealing experience with the public. I also trained to do therapeutic massage for elderly arthritic people. During that time, I got increasingly interested in science and began to concentrate more on biochemistry. Eventually, I changed my major to experimental psychology. And I also became interested in going to med school. For one of my first jobs in a hospital, I was on two different wards: one was with the geriatric patients and the other was with the children in pediatrics. That was really difficult for me because I would come in some mornings and the baby that had been in the crib wasn't there anymore."

Barbara pauses for a moment, remembering. Then she adds, "The point is, I had a broad spectrum of experiences and I think that's what a lot of young people don't get now. They don't know what they want to do necessarily, but they don't get to try out different things. They may not yet have a particular passion, and they really should have the opportunity to consider different avenues, so they can discover their deepest interests."

"I had a broad spectrum of experiences and I think that's what a lot of kids don't get now."

For Barbara, after her exploration of all these different fields, she returned to her artistic side by developing what would become a key passion: interior design and space planning. A proud member of ASID (American Society of Interior Designers) and president of her own firm, Imaginings Interior Design, Inc., for more than thirty years, Barbara has, of course, demonstrated her skills in her stunning and innovative restaurant designs. She also does distinctive interior design for homes and is an award-winning product designer.

For some, the discrepancy between her college studies and her design work is confusing. Barbara laughs. "People would say to me, 'What do you mean you were studying science and medicine, and now you're doing this? Why did you go to school for so long and then change?' Well, I can read makeup packages and know what's in them. With my ill friends, I know which doctors to send them to. I can understand the material and I can help." Additionally, it is her varied education that enables Barbara to access both right-brain and left-brain skills: the analytical, systematic thinking developed in her science courses, and the creative, open-ended, imaginative thinking developed in her training in various arts. "As my mother once said," she remarks. "No education is ever wasted."

When Barbara and Wolfgang met, he was still a chef at Ma Maison. She encouraged him to put himself forward, even setting up TV appearances for him.

"As my mother once said, 'No education is ever wasted.'"

Through this process of creating PR opportunities, along with her unique restaurant designs, Barbara helped form the foundation of what would become the Wolfgang Puck "brand." Her skills in interfacing with the public were a big factor in this. Barbara and Wolfgang made a point, for example, to interact with appreciative patrons at their popular restaurants, which soon became the "hot spots," the places to be and be seen. The power couple gained distinction as iconic figures in the restaurant industry. And starting in 1994, their Wolfgang Puck Catering Company created the special menu for the internationally famous Academy Awards party known as the "Governor's Ball," a tradition that continues to this day.

Barbara was always present in the restaurant dining room and was also involved in a good portion of the day-to-day running of the business. She explains, "Owning and operating restaurants requires the ability and the desire to fulfill many different roles. I was reviewing contracts. I was writing business presentations. I was part of the real estate committee at the former Wolfgang Puck Food Company (presently Wolfgang Puck Worldwide). I also headed up the design and architecture wing of the food company. Oh, and I was having babies too!"

Women Plan and God Laughs

Indeed, Barbara, like many women, has faced the challenge of having a high-powered job while raising children. If there is anything a mother learns, it is that the best laid plans are often completely disrupted by little beings with minds of their own. As Barbara puts it, "You can plan whatever you want with the kids and lay out the clothes and try to get them to school on time, and then one of the children has a meltdown and yells, 'I'm not wearing that!' and the other one has a runny nose, and suddenly your day has changed. As a mother you have to be constantly making Plan B and Plan C; you have to have contingency plans. "But," she laughs, "I once heard someone say, 'The reason women make good leaders is they are always dealing with one cookie and three kids.'" There is little doubt that in today's world, with its uncertain economic environment and shifting demands, that the value of flexibility cannot be overstated.

"I once heard someone say, 'The reason women make good leaders is they are always dealing with one cookie and three kids.'"

Always Expanding

Barbara has never been one to rest on her laurels. Like all Renaissance women, she has continually expanded into new arenas and ventures. For example, as a writer, she has co-authored, with Tricia LaVoice, *Wishes for a Mother's Heart*, an inspirational and empowering book for women, and has penned a number of articles for the *Huffington Post*. And, as mentioned, she wrote a poem that was etched into glass panels at Spago, Beverly Hills. That poem, *The Flame of Life*, is a testament to the "flames" that burn in each of us, that inspire us to action and appreciation, as illustrated in these sample lines: "The flame of life creates/the flame of love inspires/the flame of passion seduces our soul/the flame of compassion heals/the flame of curiosity & knowledge illuminates."

The poem became the inspiration for another creative endeavor, the design of her "Flame of Life" dinnerware, beautiful china in a vibrant palette of colors, featuring single lines of the poem on each piece. Sales of the dinnerware have helped fund myriad charities, many of which Barbara has supported over the past 30 years. She is also in the process of designing a line of home furnishings and accessories.

Additionally, Barbara has been active on the lecture circuit, speaking at events for the American Society of Interior Designers, the Young Presidents Organization, The Women's Conference, and at such educational institutions as UCLA, California State University at Northridge, and the Interior Design Institute of Newport Beach.

And if these things aren't enough, she started her own podcast, "Exuberant Living," where she interviews exceptional artists, innovators, and business people. She has also formed a production company, Filmanthropic Group International (FGI), with Jordan Roberts, with the goal of creating socially conscious movies and television, as well as generating funds and awareness for their causes.

A Charitable Heart

A major portion of Barbara Lazaroff's life is devoted to social and charitable causes, fundraising, and philanthropy. She continually seeks ways to give back and to create a better world.

"I think the desire to make things better (without sounding corny about this) has existed in me since I was a little girl." She laughs at a memory: "It was a problem because my mother was also very giving, and she always wanted to help people. This inspired me to come to the aid of others, even to the extent that, on various occasions, I brought strangers home. My mother told me, 'Honey, you just can't do that, you can't just pick people up!'" Ironically, years later, Barbara's son would do the same thing. "I would have my older son in the car and we'd be headed to his school and we'd see someone in the street and he'd say, 'Mom, they look hungry, let's pick them up and take them home with us; we have another room.' And I would have to explain why we couldn't, without wanting to totally dampen his desire to help."

Maybe Barbara no longer brings people home, but her contributions both in time and money to causes and charities have been substantial. The many organizations she has been involved in include Aviva Family and Children Services; The American Cancer Society; The Zimmer Children's Museum; The Israel Cancer Research Fund; The Sheba Hospital in Israel; The Fulfillment Fund; Big Brothers/Big Sisters of America; hunger organizations such as Mazon, and Meals on Wheels; and multiple AIDS organizations such as Alliance of Housing and Healing, and Project Angel Food—just to cite a partial list.

Her involvement often includes innovative ways to raise funds. She and Wolfgang Puck, for example, founded the American Wine and Food Festival that raised many millions for Meals on Wheels and went on for twenty-nine years. For the Zimmer Children's Museum's "You Think" program, which helps inner city kids, Barbara asked major artists such as David Hockney, John Baldessari, and Robert Rauschenberg for artistic donations. Talking about the program, Barbara says, "Many of the kids in the program were bullied at school before bullying got as much public attention as it does now. Some of them couldn't relate to their peers or felt seriously marginalized. The program teaches them to be able to look within themselves and see what their gifts are." For the Aviva Foundation,

"The program teaches them to be able to look within themselves and see what their gifts are."

although it took 4 ½ years to do so, Barbara succeeded in raising a million dollars of in-kind donations to repair and remodel one of the Aviva homes.

To Barbara, it is simple: "If one person suffers, we all suffer." And she works hard to put a dent in that suffering.

The Power of the Feminine

"Women birth both babies and ideas," explains Barbara. "Not to say you can't be a full woman without being a mother. You can 'mother' in different ways. That maternal approach is often what works well in business. I think that showing respect and appreciation along the way for the people that work with you and support you is vitally important. I heard these lectures recently that spoke about the

"Women birth both babies and ideas."

idea that real progress in a venture or a business happens through nurturance. That doesn't mean spoon-feeding someone; it means giving positive feedback on a job well done. You need to acknowledge people and to value their ideas, even when you don't use them. You need to make them feel that they are contributing and that they have a sense of place and purpose." This kind of approach, she insists, should go well beyond the workplace. As the film *Femme: Women Healing the World* (on which Barbara was a co-producer) contends, there needs to be a worldwide shift away from the predominantly masculine values that have held sway for so many centuries. "I think that more and more women are needed to illuminate serious world issues such as hunger, abuse, human trafficking, the environment, and war," Barbara stresses. "We were born as caretakers, as nurturers. From our womb come the children that inhabit this earth, and many of us have an innate desire to protect not only our own children but other children as well. I think if more women were in politics, more women were controlling situations, we'd have less people going off to war, because women wouldn't want to send their children and other people's children off to war. We'd also be protecting our environment more, because we understand that this earth is precious, and that we need to safeguard it because it sustains us."

"I think if more women were in politics . . . we'd have less people going off to war, because women wouldn't want to send their children and other people's children off to war."

Barbara adds, "I've always been an advocate for women in business, politics, the arts, and in every sphere of life. I was one of the original founders of Women Chefs and Restaurateurs, which supports women in the hospitality industry and provides mentorships and scholarships for women in the field. I was a member of the now defunct but once very powerful organization, Hollywood Women's Political Committee, that helped elect women to various political positions around the U.S. I got very involved in the Big Sisters organization. And in my personal life, by the way, I have 24 Goddaughters that I've helped in various ways."

The Challenges of Caretaking

Barbara has also, as many women have, needed to take care of, at the same time, both children and aging parents. "This whole sandwich generation can be very stressful," she says. "Simultaneously raising children, while caring for elderly parents, especially if they have a prolonged illness, is enormously challenging." When asked how much taking care of others has impacted her work life, she answers, "Hugely. It has actually sidetracked my career in many ways.

There are times you can't work, you can't move ahead, you can't leave town. During one particular year-and-a-half period, I had eleven design offers from eleven different restaurants—one in London, the rest all over America—but I couldn't leave. It was a time of taking care of my children. And then I thought, as my sons got older, it would be easier, but the high school years had their own challenges, and, once they graduated, there was all the organizing with them so they could get into college. It becomes overwhelming. And, of course, if you're also taking care of parents, not only do you need to spend time with them but you also manage their appointments, along with researching all the medical options for their care. You can't sleep at night; you're worrying about it all. So yes, it can deeply affect your ability to work. It impacts every aspect of your life. A lot of young people working in our restaurants don't get it. One of our staff who lost her father started to understand. And then, once they start to have children, they say to me, 'How did you do it? How did you build these restaurants and have kids?'"

"They say to me, 'How did you do it? How did you build these restaurants and have kids?'"

Strategies

So how then, in the midst of all these life challenges, did she accomplish so many extraordinary things? What were the values and strategies that saw her through and that she would advise young women to cultivate?

"Organization," she says. "Lots of people have dreams, but it is those people who say: I have this dream and I'm going to actually make it happen, I'm going to step over that line, I'm going to take that first step, who accomplish something and distinguish themselves from the people who are just dreamers.

"Creativity is also essential. A lot of people associate creativity only with the arts and entertainment. But there are many ways to be creative. Take medicine for example. Free-thinking researchers and doctors can come at problems by combining facts, trial and error, and intuition to create a template of what might be going on with a patient, to establish a new protocol, or to discover a potential cure. For example, the decoding and analysis of the human genome is at the frontier of groundbreaking discoveries about medicine and humankind. That's one of the things that interested me about medicine. I believe, for example, the answers to cancer are out there. In every field, really, people just need to open their minds and be creative.

"A lot of people associate creativity only with the arts and entertainment. But there are many ways to be creative."

"Another key element of success in any field is tenacity. Many people have potential, talent, or exceptional intelligence. But it also requires doing the work and having the emotional stability to handle failure and to forge forward. In our business, we've made millions and lost millions. We came within a breath of losing the house I presently live in. But failure can be a very good thing. You often learn far more from your failures than your successes. They teach you what doesn't work. If you learn lessons from your failures and take them to heart, you become stronger, smarter, and more focused.

"And, of course, education!" she asserts. "It's essential! Education is the one thing they can't take away from you. You have to *prepare* yourself to be able to fulfill your dreams. My personal strategy for life was to be sure I would be able to take care of myself and my kids with or without a man."

"Education is the one thing they can't take away from you."

Barbara acknowledges, however, that even the best laid plans cannot always protect you from life's vicissitudes. She never expected, for example, that her marriage to Wolfgang Puck would fall apart. As she puts it: "It was a betrayal on the part of my husband, who was also my business partner and, I thought, my best friend. What complicated the situation further was that the affair was with one of our employees. My deepest concern was the effect it would have on our two sons, and for that reason I tried multiple times to keep the marriage together. At the same time in my life, I discovered that a close girlfriend had an advanced-stage cancer, and I began to help care for her. A couple of years later, she passed away, and, shortly after that, my beloved mother developed terminal lung cancer, which became a three-and-a-half-year battle. So understand," she stresses, "you're going to get sidetracked, so you need to have your contingency plans in place. At those impactful crossroads, I had to redesign essential aspects of my life plan."

Barbara adds some very practical pieces of advice: "You have to know and be prepared for the fact that some things will be timed-out. You can only be a prima ballerina up to a certain point. There's only a certain time you can be a world class athlete. There are some things you have to be realistic about, and some opportunities you will miss. And really think about what your strengths are and what your weaknesses are. If you want to do something and it requires things you're not good at, find someone who is; partner with the right person. I'd also say to be trusting but not completely naïve. And opening yourself up to correction is important. A lot of people see correction as criticism. But it's a maturity issue. Know that every time someone says, 'Well, I actually didn't like that' or 'This is how it should be' or 'You really need to work on that,' it's not necessarily a slap in the face. It's often somebody putting their hands under your armpits and helping to lift you up a little bit. Take it as a learning directive. Ultimately, you need to be able to make choices that

"[Constructive correction] is often somebody putting their hands under your armpits and helping to lift you up a little bit."

will create balance and harmony in your life. So strategy comes with making goals and a plan. Make a plan!"

And with that excellent set of advice, our time with Barbara has come to an end. During our hours together for the interview, she fed us pizza (Wolfgang Puck brand, of course) and made us tea and even insisted that one of us, who was under the weather, lay down and rest.

No doubt Barbara Lazaroff is a force to be reckoned with. She is strong, intelligent, and outspoken. She combines astonishing creativity with fine-tuned business acumen. Her interests and accomplishments are varied and far-reaching. Her dedication to work and to the causes she believes in are unflagging. And yet, if you ask her what she'd most like to be remembered for she will answer, "As a good parent." There's a lot to learn from Barbara Lazaroff, but this, perhaps, is the most important lesson of all.

Ren Gems

Barbara Lazaroff

"You can become your failure by giving up, or you can grow into success by moving forward with lessons learned from missteps or unforeseen circumstances."

"Don't just ask, 'What can I do?' If you see a need do something, do it with heart and do it now. Any positive deed is more powerful than good intention with no action."

"Money can corrupt, money can create. We each need to decide on which side of the golden coin we stand."

"Reputation and character are constantly confused; they are not interchangeable. Reputation can be bought and calculated. Character is learned, earned and honed."

"Being a mother is a tough, joyful, rewarding, often unappreciated, exhausting, exhilarating, never-ending, and life-expanding responsibility. Sound confusing? It is, and yet we all know how important that particular CEO position is; we raise the future of the world."

13

JEANNE MEYERS, RITA STERN MILCH, KAREN PRITZKER

"There are people who are beacons of light through the darkness."

Jeanne Meyers: TV and film producer and director, former news director for *NBC News from Moscow*, co-founder and director of The MY HERO Project

Rita Stern Milch: visual artist, film editor and producer, co-founder and graphics arts contributor of The MY HERO Project

Karen Pritzer: writer, magazine editor, film producer, education advocate, philanthropist, co-founder of The MY HERO Project

In the mid-nineties, news outlets were bombarding the public with updates from the O.J. Simpson trial. The Bill Clinton/Monica Lewinsky scandal was on the front page. Reality TV was gaining a foothold. Gossip and innuendo permeated mainstream TV.

Two working mothers, Jeanne Meyers and Rita Stern, who had known each other since childhood (and had attended the same progressive K-12 school) found this unacceptable. They were both mothers of school-age children and wondered why these pitiful role models were all the media was offering up. What about the real heroes and their stories of inspiration, hope, and social justice? Where were the positive role models out there? Why was no one talking about them?

Since both women had backgrounds in filmmaking, they decided to create a television pilot for a children's series. They called it "My Hero." It was a children's magazine, in the style of 60 Minutes. In it, children interviewed real-life heroes, told inspiring stories, and author Michael Crichton spoke about environmentalist George Schaller.

Jeanne and Rita eagerly approached the networks, but no one was interested. It seemed good news didn't sell. Unwilling to give up their dream, they explored the possibility of showcasing the My Hero *content on a new platform called "the Internet." By this time, Karen Pritzker, another graduate of their K-12 school, had come onboard. She believed the Internet would be the next big thing and encouraged the move.*

Twenty years later, The MY HERO Project (which can be found at the site myhero.com) is an abundant and inspiring online resource of good news, and contains more than forty thousand stories and essays, thousands of works of art and more than three thousand short films. The entries come from educators, students, professional filmmakers, writers, and artists. The site (which was visited by over 20 million people last year) has stirred hearts, encouraged action, and changed lives—all because three mothers, twenty years ago, refused to believe that bad news was the only kind of news people wanted to hear.

Jeanne Meyers and Rita Stern Milch sit down for our interview in Santa Monica, and we phone Karen Pritkzer, who speaks to us from New York. Each of these women lead rich, multi-faceted lives. Jeanne is a graduate of the American Film Institute's producing program. She has worked as a producer for NBC and is a documentary film director and producer. She founded and managed Brown University's Media Services and has developed feature films. Rita Stern Milch is a documentarian, visual artist, film editor, and producer who has also developed feature films. Karen Pritzker is a writer, magazine editor, businesswoman, film producer, philanthropist, and education advocate.

Early Memories

It is an interesting and noteworthy fact that Jeanne, Rita, and Karen all attended the same K-12 school, Francis Parker, in Chicago. Parker was a small, progressive private school that emphasized hands-on learning, critical thinking, media, and the arts. It was here that Rita and Jeanne first explored their mutual interest in filmmaking and social issues.

"When the 1968 Democratic convention was held in Chicago, I was a teenager," says Jeanne. "I was very influenced by that event. One night during the convention, my father drove us home right through the protesters' encampment in Lincoln Park. We saw young people camping out on one side of the street, and the Chicago police lined up with bully sticks on the other side of the street with orders to remove the protesters from the park. When we got home, we turned on the TV and watched the drama unfold. Strangely, the presentation in the news was not what I had experienced. In fact, Rita and I had been in the park earlier that day, and we observed young people playing music, having fun, and wanting peace. But the news was telling a different story. So, I became aware of how the camera can tell a certain kind of story, and what that means."

Jeanne: "[In 1968] We saw young people camping out on one side of the street, and the Chicago police lined up with bully sticks on the other side of the street."

Jeanne and Rita were in a media class at Parker at the time. "We had a teacher that let us make films as our final project," says Jeanne.

"Rita and I made a documentary on Super 8 film. It was sort of a surrealistic peace-loving kind of film. At one point," she laughs, "the film fell apart and Rita had to splice it back together again."

Rita adds, "The last image got caught in the projector, so the bulb burnt it, and it looked like a slow burn from the center outward. . .a visualization that the center cannot hold. It was the perfect ending. A happy accident."

> Rita: "The last image got caught in the projector, so the bulb burnt it, and it looked like a slow burn from the center outward."

"So there became a love, right then, of using film to tell stories," says Jeanne. It was particularly important, she stresses, to tell positive stories. "My parents' religion was important to me. I had a young and inspiring Rabbi, and I gravitated towards life and peace and love."

Karen Pritzker, who attended Parker a few years after Jeanne and Rita, was also interested in telling positive stories from a young age. As she describes in the foreword of The MY HERO Project book that she edited, *My Hero: Extraordinary People on the Heroes Who Inspire Them*, "I was ten when I got the idea of starting a 'good news' newspaper, filled strictly with news of good works. I realized even then that real-life stories of sacrifice, heroism, and courage make great copy."

Pursuing Their Passions

Jeanne attended Brown University and threw herself into filmmaking. "My Dad had bought me a port-a-pack, which was expensive at the time. A port-a-pack was the first half-inch reel-to-reel video documentary tool that people were using in the seventies. It was really heavy but it was theoretically portable, and no one at Brown had one, so I started to do some documentaries for different people in the school. I also studied experimental film at the Rhode Island School of Design (you were allowed to take classes at RISD if you were at Brown). I was interested in ways in which you could make art with film, in addition to the documentary work."

Rita started drawing and painting as a young child. "My grandfather says that he remembers me as a little kid sitting on the floor drawing while my brother and sister were teasing me," she says. "I went to the Art Institute of Chicago as a child—their Young Artists Studio program—and I studied painting as a student at Parker." After graduating high school, she attended Yale University and studied fine art. There, she met her future husband, television writer/producer David Milch, who was a professor at the university at the time.

Meanwhile, Karen, upon graduation from Parker, attended Northwestern University. There, she began to develop and hone her interest in writing and editing.

Jeanne, after receiving her B.A. from Brown University, got a job with *Communications for Change*, an organization doing social documentaries in Chicago. They also hired her boyfriend, who would become her husband. Together, they made documentaries for non-profit organizations. When her husband went back to Brown University to finish his degree, Jeanne approached the Dean about the need for a campus media center. The University hired her to build and run it.

She continued making documentaries but found herself longing to stretch. "It just seemed like there was more to see in the world," she said. "So my husband and I went to NBC news and told them we were going to go around the world, and we were going to do so whether they supported us or not, but they should get an option on the documentaries that we made during our travels. By this time, we had won some awards for our documentaries, and we had a reel that was impressive, so the head of the news magazine at the time said, 'Sure.'" She laughs. "He didn't have much to lose; we were very reasonable. So we went around the world and did some short documentaries for the NBC news magazine. They then asked us to try living in Moscow to run the production of the NBC news from Moscow. We agreed and happened to get the last two visas into Moscow just before Brezhnev died."

However, the job was less than ideal. "Here we were, doing a nightly news broadcast from Moscow, and the stories that they wanted were all pretty much the same," Jeanne says. "They weren't interested in the kinds of stories I wanted to tell. They wanted to see everybody with their hands up at the Politburo. They wanted to see people waiting in long lines for food. There were a lot of Cold War sentiments around, on both sides. I was even arrested there for doing a story showing Russians waiting in line to purchase the Rubix Cube!" By the time Jeanne returned to the States, she had decided to explore narrative filmmaking and applied to the American Film Institute in Los Angeles.

> *Jeanne: "They weren't interested in the kinds of stories I wanted to tell. They wanted to see everybody with their hands up at the Politburo. They wanted to see people waiting in long lines for food."*

Rita, after college, became a film editor. "I had worked, the summer before college, in a production company, and I just fell in love with the process of making movies," she says. "Editing particularly appealed to me because, as someone who likes to be alone with a canvas, editing felt similar in that you are in the room trying to give shape to raw material. It's not about meetings. It's not about deals. It's about the film and the work. So I started to work as an apprentice and then made my way up through the union, working in both New York and Los Angeles."

She also produced the Emmy-winning documentary *Abortion Clinic* for Frontline. The film was inspired by her mother's experiences working in an abortion clinic in Chicago. Around this time, her husband was offered a writing job on the TV show *Hill Street Blues*, which brought them out to Los Angeles full time.

After Karen graduated from college, she moved to New York, determined to be a working writer. "I was lucky enough to get a job at *Working Mother* magazine as an editor and a writer," she says. "Although I wasn't a mother, it was a great opportunity because the magazine was growing, and I was able to work with a lot of fantastic writers. My boss was also an amazing person. During her mothering years, for example, she organized *Mothers Against Vietnam*.

"The columns I wrote for the magazine examined the unique challenges of raising children while also working," she continues. "If, for example, you are toilet training in your home, that's one discussion, but if you are toilet training, and you're a working mom, and you have to communicate with the folks at the day care center or with your nanny and your husband, it's actually a whole different discussion. These issues were not just personal, they were also political. For example, I was creating a directory with information about daycare, and so I was on the phone discussing the whole daycare situation with lots of people. It was a real hot-button topic. Access to quality daycare was so important. People couldn't work if they didn't have it."

Karen: "I was on the phone discussing the whole daycare situation with lots of people. It was a real hot-button topic. Access to quality daycare was so important."

An interesting by-product of her job at *Working Mother* was the fascinating people she met. "When I decided to create a really great list of kids' books," she says, "I would ask children's book authors what their favorite kids' books were. I had wonderful correspondence with Dr. Seuss and an amazing conversation with Madeline L'Engle. I ended up becoming pretty friendly with her and had a number of encounters with her over the years." (Karen, in fact, would later contribute an article about Madeline L'Engle to MY HERO.)

She also spent time tutoring inner city kids in Harlem. "I thought it was something important I could do," she says. "Harlem was literally twenty blocks from my house, but it was a whole different world."

When Karen married and her two daughters were born, she decided to cut back her hours at the magazine to have more time with her family. She started doing freelance work, writing for such magazines as *Seventeen, Success, Newsday,* and *Kirkus Reviews.* Her marriage ended in divorce, but she later met her current husband, Michael Vlock. They married and moved to Connecticut, and Karen had two more children with him.

When keeping up with freelancing became more challenging, she began, instead, to volunteer her time teaching journalism and writing in the public schools. She also joined the board of the Long Wharf Theatre. "With the theater, I did a lot of outreach and brought theatre artists to schools, as well as created curriculums for schools related to plays we were doing," she says.

In addition, with a friend of hers, Karen founded the organization Read to Grow. "My friend, who had arrived in Connecticut to open a bookstore, was appalled to learn how many kids didn't have books in their homes. We both knew that to become a good reader, speaker, or thinker, you have to be exposed early to books. Children without books in the home were going to kindergarten with half the vocabulary of children from homes that had books. The idea behind Read to Grow was to give a newborn baby in the hospital a book and a library card. We also got people to donate books that we gave out to siblings and to schools. We had kids giving books, for example, as their Bar Mitzvah projects.

Karen: "Children without books in the home were going to kindergarten with half the vocabulary of children from homes that had books."

"We collected literally truckloads of books," she says. "There were readers who might be in sixth grade but only reading at a third grade level, and they were interested in, say, a sports hero. We would find and sort books according to level and interest, and teachers or tutors could come and pick out the books their students would like. It would just be a gift. Connecticut is so small and New Haven is so small that you could have an idea like this and you could get it done. This year, Read to Grow celebrates its 15th anniversary."

Jeanne describes to us her first year at AFI: "I was told to come prepared with projects to develop. I read hundreds of short stories, and I found one story in a 1950s *Galaxy Magazine* written by Damon Knight entitled "Special Delivery" about a baby who is talking inside his mother's womb. I produced this short story as a short film at AFI."

Jeanne was invited back to a 2nd year at AFI, but, when she became pregnant, she decided to forego the opportunity and to work instead on her own projects. She and Rita found themselves in similar phases in their lives. Rita says, "We were both pregnant. By the time Jeanne was in AFI, I had moved out to LA from

Rita: "By the time Jeanne was in AFI, I had moved out to LA from New York, and I was cutting an AFI film for Paul Schneider. So we were in the same place at the same time, both having babies!"

New York, and I was cutting an AFI film for Paul Schneider. So we were in the same place at the same time, both having babies!"

"Later Rita and I developed that short film *(Special Delivery)* into a treatment for a romantic comedy," says Jeanne. The two women do not discuss any details of that project. However, a *New York Times* article, dated June 14th, 1991, recounts, "A $20 million lawsuit charging that Tri-Star Pictures and the director and writer Amy Heckerling stole the basic premise and large chunks of her 1989 hit, 'Look Who's Talking,' from a student project given to her three years before the film's release has been quietly settled." The article continues, "Court records indicate that a settlement was quickly reached in recent weeks after Judge Byrne issued an order on April 3 turning down Ms. Heckerling and Tri-Star's efforts to seek a dismissal, saying that the facts of the case not only show 'substantial similarity' between the two works but also 'suggest copying.'"[79]

During this time, Jeanne and Rita also developed a script called *Mother Lode*, involving a working mother and her grown daughter. "It is about seeking approval, seeking forgiveness, and trying to balance career and children," Jeanne explains. This subject is as relevant today as when they wrote it.

Where Are the Heroes?

In 1994, the O.J. Simpson trial hit the airwaves. (And a year later, the Bill Clinton and Monica Lewinsky scandal would rule the media.) Jeanne's children were eight and ten. Rita's were six, nine, and eleven. "Television was covering the O.J. Simpson trial 24/7," says Rita. "That kind of tabloid programming was the impetus for The MY HERO Project."

"Our objective was to create an alternative," adds Jeanne, "to create an archive in the media where young people would be able to find stories of hope and inspiration."

"When we started," adds Rita, "It was the beginning of reality television and of people being famous for doing nothing, like Paris Hilton. We wanted to celebrate people who were working to make the world a better place, not just going to parties."

"It was sort of like that movie *Field of Dreams*," says Jeanne. "'If you build it they will come.' We figured we couldn't be alone in this desire. We couldn't be the only ones feeling like this was needed. It's easy, sometimes, in this post 9/11 world to be pessimistic, and it can be a struggle to find inner peace. But there are people who are beacons of light through the darkness."

> Jeanne: "It was sort of like that movie Field of Dreams. 'If you build it they will come.' We figured we couldn't be alone in this desire."

Around this time, their friend, Jonathan Alter, who was Senior Editor for *Newsweek* (and who had been another Parker student), said they should talk to Karen Pritzker. He remembered she had wanted to do a good news newspaper in elementary school and thought she would really get what they were doing. "So we went and talked with her," Jeanne says, "and she loved the idea. She then gave her first donation to support what we were doing. We had already produced our MY HERO TV pilot, which was actually quite good."

"And there was a brief moment," adds Karen, "when the FCC was saying, we can't have all Saturday morning cartoons and maybe we should have something a little more uplifting. So Rita and

> Karen: "There was a brief moment when the FCC was saying, we can't have all Saturday morning cartoons and maybe we should have something a little more uplifting."

Jeanne thought they could sell their pilot, but there were no takers."

Jeanne says, "A former student who had worked for me at Brown University, Tony Mendoza, told us about this thing called the 'Internet.' He told us that our idea for MY HERO might actually work well there." Encouraged by Karen, who now had officially joined their team, they soon began to realize the potential of "the world wide web" for culling and disseminating stories.

"So we worked on launching the MY HERO website," Jeanne explains. "We launched it in 1995 with the help of a small company called Digital Genesis. Then, I went to the Laguna College of Art and Design to talk to Professor Gary Birch, who was running the multimedia class, and I explained to him what we were trying to do. He invited me to audit his class." And it was in that classroom that Jeanne met MY HERO's future web designer. "There was this thirteen-year-old kid named Nathan Smith," Jeanne explains, "who was teaching the class with Gary. Well, Nathan helped design our website, and he has been doing so ever since. He's now in his 30s and has two kids."

The women began modestly, with a simple website that had a "guest book." People could sign in and write about their heroes. "Early on," Jeanne says, "Harold Wood from the Sierra Club wrote a blurb in our guestbook about John Muir as his hero, and then a packet of stories arrived from a school in Hong Kong. We realized there were people out there who wanted this."

Karen contributed her interview with Madeline L'Engle and

Jeanne: "Early on, Harold Wood from the Sierra Club wrote a blurb in our guestbook about John Muir as his hero, and then a packet of stories arrived from a school in Hong Kong. We realized there were people out there who wanted this."

wrote additional pieces. Harold Wood wrote a longer essay for MY HERO about John Muir, and they linked it to the Sierra Club site. Although MY HERO was largely intended for kids to contribute, "it became clear," says Jeanne, "that the storytelling could come not only from kids but also from professionals, who were experts in various things, or from writers who would take the time to interview people we really wanted to highlight."

Karen arranged for MY HERO to do an installation at the Chicago public library on its family day. "We were having kids type their hero stories into the MY HERO guest book," explains Jeanne, "and they were writing things like, 'My Mom is my hero,' and then the mom would see it and start crying. Karen really understood that MY HERO is a library and belongs in libraries."

Karen was able to help from her home on the East Coast. "The fun part of working with Rita and Jeanne was that I had three little kids and was an insomniac, so I would be up at night, and, for me, it was so nice to be able to work in the middle of the night or during the day when the kids were napping or at afterschool practices," she says. "I was able to contribute many of the jobs that needed to be done—writing, editing, rewriting, checking the guest book, etc. I could see, having worked at a magazine for so many years, that this was like a magazine but was also a new place and a new way of doing things, and I had a lot of ideas about how we could share what we were doing."

The next step was to get teachers involved. The MY HERO team approached teachers and invited them to participate by having their students write stories. Rita says, "It was great for kids because it gave them a sense of ownership and authorship.

Rita: "It was great for kids because it gave them a sense of ownership and authorship."

By having their essays on our website, that the whole world could see, it was like getting published." MY HERO also provided a web-design template with room for five paragraphs, five pictures, and five links, teaching the basics of a five-paragraph essay, while also using media. "The students could prepare their essay and go onto MY HERO and build their own webpage," says Rita. "It was the first webpage that most of these students had ever built. My daughter was in fifth grade at Crossroads School at the time, and it was her class that did the first student webpage about their hero."

"Additionally, a huge piece of what we were doing was helping teachers use the web," says Karen. "Jeanne would bring flyers and demonstrate MY HERO at technology education workshops for teachers. Teachers knew they had to learn about the web, but,

> Karen: "A huge piece of what we were doing was helping teachers use the web."

at least in the beginning, it wasn't very user friendly. Our site was something that was very accessible, as well as being something they could care about. We were educating teachers to get over their fear of the Internet. Our project was making new technology easier for teachers to use. Jeanne would get a phone call from a teacher, for example, asking, 'How do I upload a photo into this story?' Because teachers were inspired to share their students' stories, they were motivated to learn how to do it."

"We were ahead of our time," Jeanne says. "And we don't know how they found us, but in 1997 we were invited to Stockholm for something called *Global Challenge*, which celebrated innovators in

> Jeanne: "We don't know how they found us, but in 1997 we were invited to Stockholm for something called Global Challenge, which celebrated innovators in technology."

technology. There, we were honored to join other innovators at a reception in the Nobel Peace Prize dining room."

Karen adds, "They had nominated ten sites who were using the Internet and doing good things with it. It was in a big exhibition hall, and we were thrilled to be part of this very cool project and to get that recognition. These awards along with positive feedback from teachers helped grow our commitment and our understanding of the impact our project was making in classrooms around the world."

"We were also invited, in 2001, to apply to a competition called Child Net," said Jeanne. "We won best prize for a non-profit children's website at their ceremony held at National Geographic Headquarters in Washington, D.C."

Hard Times

Jeanne, Rita, and Karen have had, in their lives, their share of challenging times. They have also risen above them and, through their experience, gained greater wisdom and determination.

When Jeanne's two sons were only three and one and a half, her husband asked for a divorce. "I had met him when I was eighteen, and we married ten years later. I thought he was the sun, moon and stars. We had fifteen years and two beautiful boys together." But suddenly, the marriage was gone, and Jeanne was a single mother of two toddlers, a shift that brought the painful realization that life isn't always what we expect it to be. "It wasn't what I had planned," she says. "That ability to switch gears and embrace the next thing was something that in my wildest dreams I could not have imagined I would need. But, you don't know what the

Jeanne: "That ability to switch gears and embrace the next thing was something that in my wildest dreams I could not have imagined I would need."

journey is going to be. You can't get stuck thinking, that's it, because you really don't know. You have to be open."

"I hadn't dated since I was seventeen years old," Jeanne says of her return to being single, "and I was lost in this new world."

A few years later, she met architect Ken Koslow, with whom she continues to have a very happy relationship. "I have a life partner whom I love and who has been involved in my children's lives for twenty-three years," she says. "I am very blessed to have Ken in my life. He is a great architect and human being and has been part of MY HERO from the start. He is someone I deeply respect and love.

"We ended up moving to Laguna Beach," she continues, "where the ocean was our front yard and where I have this incredible community of people who have helped support MY HERO as well."

Rita went through some very difficult times of her own. Her husband David Milch, the brilliant television writer and producer (of *NYPD Blue* and *Deadwood*) suffered from bi-polar disorder and addiction. "Bi-polar disorder is a frightening thing," Rita says. "The person can be very charming but also very scary, especially in terms of temper. When David was manic, he'd be up all night. He'd have incredible ideas, and he'd want to call the White House because he figured he had the solutions to everything! And when he was down, it was such a steep drop. His addiction was really a form of self-medication."

Rita: "When David was manic, he'd be up all night. He'd have incredible ideas, and he'd want to call the White House because he figured he had the solutions to everything!"

She sighs. "He is brilliant, a genius, but dealing with those things while raising children was daunting. It was a long journey to come to some understanding."

That understanding finally arrived when David started having heart problems. His post- cardiac-therapy doctor diagnosed his bi-polar condition and started him on medicine which brought big positive changes. David's next step was addressing his addiction through Alcoholics Anonymous. "It was hard," Rita says, "but we got through it. All the kids survived. I think they actually learned a lot from witnessing that. They got a very revealing look at the world at a very young age. And, for David," she adds, "people who suffer like that are very empathetic. That's why he attracts so many people, so many lost souls. I mean, he can see right into them and they feel understood. There's the crack that lets the light in. He has been a mentor and a writing teacher to so many people. As a former professor, that's always been an integral part of who he is."

"And," Jeanne comments, "David's undying love for Rita and his kids was always there. In my time, so many people haven't stayed married, and it's a real tribute to Rita that she did, that she survived the whole journey."

Karen describes her difficult times as "falling down a rabbit hole," when she realized that three out of four of her children were dyslexic. She herself had grown up dyslexic, although she was never diagnosed. "My undiagnosed dyslexia made school a real challenge," she says. "My teachers thought I was simply careless or lazy. In college I had to spend every weekend in the library to keep up and work much harder than my classmates. It was the same at my job. I had to work longer and harder. Still, I was able to get very good grades in college and publish numerous articles."

It took a number of years for Karen to realize her older daughter suffered from the same condition. She wasn't diagnosed until her twenties. "They kept wringing their hands about her. During her third-grade conference, the teacher said, 'We don't know what to do for her. Her spelling is so poor, and she seems to struggle with tests.'

This is a kid who is currently blazing through academia, first at the University of Chicago, and now at Columbia, where she is getting her doctorate in American history."

The discovery in her next child's case came more quickly. "When my son, who is 12 years younger, couldn't read stop signs and didn't recognize his own name, I knew it was the same thing," Karen says. "When he would read to me from a book, he would say, 'The obese cat sat on a rug' and, of course, it was 'The fat cat sat on the mat.' He couldn't read at all. He was just looking at the picture, but his version was so much better. It was clear my son was really smart, but he wasn't reading, and, understanding my daughter's struggles, I wanted to intervene early with him."

"But it was frustrating," she says. "When your child is diagnosed with dyslexia, they give you, literally, a forty-page document that is near indecipherable. I would say, 'Can you tell me in four sentences what the problem is?' They couldn't do it."

Karen: "When he would read to me from a book, he would say, 'The obese cat sat on a rug' and, of course, it was 'The fat cat sat on the mat.' He couldn't read at all. He was just looking at the picture, but his version was so much better."

Searching for answers, Karen found Doctor Sally Shaywitz at the Yale Center for Dyslexia and Creativity. "Sally is an amazing person," Karen says. "She is my hero."

Dr. Shaywitz has devoted her career to better understanding children and adults with dyslexia. Her research into the neurobiology of the condition is exhaustive, and she has written more than 200 articles and a bestselling book (*Overcoming Dyslexia*) about the subject. With her husband and co-director of the Center, Dr. Bennett Shaywitz, she developed a model of dyslexia that emphasizes the higher levels of critical thinking and creativity surrounding the condition.

Karen wanted to find ways to support Dr. Shaywitz's work. "And I wanted other parents to have what I had," she says, "which was much more knowledge, front-loaded." Karen became deeply involved with the center, helping to create a highly informative website. "It is a really amazing site that provides so much more awareness for people," she says. "Sally is deeply understanding of the science, and she, herself, is a wonderful writer and

Karen: "I wanted other parents to have what I had, which was much more knowledge, front-loaded."

communicator. But she had to spend a lot of time in the lab and with patients, and there wasn't time for her to do as much as she would have liked, so I have been able to aid her in a lot of ways."

One of those ways was producing a groundbreaking documentary film, *The Big Picture: Rethinking Dyslexia*. The website for the film describes it this way: "*The Big Picture: Rethinking Dyslexia* provides personal and uplifting accounts of the dyslexic experience from children, experts, and iconic leaders, such as Sir Richard Branson and financier Charles Schwab. Directed by James Redford, the film not only clears up the misconceptions about the condition but also paints a picture of hope for all who struggle with it."

Big Picture aired on HBO and was an official selection of The Sundance Film Festival and other festivals. One mother said her child watched the film and saw himself in it. Afterwards, he stood proudly and announced, "I am dyslexic!"

Karen tells the story of a colleague whose father sent him the film. "He said he wanted his kids to watch the movie so they would understand him. He had felt so stupid. Even though he ended up running a division of ABC, as a kid he had gone undiagnosed. It's very heartwarming when people understand what they have, there is a name for it, and someone really gets what happened to them." The film is used in schools and community groups throughout the nation. Along with Karen's other outreach and development programs, the film has also been the impetus for new legislation.

Karen was also executive producer of another James Redford documentary, *Paper Tigers*, which addresses the toxic effects of childhood trauma. "When teachers and health care professionals understand the traumas that the kids have been through, it can really make a difference," Karen says. "The film was the runner up at the Seattle Film Festival, as well as appearing at other festivals. Organizations like Prevent Child Abuse America and The American Academy of Pediatrics have embraced it and are using it as a teaching tool."

Impact of The MY HERO Project

The MY HERO Project has had long-lasting and reverberating effects. "I can see the positive impact of MY HERO on the lives of young people I've watched grow up with the project," says Jeanne. "It has been a joy, for example, watching Slater Jewell Kemker. I handed her a video camera when she was five, and she wouldn't give it back. She started reporting for MY HERO, writing stories, making art and short films. Now she's twenty-three and making a feature film on youth activists and climate change that's funded by the World Bank. Slater has been mentored by MY HERO staff as well as some amazing heroes."

Another extraordinary young person who has grown up with MY HERO is Mohamed Sidibay. At three years old, Mohamed, a native of Sierra Leone, watched soldiers kill his parents. They forced him to become a child soldier in their army. "When he was ten, and the war was coming to an end, he finally escaped," explains Jeanne, "and, one day, he was playing on the beach and didn't want to go to school, and a kid who was involved in a project that we're partners with, iEARN.org, told him iEARN was not like other schools. You can connect with people around the world, and it's really cool." (iEARN is a non-profit organization made up of more than 30,000 schools and youth organizations in more than one hundred and forty countries. The organization enables teachers and young people to work together online.) "So Mohamed reluctantly joined the program," Jeanne continues, "and he became their star student! Then, students in Canada decided to embrace Mohamed as their 'Hero,' and they helped fund his education." In May of 2015, Mohamed Sidibay graduated from George Washington University with a degree in peace and conflict resolution.

Mohamed is now a teacher for the World Teacher organization. In October of 2015, he spoke at the United Nations. He uses MY HERO

Jeanne: "Students in Canada decided to embrace Mohamed as their 'Hero' and they helped fund his education."

in his classroom and continues to work as an ambassador for The MY HERO Project. "He was the keynote speaker at the iEARN educational conference in Brazil this past summer," adds Rita. "Mohamed has always been charismatic, even as a kid, but now he's such a great speaker, he really moves people. He's funny, he's charming, and he really gets the message out about the power of education to transform lives." (To learn more about Mohamed, go to: http://myhero.com/go/ Mohamed_Sidibay)

Another remarkable young hero was Mattie Stepanek, a poet who, before his death of mitochondrial myopathy at age 13 in

2004, became a respected motivational speaker and an inspiring advocate for peace. In 1997, Rita and Jeanne attended a workshop hosted by Children's Hospice International to encourage staff to use MY HERO's resources to shine a light on brave children facing big challenges. During the workshop, Jim Hawkins, a Children's Hospice volunteer, wrote this entry in the My Hero guestbook:

"Little Mattie has somehow acquired more wisdom in his short life than most of us do after decades of living. Through his poetry, he expresses wisdom in a way that touches anyone's heart. With his unabashed enthusiasm for life, Mattie has charmed everyone who has crossed his path. Mattie has inspired many people, young and old, to overcome every obstacle they may encounter and strive for their goals with dignity and humanity. THANK YOU, MATTIE!"

"Mattie was only five or six at the time," Jeanne explains, "and already a wonderful poet. His disease was a rare form of muscular dystrophy. Mattie's three older siblings had died before the age of four of the same condition, which had not been diagnosed until after they all were born. We asked his mother, Jeni Stepanek, how we could help. She said they could use a computer so Mattie could start to self publish his poems. We reached out to Children's Make-A-Wish Foundation, and they supplied Mattie with a computer and printer, and we posted his wishes online on MY HERO."

Jeanne: "Mattie was only five or six at the time and already a wonderful poet. His disease was a rare form of muscular dystrophy."

In July of 2001, at the age of 11, Mattie released his first volume of poetry, *Heartsongs*, which explored issues of love, peace, and spirituality. The book made The New York Times best-seller list.

Mattie's other wishes were to meet his heroes Jimmy Carter and Oprah. "All of these things came true," says Jeanne, "not only because of MY HERO, but we were part of the story." In September of 2001, while Mattie was in the hospital, staff members set up a phone conversation with President Jimmy Carter. A month later, he was invited onto *Good Morning America*, and he had a surprise in-person meeting with President Carter. On October 19, Mattie was featured on the Oprah Winfrey Show. Oprah admired, given the recent events of 9/11, the way he still saw "miracles everyday" in his life. Later, she would say of him, "Mattie would be the single biggest relationship that ever developed out of a show. When I saw him and met him, my heart melted."[80]

Mattie would go on to publish three more books of poetry before he died, just shy of his fourteenth birthday. Jimmy Carter delivered the eulogy at Mattie's funeral service held on June 28, 2004. In it he said, "My wife and I have been to more than 120 nations. And we have known kings and queens, and we've known presidents and prime ministers, but the most extraordinary person whom I have ever known in my life is Mattie Stepanek."

Jeanne says, "When Mattie died, our guest book had one hundred pages of entries by people around the world who were impacted by this young man and who continue to be."

Mattie Stepanek's legacy has continued through the Mattie J.T. Stepanek Foundation, which advocates ways to promote and practice peace. Jeni Stepanek, who is executive director of the Foundation, had gone on to earn her PhD in early childhood special education. She works as a consultant, an inspirational speaker, and a peace advocate, guiding hundreds of teens in more than 40 countries and on six continents to become global leaders for peace. "These are the ways Jeni has honored the memory of her extraordinary son," says Jeanne. "They call her 'Mama Peace.' She's lost all of her children but she has created a family of children from all over the world whom she mentors and who bring her peace."

Karen gathered many inspiring hero stories in *My Hero: Extraordinary People on the Heroes Who Inspire Them*. The book brought together heroes who contributed chapters about whom they considered *their* heroes. Karen describes in the foreword how her own inspiration came from stories of bravery and heroism told around her parents' dinner table. "Stories like these . . . showed me how courageous, honorable, giving, and fair people could be, even,—perhaps especially—in bad times."[81] Among those featured in the book are Elie Wiesel, Paul Newman, Dana Reeve, Magic Johnson, Kathy Eldon, Erin Gruwell, Billie Jean King, and Muhammad Ali.

One exceptional woman who contributed a chapter and was also the hero who inspired another contributor (Frances Moore Lappé) is Wangari Maathai. Maathai was the first

> *Karen: "Stories like these . . . showed me how courageous, honorable, giving, and fair people could be, even—perhaps especially—in bad times."*

woman in Africa to get a PhD, and was a recipient of the Nobel Peace Prize in 2004. Aware of the crisis of shrinking forests in Kenya, she founded the Green Belt Movement, which mobilized thousands of Kenyans, mostly women, to plant more than 30 million trees.

"When I want to encourage teachers and students to use MY HERO," says Jeanne, "I tell them, 'Well, you don't know about Wangari Maathai, but you should.' And so, some people have made murals about her. Others have made art and films about her. On our site she is also featured narrating a fable called *The Hummingbird*. It is an excerpt from the feature documentary *Dirt! The Movie*. So we have all of these layers of stories that come together around an unsung hero." (To see more about MY HERO projects about Wangari Maathai, you can go to http://myhero.com/go/Wangari_Maathai.)

Outreach—MY HERO Special Events

When broadband came on the scene, Karen suggested MY HERO sponsor its own film festival. Jeanne explains, "When you want to shine a light on inspiring content, it's really helpful to have a festival, where prizes, trophies, and recognition are given. We now have an amazing short film festival with films submitted from all over the world. They are made by everyone from third graders to Frank Marshall (who was nominated for Academy Awards for producing Steven Spielberg's "Lincoln" and other major feature films)." At the festival, Marshall received the Ron Kovic Peace Prize and the MY HERO Best of Fest Award for *Right to Play*, a short film he directed that showcases Olympian Johan Olav Koss and his organization that helps child soldiers reform through sports.

Jeanne: "We now have an amazing short film festival with films submitted from all over the world. They are made by everyone from third graders to [Academy Award nominated] Frank Marshall."

"We've built a library of more than 3,000 short films in the last ten years," says Jeanne. "The woman who directs the festival is Wendy Milette. She was teaching my children when they were in an alternative public elementary school, and she would emphasize things with her students like protecting the environment and working for peace, using music and art. After we started talking about a MY HERO film festival, we ran into her. She had just finished her master's at the USC School of Cinematic Arts, so we brought her on to direct our film festival and media arts education program. This has become a major forum for outreach to our local and global community." (To see information about their festival winners, go to:

http://myhero.com/Winners.)

Along with the film festival, Rita notes other MY HERO projects that have been particularly gratifying for her. "We do an annual Poetry-Jazz salon in April, which is National Poetry and Jazz Appreciation Month. We get an array of poets, musicians and students to come play and read. This year the theme was 'A life in poetry and poetry in a life.' We started with nursery rhymes and went through to T.S. Elliot. Poems that represented each phase of life were read by people in that phase of life." (You can see clips of these poems at http://myhero.com/go/Poetry_Salon15.)

"The music event that MY HERO and Creative Visions Foundation hosted this year was also very moving," says Rita. "It was a celebration of music arts educators, and included groups like *Guitars in The Classroom*, *Playing for Change*, and *The Harmony Project*. We also screened a wonderful feature documentary called *Imba Means Sing*, *The Story of the African Children's Choir*. That organization takes kids out of villages and poverty, and transforms their lives."

Rita: "[For the Poetry-Jazz Salon] this year the theme was 'A life in poetry and poetry in a life.' We started with nursery rhymes and went through to T.S. Elliot. Poems that represented each phase of life were read by people in that phase of life."

Additionally, this past year, MY HERO, with support from The American Association of University Women (AAUW), began producing a video series called *Women Transforming Media*. The series features, among other extraordinary women, two of our RenWomen, Kathy Eldon and Eva Haller. (See the videos at: http://wtm.myheroblog.com.)

"Being part of MY HERO," says Jeanne, "has been a deeply

meaningful experience. Just to be able to witness pieces of history and to be a small part of that is profound. That's the beauty and the opportunity of this work."

Life Outside of MY HERO

The three women of MY HERO also have lives outside of the project. Besides, of course, raising their children—who were often involved with MY HERO projects—they devote their time to other careers and ventures.

Karen's father, a member of the notable Pritzker family, was President of Colson Associates, Inc., which deals in medical devices companies, among other things. "Before my father died," Karen says, "I was very involved as a board member of Colson, but he really was running it. Now, it is my sister and I, and the management team. It's fascinating to meet people who are thinking of new ways to help people lead more productive and healthy lives.

"One aspect of being a Renaissance person for me," Karen says, "is that my financial resources have created opportunities for me to get very interested in and be supportive of other people who do amazing work. So I have been able to fund and start really interesting initiatives." For example, besides her continued involvement with the Yale Center for Dyslexia and Creativity, she works with the Seedlings Foundation, which, she explains, "fosters an educated and engaged citizenship by supporting programs that nourish the physical and mental health of children and families."

Karen talks of another key project: "I have partnered with innovative individuals to help create *The Connecticut Mirror*, a not-for-profit website that reports on the activities of our legislators and government officials. With so many newspapers folding or retrenching, there are fewer eyes on the actions of our government officials. *The CT Mirror* does that with a first-rate staff, and provides a check and a deeper understanding of the issues facing our state. This helps voters make better and more informed decisions."

Rita is deeply involved in her art career. "Painting has been a constant part of my life," she says. "It's about preserving my sanity. It's how I express something that needs to get out. I'm driven to paint, and it is a calming and meditative process for me." She has shown

Karen: "With so many newspapers folding or retrenching, there are fewer eyes on the actions of our government officials. The CT Mirror does that with a first-rate staff."

her work in multiple solo and group exhibitions throughout the years. Her most recent show was in August of 2015 at SOVAC Gallery in Venice Beach, California. (View her work at http://ritasternmilch. com.)

Jeanne's alternate universe includes a film project in the works. "I have the multi-media and motion picture rights to *The Twenty-One Balloons*, the Newbery Award winning book by William Pène du Bois," she says. "I get calls from people who want to buy the rights from me so they can write or produce a film themselves; it's a very popular children's book. You can see the flash storyboard for our feature film project, which captures much of the flavor of the book and its author's beautiful art work, online at: http://bigviewpictures. com."

Advice to RenWomen in the Making

So what would these three remarkable RenWomen tell young women who want to live abundant, inspiring lives?

The first thing I would say," Rita remarks, "is when you find that thing that, while you're doing it, you lose all track of time, follow that light, whatever it is. That's your path. Try to shut out the critical voice, which is usually quieted by action, and make time for yourself. That's something we, as women, often forget to do. We are so busy taking care of children, parents, animals, and other people, that we forget to take care of ourselves."

Rita: "When you find that thing that, while you're doing it, you lose all track of time, follow that light, whatever it is. That's your path."

Karen adds, "Have a sense of curiosity! You should be someone who is interested in the world around you, not just the fashion world, or even just literature, but also what's happening in science and in other cultures. In other words, don't just be curious, but follow that curiosity to continually learn and understand new things. Also, go with your strengths, which can shine in many different arenas. And have fun in your life. Be engaged! That's what's important!"

Karen: "You should be someone who is interested in the world around you."

Jeanne advises, "Stay flexible and firm. Firm in your belief, but also flexible in the way you write your life. The way you think things will work isn't always how it plays out, so you really have to be able to adjust and to do so graciously. Still, hold on to your dreams, and be firm in trying to realize them, even if it's just a little bit everyday."

"In the end," Rita says, "there are two great motivators – fear and love. If you are motivated by fear, you turn inward, but if you can allow yourself to be motivated by love, you can be expansive."

Jeanne: "Stay flexible and firm. Firm in your belief, but also flexible in the ways you write your life."

Present Challenges and Future Dreams

It is, indeed, love that motivates Jeanne Meyers, Rita Stern Milch, and Karen Pritzker. It is love that compels them to tell uplifting stories, to point to the good in the world, and to show the humanity that unites the human race. But, despite its many successes, keeping MY HERO going and supporting the needs of this growing multimedia project is a constant challenge. "I love MY HERO," Jeanne says, "I wake up every morning, ever since this journey began, thinking that at some point it'll get easy, but there is always so much needed to both sustain and grow it, and to engage a wider base of support for something that reaches so many people. There are the wonderful media makers, designers, programmers, and editors who work for MY HERO who have become part of our extended family. There are the teachers and students who represent the project and mentor others, and then there is our beautiful precious online library. I'd like

Jeanne: "I wake up every morning, ever since this journey began, thinking that at some point it'll get easy, but there is always so much needed to both sustain and grow it."

to know that this team and these resources will, ultimately, have a permanent home. We have roots that are long and wide, and, as 2015 was our 20th Anniversary, we believe this is good time to secure a future for MY HERO."

She sums things up by saying, "MY HERO is a vast virtual library used in schools, organizations, and homes around the world. My dream is that we create an endowment so that the library can continue to grow and we can build on that. So I wake up every morning and I try to figure out what letter I can write, and to whom, that will make that happen."

All are invited to take part in The MY HERO Project. Visit the web site (http://myhero.com) to share your own hero stories with the world or to find more stories of hope and inspiration from this ever-growing internet archive of stories, art, films, and music celebrating heroes around the globe.

It has been a pleasure talking with the exceptional Jeanne Meyers, Rita Stern Milch, and Karen Pritzker who are heroes in their own right and the beating heart of The MY HERO Project.

Ren Gems

Jeanne Meyers

"Wherever you are, take time to watch the sunset and be grateful for another day."

"Remember, on land and in water, to float you must breathe and relax."

"God bless Malala and her Books Not Bullets movement. It is the greatest calling of our time to listen to this young girl."

"There are beacons of light in this world, and they keep illuminating a path for us."

Ren Gems

Rita Stern Milch

"It is good for our children to see us working at something that is trying to help others. It teaches them perspective and priorities."

"I think many women, especially those who have been out of the work force, don't acknowledge all the different things that they are good at."

"Someone once said, 'Absent action, all animals are sad.' Painting is my action."

"Someone also said, 'Showing up is half the battle,' and it's true. Show up, be ready to work hard, and stay flexible. That will take you far in any endeavor."

Ren Gems

Karen Pritzker

"My father always said, 'You should always leave a place better than you found it.' This philosophy has animated everything I do. I can't change the world completely, but I can make some things better than I found them."

"Motherhood is a bright line between being self absorbed and thinking about the needs of someone dependent on you."

"The future is wide open to those with curious minds and open hearts."

"Everyone deserves a roof over their head, and access to medical care, education, and productive work!"

14

"I never in my life thought that I could not do everything I wanted."

PhD in psychology, therapist, biofeedback expert, professor, dissertation advisor, author, photographer, leader of study trips to Africa, China, India, Russia, Tibet & Nepal; former Wall Street stockbroker

It was Wall Street in the mid 1950s. 20-year-old Lita Rawdin had been hired as a secretary for two brokers, but she didn't plan to stay a secretary for long. She knew she had what it took to be a trader. But since, other than one woman who had bought a seat on the exchange, the only women working on Wall Street were secretaries and switchboard operators, she figured she'd have to be resourceful. She put together a plan to make herself invaluable to her bosses and convinced them that she could help writing orders when they were too busy. But for that, she'd need to get the proper certification. Well, she got the go-ahead and, once certified, there was no stopping Lita! She began bringing in her own accounts and, in no time, she was working the market just like the boys' club around her!

Lita Rawdin Singer sweeps in for our one o'clock interview. She is all fire and energy, passion and poetry. The first thing she does is quote from the 13th-century Persian poet and Sufi mystic Rumi:

"You have no idea how hard I've looked for a gift to bring you. / Nothing seemed right./What's the point of bringing gold to the gold mine, or water to the Ocean?/ Everything I came up with was like taking spices to the Orient./It's no good giving my heart and my soul because you already have these./ So, I have brought you a mirror. Look at yourself and remember me." Rumi poetry has inspired her life and she uses it often to inspire others. As a therapist for much of her professional life, she is more used to listening to others than talking about herself, but as we settle down for the interview, she is honest and frank about the many varied pathways she has traveled in her close to 80 years.

Lita has been a Wall Street broker, a therapist, a biofeedback specialist, a much beloved professor and advisor to countless graduate students. She has led professional study tours for therapists to China, Tibet, Nepal, Africa, Russia, India, Indonesia, Bali, Thailand, Singapore, Latvia, Australia, New Zealand and throughout Europe. She is a musician, a gifted photographer and painter. She has authored two books: *Adam Was Trapped Eve Was Framed: Five Steps to Relationship Freedom*, and *Cancel the Pity Party: Five Steps to Creating Your Best Life*. (Her daughter Stephanie Dawn Singer and grandson Brandon Singer also made contributions to the latter book.) Lita has often heard herself referred to as a Renaissance woman, so she was particularly pleased to be a part of our book.

Lita's childhood and cultural heritage served as both a spur and a deterrent to the woman that she would become. These two opposing elements were particularly embodied in her mother, who had come to the United States from Latvia in 1928. She was a brilliant and talented woman, who was a concert level pianist and spoke seven languages. She introduced her daughter to the arts and to classical music. "When I was a little girl," Lita says, "on Saturdays at 1pm, on the radio, there was 'Texaco Presents the Metropolitan Opera!' And they would play, for example, Risa Stevens singing *Carmen*. My mother would sing, and I would sit there, six years old, with a book that had little pictures of the composers. I would cut them out and write down all the things that they composed. I often went with my mother to the opera, and they didn't have the translations, and I didn't know what was going on, but I listened to the music, and I loved it. I did it because my brothers weren't interested and also because it was important to my mother."

"My mother would sing, and I would sit there, six years old, with a book that had little pictures of the composers."

On the other hand, as gifted as her mother was, she did not live up to her full potential. She squandered opportunities, for example, she might have taken advantage of for creative advancement. "When she came to the United States," Lita explains, "she had a letter of introduction to Sergei Rachmaninoff! She was that great! But she didn't call Sergei. The problem was—in a cultural Jewish household in the 1920s—women were nothing. Personally, I would have gone to his house. Found the address and gone to the house!"

Lita has a twin brother. "But," she says, smiling: "I was born first, I walked first and I was bigger than him." She also had a brother who was two years and nine months older. Because of the cultural household, her mother often made her daughter feel less than, while treating her sons with deference. As Lita describes it, "She was always criticizing me. I was never given any validation." Her relationship with her father was different, however. "My father was a socialist from New York," she says. "Very educated. He got newspapers from all over the world, and he sat and talked to me. Not to my mother but to me. He talked about politics, and he talked about economics and cultural differences between peoples of the world. So I got that attention and recognition of my intellect from him. But with my mother, I had to minimize myself."

Still, Lita had too much drive and energy to be kept down. As she puts it, "I never thought I could not do everything I wanted. If someone said I couldn't, I would think, *What are you, out of your mind?*"

Her family lived in Brooklyn, New York. As a teen, she attended Abraham Lincoln High School. "That's where Arthur Miller went," Lita remarks. "And Louis Gossett Jr. A lot of people went there. I loved it. I got involved in theatre; I played piano. I was always in the auditorium holding the flag. I ran for this; I ran for that. I was always up there! Why? I just did all the activities that were of interest to me. It never was a question of should I or shouldn't I? It was exciting. It was a challenge."

> *"I never thought I could not do everything I wanted."*

Watch Out Wall Street, Here Comes Lita!

With that same excitement, once out of high school, Lita started looking for work. She first found positions working for attorneys on Wall Street. But what really interested her about that famous street was the stock market. "It fascinated me," she says. "I would get up in the morning, and I would read *The Transcript, The Wall Street Journal, Barons,* and *Reuters,* and I just loved it." But as a woman in the 1950s, how was she to break into what, at the time, was an all-male bastion?

"Well," she explains, "I was smart. I knew I had to play the game. So I applied first as a secretary. Herbie Meyers at Merrill Lynch hired me to be a secretary for two brokers. Now, in order to write orders, to be able to trade, a person had to get special training and be registered, which of course, I wasn't. So I made the argument to Mr. Meyers that the men I worked for were very busy, and when they didn't have time, I could help with their orders. Of course, for that, I needed to have a certificate number—otherwise the orders wouldn't go through. So he said okay, and I went and took the necessary classes to get registered. When I got back, I started pushing. I had my number now and soon I had some of my own accounts. And then, I said I wanted my own little space. I started really working the market. If you saw the film *Wolf of Wall Street*, which took place in the 80s, some of that was also happening in the 50s. For example, they talk in that film about 'pump and dump,' and that's what they also did back then. There were these "pink sheets" with all the penny stocks. We would buy them and then a client would pick out a stock, buy it, pump it up by making up stories about it—thus getting it to go higher—and when it got to where he wanted, he would sell it with a big profit. Since they were all penny stocks, they would go from, say, 25 cents to 95 cents, but if you bought a lot of them, you could make some good money! It was a way of manipulating and playing the market then, and the truth is, they still do it today."

Lita may have been working the market, but the men around her weren't happy about it. "To them, women were secretaries or switchboard operators; they were not stockbrokers," Lita says. "The only other woman there was Muriel Siebert, who had purchased a seat on the exchange." She remembers someone walking in asking for Mr. Rawdin. "I said, 'I'm *Miss* Rawdin.'

"To them, women were secretaries or switchboard operators; they were not stockbrokers."

'Oh,' he said, 'I thought you were the secretary.'"

Of course, when Lita wasn't getting hostility from the men, they were propositioning her. "I was gorgeous and thin, long legs, short skirts, heels, and very smart. But I never messed around," she says. "It wasn't in my vocabulary. I knew how to spar with the boys, but there was no way I was going to bed with them. I just did my work."

Wife and Mother, Lita Style

During this time, Lita met Larry Singer, a sound editor. They married in 1956, after which Lita continued to work her Wall Street job. But in 1960, Larry got a job in Hollywood and they picked up stakes and moved to Los Angeles. Lita, now pregnant, gave birth to her son, Randy, in January of 1961. She decided, since she was home with one child already, not to string out having children. One year later, her daughter Stephanie was born. And two years after that, Serena came along. But as much as she adored her children, being a full time mom was just not for her. When her youngest was two and a half, with the help of a great live-in, Lita went back to work, accepting a position at Shearson Hammill, a brokerage and investment banking firm. Given societal attitudes at the time, she got a lot of push back for this. "In the culture I lived in—it was the late sixties, early seventies—friends would say, and my husband, too, 'How can you go to work and leave your family? What kind of woman are you?' I loved my kids, they're wonderful. But if I had stayed home, I would have gone crazy."

"Friends would say, and my husband, too, 'How can you go to work and leave your family? What kind of woman are you?'"

When the children were 11, 13 and 14, Lita decided to enroll in college. "I was always interested in psychology and how the brain worked," she says. "Even when I was on Wall Street, the psychology of the market, of why people buy, and how emotions affect people's decisions intrigued me."

So she completed a B.A., and then a master's and a PhD in psychology. Having also an avid interest in the interplay between the mind and the body, she simultaneously trained in biofeedback through the Biofeedback Society of California.

Getting Her Wings

This began, of course, a whole new chapter in Lita's life. After completing her studies, a friend introduced her to the psychologist Patty House who co-ran the House Clinic with her doctor husband, John. Patty and Lita conducted studies using biofeedback for tinnitus, which resulted in positive outcomes and in many clients coming into their practice. "I also had a lot of clients because there was something about me that people just connected with," Lita explains. "And I always had doctor referrals because of my mind, body and spirit work. I provided the adjunct biofeedback, relaxation, and stress reduction that doctors appreciated."

"I also had a lot of clients because there was something about me that people just connected with."

In 1982, Lita and Larry divorced. There had been infidelity during the whole marriage, and when they went to couple's therapy, it became clear to Lita that she could not live in that situation anymore.

As she put it, "I got divorced in '82, and I got my wings in '83." As a happily single woman now, her life became even more expansive as she added teaching and travel to her thriving practice.

Lita began teaching psychology at the California Graduate Institute. She taught there for fifteen years, from 1982 to 1997. Her popular classes were always full and, in 1990 and 2000, she received the Distinguished Professor Award, which cited her as "a great teacher whose heart and soul and intellect impart gifts of love and knowledge to students and faculty alike."

In 1983, Lita began to take psychologists on "Healing Study Tours" to various locations, including China, Peru, Tibet, Africa and China. Her goal was to open her colleagues' minds to other cultures and other ways of healing. In addition, she also lectured at universities in Russia, China, and Turkey on biofeedback and stress reduction. "I have travelled all over the world," she says. "I've been to Bali, I've been to Tibet and met with the Dalai Lama, and I've visited the Shamans and the healers of Africa. I have seen the wonders of nature and the spirit. Do you know that in Bali, there is no word for art? 'Art' and 'life' are the same word."

"I've been to Tibet and met with the Dalai Lama, and I've visited the Shamans and the healers of Africa."

In her book *Cancel the Pity Party*, Lita talks about some of these travels to remote areas of the world, and how they gave her a new perspective: "The indigenous consciousness holds the key not only to understanding our most primal selves, but also to healing issues at the deepest level of self. These native people seem to have found the balance that we in modern society have lost."[82]

She describes one particular trip to China she found particularly intriguing. "In October 1988," she says, "I was invited by the head of the Shanghai Psychological Association to teach a class in assertiveness training at the Shanghai Normal University. *Normal*, in China, refers to a teaching university. This was right after 1988 with those kids standing in front of the tanks in Tiananmen Square! I taught them assertiveness training, which the translators translated as 'Brave Training.' I ended up having a class with sixteen men in it.

Why were they there? Because they felt they were too aggressive. They wanted to learn how to say what they wanted in a non-aggressive way. Assertiveness training is a very practical and important thing that, of course, women also need to learn."

When Turkey had a major earthquake in 1999, Lita was invited by the Turkish Psychological Association to work with mental health professionals there to help them deal with trauma, shock, and PTSD.

The Power and Wonder of Photography

Lita, in true Renaissance fashion, has a highly evolved creative side. She developed, in particular, a passion for photography in the 1970s. Through the subsequent years she purchased cameras and attended workshops with such photographers as Kim Weston, John Sexton, and Michael Kenna. Michael taught Lita the special art of night shooting. Lita has an evocative black and white photograph of a stark pier at night stretching out into a flat motionless sea that was taken under Michael's tutelage. "We were in Boynton Beach Florida," Lita explains, "and he said, 'Let's set up. This is how you do it, Lita.' Because he does a lot of night shooting, he is a very isolated kind of guy. He's very internal. He says it takes him nine hours to find a place, get the location, get the best light, and then he waits for the right moment."

During this time, Lita was also fortunate to meet and get to know two famous women artists: potter and ceramicist Beatrice Wood and photographer Ruth Bernhard. Lita and Ruth (who was over 100 years old!) became fast friends. "I would call her up and say, 'Ruthy!' and she'd say, 'Lita!' and I'd say, 'How are you doing?' and she'd say, 'As opposed to what? I'm not flying with the angels yet.' Her father was Lucian Bernhard, a well-known German expressionist poster painter. Ruth would take me on 'light walks.' 'People don't see the light,' she would say. 'People don't listen, and they don't see.'"

After meeting Beatrice Wood, who happened to also be a centenarian, Lita asked and received permission to photograph her. "As I was taking the picture," Lita says, "I asked her, 'What has kept you so beautiful?' She answered, 'Young men and chocolate!'"

> *"As I was taking the picture, I asked her, 'What has kept you so beautiful?' She answered, 'Young men and chocolate!'"*

Lita's photography found particularly rich expression during her many travels. She took, for example, a stunning series called "Women of the World," which portrays women from locations as far flung as Tibet, China, Africa and India. She has had a number of exhibitions of her photography including shows at Paramount Studios, Antioch University, UC Santa Barbara, and the Santa Barbara Jewish Federation. "The traveling, the photography, they both became such important parts of my life," Lita affirms.

Five Steps to Finding the Best Life

Over the years, Lita developed a five-point system for helping her clients live happier, more meaningful lives. Much of this is detailed in her book *Cancel the Pity Party: Five Steps to Creating Your Best Life*. "First is mind," Lita says. "The mind is what you say to yourself. What is the voice in your head saying? For example, is it saying negative things like 'You're dumb' or 'What do you know?' Step one is to train yourself to observe what the voice is saying and replace the negative thoughts with more positive ones. You have a story

> *"You have a story you tell yourself about yourself. But you can change your story."*

you tell yourself about yourself. But you can *change* your story. I tell my clients, 'Don't be the victim. You had a terrible life? Well that was then. Take the high road, and let it go. It's up to you to change the voice in your head.'"

Lita explains that working with the body is the next step. In her book, she notes, "In 1975, American physician Herbert Benson established that just as there is a human stress response, with negative effects on the body, there is also a relaxation response, with a healing or restorative impact on the human physiology and mind."[83] In her practice, she uses relaxation techniques and biofeedback to teach clients to relax and to self-regulate, both physically and emotionally. "People don't want to take pills anymore," she remarks, "which is a good thing." Lita also combines biofeedback with mindfulness, which is present-moment awareness and acceptance of what is. As she explains in her book, "Mindfulness allows people to become truly aware of the present moment, tell the difference between what they can and cannot change, and then focus their attention on the things they can change."[84]

Step three involves the brain. "More recently I've incorporated neurofeedback into my practice," Lita says. "Neurofeedback is most specifically targeted at the brain waves called *delta* waves. This recalibrates the brain to help an individual be calmer and more attentive; it can even lessen the pain of migraine headaches. Neurofeedback also teaches a person to train his or her own brain, by using and recognizing the different brain waves: alpha, beta, and delta."

The fourth step in Lita's system is developing one's spirituality and opening oneself to the rapture of nature. In *Cancel the Pity Party*, Lita writes, "What does it mean to be spiritual? It means you are conscious of relating to your spirit and soul rather than just to the practical aspects of your physical reality." She defines soul as the "essence of our inner being," and spirit as "the flow of energy that connects our soul

"What does it mean to be spiritual? It means you are conscious of relating to your spirit and soul rather than just to the practical aspects of your physical reality."

with universal energy."[85] One of her most significant influences in the spiritual field is the Austrian neurologist and psychiatrist Viktor Frankl. Frankl was a concentration camp survivor who turned his harrowing experiences into a discovery of the power of the human spirit to transform any experience into spiritual growth. In 1994, Lita attended a talk by Dr. Frankl. She recalls that he began by telling those assembled: "Teach spirituality—it is the antidote to violence, emptiness, depression and aggression." His emphasis on discovering a meaningful life has deeply affected Lita's practice. She seeks to help her clients find meaning that runs deeper than mere hedonistic pleasures and materialism.

The other conduit into spiritual awareness, Lita contends, is a connection with nature. As she puts it in her book, "Experiences in nature aid in self-restoration, and this becomes an inner meditation, not an outer striving."[86] Lita advocates taking ourselves into nature as a means of connecting with the beauty, awe, and peace with which the natural world can fill us. "Once you see the sunset," Lita says, "life is never meaningless again."

Step five is the heart. Or more specifically, learning to open the heart. As she remarks in her book, "If you observe your heart, you know what it feels like when it is open and what it feels like when it is closed. . . . You need to

"If you observe your heart, you know what it feels like when it is open and what it feels like when it is closed."

examine your everyday experiences to understand why you are closed. As events happen, they come in through your senses and have an impact on your inner state of being."[87]

Lita uses two powerful tools to help people both recognize when their hearts are closed and to learn how to open them. The first is using mindful awareness. "Imagine," she says in her book, "if you were so fully present during each experience of life that life was touching you to the depth of your being; every moment would be a stimulating, moving experience, because you would be completely open."[88] Lita works with people to connect them to this powerful NOW, to help them to allow life, as it is in each moment, to flow through their hearts.

The second tool is poetry—in particular the poetry of that favorite poet of hers, the remarkable 13th century Persian Rumi whose insights into human nature and spirituality still touch so many people in our modern age. In fact, in 2014, the BBC called him "the most popular poet in the U.S." Among other subjects, his poems look deeply at the subject of love, in all its forms, from sexual desire to companionship. As Lita queries in her book, "What is it about Rumi's poetry that is so compelling that it has the capacity to open hearts? This question in particular interests me because people who come into my office today are involved in fields like law, engineering, information technology and insurance. . .[Yet]

"What is it about Rumi's poetry that is so compelling that it has the capacity to open hearts?"

Rumi is able to reach them, even those who never liked poetry." As one of her clients said, "The more I read Rumi's poetry, the more aware and conscious I become of my personal process and the depth of my being."[89]

Lita explains, "When you are able to live with an open heart, each moment will change you. . .The heart is the place through which energy flows to sustain you. This energy inspires you and raises you. It is the strength that carries you through life."[90]

Working It Out

The insights Lita has gained through her therapeutic practice, her creativity, and her travels have inspired her not only to turn these into books but also to develop and lead a number of retreats and workshops. One of these, "A Woman's Journey Within," served as an opportunity for women to gather together and deepen their creative explorations. Her Goddess Groups are designed to help women and girls explore and find the "goddess within." She also has Teenage Groups to help teenage girls and boys learn how to communicate, how to decide what they want to attain, and how to find and work with tools to get there. Her Couples Groups are for couples to explore and better understand themselves and their relationships. As a guiding text, she uses her book, *Adam Was Trapped, Eve Was Framed, Five Steps to Relationship Freedom*, which contains wisdom from her many years of working with couples.

Lita feels, in particular, that we will not have a balanced society until the sexes can recognize and allow the masculine and feminine, the *anima* and the *animus,* to be balanced within themselves. "It's about equality; it's not about supremacy," she says. In *Adam Was Trapped, Eve Was Framed* she uses the everyman and everywoman figures of Adam and Eve to show how the strict delineation of the roles of the sexes has not benefited anyone, even, ultimately, those in the power position. "Both Adam and Eve feel unappreciated," she states in the book. "Adam is trapped into the position

"It's about equality; it's not about supremacy."

of being the provider/protector, and Eve is framed into the role of caregiver. This paradigm is out of balance for both partners."[91] As Lita further explains in our interview, "It's a sad thing. We need to say to each other, 'I want to be able to be me and for you to be you. Let's stop fighting.' I have a lot of empathy for the men who come to see me. When there is divorce, women tend to thrive, and the men fall apart."

Interestingly, Lita is seeing some shifts in the traditional male/female roles. "What I've noticed recently in my practice are more 'Mr. Moms' at home taking care of the kids, while she goes off with her attaché case to work. I'm also seeing more men taking care of elderly parents—taking them to the doctors, etc.—in other words, men being more nurturing." But we may still be some ways off from considering outside work and domestic work as having equal importance. Still, she asserts, "It is a model worthy enough to pass on to one's progeny, free from gender bias and inequality."

Focusing on What Counts

In Lita's work, she emphasizes with her clients the importance of the deeper values. "The Dalai Lama talks about how man suffers because he spends his life trying to accumulate money, and then he gets sick doing it, and then he spends the money trying to get better, and then he dies never having lived." Lita stresses that we need to evaluate what really *matters* in our lives. "I say to clients, 'We are floating through a vast universe on this thing called Earth, and you are upset because your daughter didn't do the dishes?'" She urges her clients to let go of anger and embrace love and empathy. "'Where is the love in your heart?' I ask them. 'Open your heart. Start to listen to the people in your life. The first word of the first poem of Rumi's seventy-six thousand poems is *Listen*.'"

In fitting fashion, Lita recently received the 2015 IRWIN Award for the Most Humanitarian Campaign of the Year, presented on October 15th 2015, by Irwin Zucker, the founder and President of the Book Publicists of Southern California.

As we finish our interview, Lita sums it all up nicely, "Ultimately, we need to inspire people, not destroy them. We've already been destroyed enough. If you don't have love in your heart, then you are not whole. Your work is learning to embrace love."

Ren Gems

Lita Rawdin Singer

"It is by accessing those inner jewels of our spiritual core that we are able to discover our true meaning and purpose in life."

"When you say you 'can't handle' a situation, chances are you will not."

"In any relationship or partnership, balance is the key. That balance stems from an equal valuing of external work and home work."

"Without contact with nature, there is something missing—it is like a type of soul death . . . as if a part of oneself is gone."

"The motivating force of life is the will to discover meaning."

15

CHRISTINE AND MARGARET WERTHEIM

"Our mother taught us to see the world as something we could construct for ourselves."

Christine: PhD in literature, professor, poet, critic, performer, museum curator, crafter, co-founder: Institute For Figuring
Margaret: science writer, science communicator, editor, exhibition curator, co-founder: Institute For Figuring

Twin sisters Margaret and Christine Wertheim were like two sides of the same coin. They had each expressed their intellect and passions in different ways—Margaret in studying math and physics and becoming a science writer; Christine in pursuing the visual and literary arts. Their brain child, The Institute For Figuring, evolved out of a twin need to show beautiful connections between these apparently disparate worlds. Many projects came out of the Institute, one of which became a stunning representation of the intersection of art, mathematics, feminism, and environmentalism. Inspired by the work of Dr. Daina Taimina at Cornell, who had crocheted models of the non-Euclidian geometry, "hyperbolic space," to give her students tactile representations, the two sisters, with a background in crochet, also began crocheting models. Margaret's models were mathematically exact, but Christine decided to play a little. While still respecting the basic algorithm, she varied the types of yarn, the colors, and the regularity of the stitch. The result was a vibrant array of curved and organic looking shapes that looked strikingly like … a coral reef! Which led to a recognition of how many forms in nature display this complicated geometry.

The sisters were asked by the Andy Warhol museum to crochet a reef as part of an exhibition on artists' response to global warning. Little did they know that this small exhibition was just the start of what would become a world-wide phenomenon, involving thousands of other women. Through the sisters' work and these international communities of women, roomfuls of colorful crocheted coral reefs were displayed in museums all over the globe. These exhibits not only spoke to the beauty of mathematics as manifest in nature but also to the crisis of dying coral reefs and to the power of a particularly female craft to educate and inspire action. The reefs have also communicated to people in a powerful and direct way, by transcending words and making the issues more than just ideas, making them also experiential, tangible, and immediate.

At first glance, Australians Christine and Margaret Wertheim do not look like identical twins. Christine has an unruly shock of red hair, and an iconoclastic way of dressing, while Margaret sports a simple shirt and straight-legged pants and has short, cropped grey hair. It appears their personalities are just as dissimilar. Margaret is quiet and articulate in a logical left-brained way. Christine is artistic, esoteric and philosophical.

Their numerous areas of expertise seem to also be at different ends of the spectrum.

Margaret studied physics and mathematics at university and has pursued a successful career as a science writer, communicator and speaker, and exhibition curator. She has been a featured Ted Talk speaker. She was an op-ed contributor (on science subjects) to the *Los Angeles Times,* and for five years, she wrote the "Quark Soup" column for the *LA Weekly.* She has written for the *New York Times*, *New Scientist*, the *Guardian* and many other publications. She is a contributing editor to the arts and science quarterly, *Cabinet.* She has written six books: *The Pearly Gates of Cyberspace: A History of Space from Dante to the Internet*; *Physics on the Fringe: Smoke Rings, Circlons and Alternative Theories of Everything*; *A Field Guide to Hyperbolic Space*; and *A Field Guide to the Business Card Menger Sponge.* She the co-author of *Crochet Coral Reef.*

Christine has a PhD in literature; is a poet, critic, performer, museum curator; and teaches creative writing and critical studies at the California Institute of the Arts. She also spent a number of years as a painter. Her experimental poetry, rich in visual and aural aspects, includes her published volumes: *+'Ime-S-pace,* (Les Figues Press 2007) and mUtter-bAbel (Counterpath Press, 2013). She is the editor of the *N'Oulipo* anthology and *Feminaissance.* She made her theatrical debut as the writer, director, performer of a sock puppet play called *Quoi.* She is the co-author of the book *Crochet Coral Reef.*

Figuring It Out

Despite their apparent divergent interests, the two sisters have found a way to combine their various skills and fields into a unique synthesis. Together they founded the Institute For Figuring. "The mission of the Institute For Figuring," explains Margaret, "is to engage people with science and mathematics by looking at the poetic and aesthetic dimensions of these fields." At the Institute, various "science + art" residents create physical embodiments of complex scientific or mathematical concepts, creations such as the geometrically inspired paper and bamboo stick sculptures of Jake Dotson or the Silurian-age inspired forms Christine made from shopping bags, earphones, and other plastic detritus. During that series, Christine held workshops to inspire others to create some Silurian forms. As Margaret explained in a 2009 TED Talk: "We're trying to have kindergarten for grown-ups." She elaborates: "We live in a society that tends to valorize symbolic forms of representation—algebraic representations, equations, codes. . . . But through plastic forms of play—people can be engaged with the most abstract, high-powered, theoretical ideas, the kinds of ideas that normally you have to go to university departments to study. You can do it through playing with material objects."[92]

Essentially, there are lots of think tanks. So why not, as Christine has proposed, have more "play tanks."

> Margaret: "Through plastic forms of play—people can be engaged with the most abstract, high-powered, theoretical ideas."

Coral Reef Project

One of the most stunning examples to emerge from IFF of this physical embodiment of mathematical theory is something called the Crochet Coral Reef project. This is a project that has been going on for ten years and, as the IFF website explains, "resides at the intersection of mathematics, marine biology, handicraft and community art practice, and responds to the environmental crisis of global warming and the escalating problem of oceanic plastic trash."[93] How, you may ask, does it do all that?

It began with the discovery in 1997 by Cornell mathematician Daina Taimina, that through crochet, one could create a model of a mathematical structure many mathematicians thought was impossible to physically model. This structure is a non-Euclidean geometry called *hyperbolic space*, and crochet, it appears, is the perfect vehicle for demonstrating its strange crenulated properties.

For years, mathematicians worked at representing hyperbolic geometry on computers. Although they eventually succeeded, it was a difficult task. When Margaret was asked by TED interviewer K. L. Mulholland why this was, she explained, "We are moving into the age of being able to simulate more and more things on computers and we are coming to realize how mind-bogglingly complex the world is which we are trying to simulate. The fall of a handkerchief in the wind is hard to simulate, and yet the handkerchief does it effortlessly. In some sense, the handkerchief knows something; it can do something that our best computer engineers can't do."[94]

The sisters met Daina in 2003. "She'd been crocheting [her models] for six or seven years," Christine says, "and she was using them in her classes at Cornell." Margaret and Christine actually had grown up crocheting, as well as practicing other feminine crafts such as knitting, embroidery and dress-making—all taught to them by their mother, Barbara Wertheim. Now they were seeing crochet used by Dr. Taimina in a most unconventional and yet very practical way—as a method to model a complex geometry in a physical object that could then be handled and played with in a three-dimensional way.

Inspired, the sisters began crocheting a number of models themselves. After a while, they began to diverge in how they approached them. "Daina's models looked a certain kind of a way," Christine explains. "Both Daina and Margaret were very interested in making them mathematically perfect. But I'm not that kind of person, so I started playing. Using pink wool and fluffy wool and sparkly wool, I changed the recipe somewhat. They were still essentially hyperbolic, but not perfectly so.

"And then I just had a pile of them on the coffee table, and I said to Margaret, 'It looks like a coral reef!' Because I wasn't

Christine: "I started playing. Using pink wool and fluffy wool and sparkly wool, I changed the recipe somewhat. They were still essentially hyperbolic, but not perfectly so."

doing them perfectly, and because I had embedded them in pink and orange and fluffy, I made them look like organic things which also made them look like corals."

This was more than a coincidence. It turns out that corals are essentially hyperbolic. There are also other things in nature that share this geometry, such as lettuce leaves, cactuses, and sea slugs. "There was a theorem among mathematicians," Margaret comments wryly, "that you couldn't have models of this geometry in the physical world. They could not see that natural structures around them were doing this. And I once asked some mathematicians, why didn't they realize this? And their brief answer was 'I guess there aren't many mathematicians out there looking at sea slugs.'"

The sea slugs, then, just like the falling handkerchief, seem to be smarter than our computers (and perhaps than some mathematicians).

Margaret: "And their brief answer was, 'I guess there aren't many mathematicians out there looking at sea slugs.'"

Besides crochet, there was another inadvertent model of hyperbolic geometry expressed through a female handicraft that, for years, was ubiquitous in people's homes: doilies! Says Christine: "The structure was in the ruffles on doilies. That ruffling that you can do with crochet and with certain kinds of lace-making techniques, women have been doing for hundreds of years, whether they knew it was hyperbolic or not. Other types of handicrafters in many cultures have been doing the same thing. You can do it with anything that is pixelated: knitting, beading, crocheting, even basket weaving."

What's remarkable about this is the distance there has traditionally been between mathematics as an abstract system, and mathematics as an expressed system, be it in nature or in crafts. It has taken women like Daina, Christine and Margaret to show that perhaps the mostly male mathematicians were not seeing the whole picture. Margaret stated in the TED interview, "The symbolic representation that has to be used [with] computers is not the only form of knowledge, there are other representations of knowledge that are just as powerful and probably even more powerful; and that is the physical manifestation of knowledge."[95]

As the sisters continued to crochet these colorful corals, the process soon expanded into issues of the environment. The twins, having been brought up near the Great Barrier Reef, were concerned about coral reefs and how, due to the influence of global warming, they are dying out worldwide. As Margaret explained in her TED Talk of 2009, "Corals are very delicate organisms, and they are devastated by any rise in sea temperatures. It causes these vast bleaching events that are the first signs of corals being sick. And if the bleaching doesn't go away—if the temperatures don't go down—reefs start to die."[96]

> *Margaret: "Corals are very delicate organisms, and they are devastated by any rise in sea temperatures."*

Ultimately, these elements of mathematics, women's crafts, and environmental awareness were joined by another key element: community involvement. It began, in 2007, with the Andy Warhol museum asking if the sisters' coral reef could be part of an exhibition they were doing on artists' response to global warning. After that small exhibition, the Chicago Humanities Festival asked if the sisters could fill a 3,000 square-foot gallery with a crocheted reef. As Margaret comments in her Ted Talk: "I naively said, 'Oh, yes, sure.' … I had no idea what it meant [to crochet enough] to fill a 3,000 square-foot gallery … And I went home, and I told my sister Christine. And she nearly had a fit … But she went into crochet overdrive. And to cut a long story short, eight months later we did fill the Chicago Cultural Center's 3,000 square foot gallery."[97] The Chicago folks also decided to get local people involved in making a companion reef, so Margaret and Christine held workshops and lectures to teach hundreds of people the techniques. And the two reefs were displayed side by side. "By this stage the project took on a viral dimension of its own,"[98] explained Margaret, as they were then invited to do similar community reefs in New York, London, and Los Angeles.

It has just continued to grow. Explains Christine: "It's now gone all over the world, and interestingly, 99.99 percent of the people who participated in our project were women. There are more than 7,000 women who have participated on the reefs that have gone on display in museums and galleries worldwide. And that actually has surprised us. I thought there would be a higher percentage of men." But she has a theory as to why this is: "The experimenting with what happens if you put the same basic formula into different materials was what I did,

> Christine: "It's now gone all over the world. . . There are more than 7,000 women who have participated on the reefs."

and a lot of women's handicrafts are about experimenting with the material embodiment of a form. So that quickly became what other women were interested in. And mathematicians were generally never interested in those material qualities. All they cared about was the form that could be reduced to the equations. It's not an accident that a woman happened to make this discovery. And then other women took it up."

Margaret adds, "One of the reasons that the reef project has been so successful and gone on so long is that it engages so many women about math and science."

"Yes," Christine says, smiling, "Whenever we do a talk, we say there's a lot of stuff to cover, do you want to hear the math behind it, and ubiquitously they all say Yes, they want to hear the math."

The Crochet Reef project has grown far beyond its original form, in that now it's made up of many sub-reefs, each with their own style, colors and environmental message. These include the *Bleached Reef*, the *Beaded Reef*, the *Branched Anemone Garden*, and the *Kelp Garden*. "Then," Margaret says in an interview with *The Believer*: "Christine . . . had the idea that we should crochet an evil sibling to our yarn-based coral reef." Called *The Toxic Reef* it is fashioned out of yarns mixed with cut up plastic bottles, cassette tapes, and other types of rubbish. *The Toxic Reef* is inspired by a zone in the ocean called the Great Pacific Garbage Patch. Christine explains, "It's the place in the ocean where currents meet and form a huge whirlpool, and it's where a lot of the garbage that goes into the sea ends up." This reef highlights the escalating problem of plastic trash pouring into our oceans and killing off marine life.

Margaret, in an interview she gave to the podcast and radio show *On Being*, points out an interesting correlation between corals and people: "The Crochet Coral Reef project is a metaphor," she says. "If you look at real corals, a head of coral is built by thousands of individual coral polyps working together. Each coral polyp is a tiny insignificant little critter with almost no power of its

Christine: "It's the place in the ocean where currents meet and form a huge whirlpool, and it's where a lot of the garbage that goes into the sea ends up."

own. But when billions of coral polyps come together, they can build the Great Barrier Reef, the largest living thing on earth and the first living thing that you can see from outer space. The Crochet Coral Reef is a human analog of that. These huge coral reef installations that we build with communities are built by hundreds and sometimes thousands of people working together . . . We humans, each of us, are like a coral polyp. Individually, we're insignificant and probably powerless. But together, I believe we can do things." It is easy to get overwhelmed by the problem of global warming and the poisoning of our oceans. "But," as Margaret remarks, "we will not solve global warming and ocean acidification if we just freak ourselves out and end up huddling in corners in fear. We must find ways to collectively act."[99] This is where people can take their cue from the amazing collective action of corals.

A Childhood Rich with Imagination

Margaret and Christine's extraordinary creative and intellectual openness were very much influenced by their childhood and particularly by their mother. "We grew up in a family of humanities," Margaret explains. "Our father was a professor of philosophy, and our mother was a Catholic mother of six who went back to university and studied sociology. She was a pioneering Australian feminist, who helped to bring in anti-discrimination legislation in Australia. She went through an enormous amount of trouble when we were children to give us what would make for an enriching experience. For example, we didn't have shop-bought toys, we had lots of drawing paper and crayons and building blocks, and we were expected to make our own toys." Christine smiles and adds, "There were times when television was banned, and Mother once said, 'Well, make your own TV,' and we did; we made our own TV in a cardboard box with a toy hand roll and scrolls of paper, and we told stories." Margaret emphasizes the importance of this approach: "What Mom did, she taught us to see the world as something that we could construct and that we *should* construct for ourselves, and actually I think that was the most amazing thing to have been given."

> *Christine: "There were times when television was banned, and Mother once said, 'Well, make your own TV,' and we did."*

A Renaissance Path

This unique upbringing was perhaps one of the reasons why, once they left home to pursue their studies and their professional lives, neither Margaret nor Christine wanted to limit themselves to a single interest. "I went to university and did physics and maths and originally thought I'd be a research scientist," says Margaret. "At universities in Australia in the early 1980s, the sciences were very very separated from everything else. It was hyper specialization. And I realized as much as I loved the science I couldn't live my life in that complete bubble. I needed a more diverse life." And so, she left research to become a science writer. "I was interested in trying to reach people who would never have a subscription to a science magazine. One sector of the population I was particularly

> *Margaret: "I couldn't live my life in that complete bubble."*

interested in reaching out to was women. And so, for ten years in Australia, I wrote a regular column on science and technology for women's magazines like *Vogue Australia* and *Elle Australia*. I suspect I'm the only person in the world who can say that." She also, before leaving Australia, spent three years making a TV series called *Catalyst* aimed at teenage girls, ages 14 and 15. "Because that's the age," she explains, "when they basically drop out of science."

In America, she continued her career as a science communicator by writing several books with topics that included exploring the fringe elements of science; dissecting the social and gender history of physics; and delving into the physical and spiritual aspects of space. Her current work with the Institute of Figuring is an extension of this desire to communicate math and science to a broad public. "Part of it came from simply being sick of people coming up to me and saying 'I bought *A Brief History of Time,* and I couldn't get past Chapter One. Please could you tell me something about physics that I can understand.' So I started thinking of ways to make science understandable."

> *Margaret: "[People were saying], 'Please could you tell me something about physics that I can understand.'"*

Meanwhile, Christine was following her own multiple interests as she pursued first painting, and then poetry (with an often philosophical or sociological emphasis), literature, and criticism. She completed a PhD in literature and semiotics from Middlesex University, London, and is currently a creative writing and critical studies professor at the California Institute of the Arts. Christine has also organized conferences on contemporary writing and often performs her own work in venues across the globe.

Forming the Institute For Figuring was, for Margaret and Christine, an innovative way of creating an interface between what, to many, may appear as entirely disparate fields. "I think the Institute For Figuring is completely a product of Chrissy and my doing it together," says Margaret. "Our work begins with the science, but it's really using sophisticated ideas from the art world about how to present it and represent it. I think it is a rare enterprise that really is based on treating the arts and the sciences genuinely equally, without one pandering to the other."

Even the name of the Institute represents its multi-aspect nature: As Margaret explains: "The organization's name is the Institute For *Figuring*, and I think the word figuring really sums it up. Because figuring is a word that encompasses figures, mathematical diagrams, and scientific illustrations. A number is a figure, we all have a figure, artists do live drawings of the human figure, and we figure things out. Figuring is a word that has intrinsic meanings in math, science, art and cognition. So the very name of the organization is meant to represent the interdisciplinary nature of it. And if you look at the acronym I.F.F, that's actually the logical symbol for *if and only if.*"

These two sisters understand the power of encouraging understanding between disciplines so that knowledge can be expanded and shared.

Margaret: "Figuring is a word that has intrinsic meanings in math, science, art, and cognition."

"I think the problem of super specialization," explains Margaret, "Is that it just simply means not only do people in academia not have common discourse, but there is no commonality with the common man and that leads to a culture in which if you want, as it were, to know the world in an officially acceptable way you have to have a PhD and that's not possible economically for our society."

Feminism: Only Half Complete

Another societal issue that both women feel strongly about is the role of feminism in the lives of women struggling to have fulfilling lives.

Their mother, Barbara Wertheim, left the Catholic church and, as mentioned, became one of the leaders of the Australian feminist movement in the 70s. She also set up the first women's refuges in the state of Queensland. "We were teenagers when our mom and her colleagues were doing feminist marches and fighting for women's right to do things," says Margaret. "But the revolution that she was part of was fighting for *two* things: for women to be able to go into the workforce and have whatever career they wanted but *also* for everybody being involved in the raising of children. That second part of the revolution hasn't really begun. And they're still working on completing the first." She adds, thoughtfully, "I think it's something we can't blame the

Margaret: "That second part of the revolution hasn't really begun."

feminist movement for failing to do. It's society that's failed."

The repercussions of only half of the feminist movement being realized has reverberated through contemporary women's lives in multiple ways. Christine explains, "One of the effects of the last 60 or 70 years has been the absolute denigration of the side of our society that has traditionally been associated with women and with the feminine, and that is the caring of people and particularly the caring of children. There has been a massive social transfer of wealth away from the caring of children, and the sick and the elderly, but particularly from the children. But everybody is a child before they are a man or a woman"

"Or," Margaret chimes in, "before they are a CEO!"

Christine smiles, acknowledging, then continues. "The raising of children still has to be managed by women, but that's not respected. Or not nearly enough. You are seen as being an important individual if you are an astrophysicist or CEO. But the most important job in the universe is being a

Christine: "The most important job in the universe is being a mother."

mother. And mothers, in fact, have always been polymaths!"

Margaret observes, "And now, young women see their mothers trying to have careers, trying to be mothers, trying to do it all, and being very stressed. And they don't want that." In the sciences, for example, Margaret points out, "The ten years after graduate school is when you really have to establish your scientific career and that usually means working very, very long hours on your research and that happens to coincide with the years of child bearing." And Christine adds that in the world of academics, "The average starting salary for a man in the humanities is $3,000 more than the average starting salary for women with exactly the same qualifications. So, in the end, for a couple, whose salary are they going to cut, even if he wanted to stay home? It's economically more beneficial for her to quit."

"We need economic incentives," Margaret asserts, "for people to take on the nurturing role. I really thought by the time I grew up that it would be something of a job sharing workplace, where everybody would have jobs, but they would all also be looking after the children!"

Endless Curiosity

We could continue talking about the sisters' lives and their perspective on important issues, but our time with them is drawing to a close. What has certainly emerged during this discussion is the twins' constant desire to learn new things, explore multiple avenues of intellectual growth, and push boundaries in both the sciences and the arts.

And in all this, they insist, persistence is the key. "I suspect all human beings have passion and drive," Margaret says, "but somehow it gets stamped out. People give up. I think the biggest issue that prevents people from being the best version of themselves is that for whatever reason they don't persevere."

Christine adds, "There is a motto our sister told us, and I think it's true. 'Always remember: You are absolutely special ... just like everybody else!'"

And with this perceptive if paradoxical statement still resonating, we leave these two fascinating RenWomen who have learned to express their own specialness in remarkably unique ways.

> *Christine: "There is a motto our sister told us . . . 'Always remember: You are absolutely special . . . just like everybody else!'"*

Ren Gems

Christine Wertheim

"What many women are doing, raising kids, is a phenomenally difficult job that is essential to our world. It's a mistake to say it's only a man's world."

"We kept our plastic for a month (and still are) and we got horrified! It makes you think, when you go out shopping, do you really want to bring home yet another plastic thing?"

"There is serious science communication going on in a project that in some sense operates like a sewing bee."

"In 2000, when *Time Magazine* put out the 100 most important things in the 20th century, our mother said they forgot the washing machine. Until then, women had to spend hours cleaning!"

Ren Gems

Margaret Wertheim

"I am a huge lover of the beauty and the poetic enchantments that exist in science and mathematics."

"The highest levels of abstraction, things like mathematics, computing, logic, etc.,—all of this can be engaged with not just through purely cerebral methods but by physically playing with ideas."

"Corals reefs are like the canaries in the coal mine of global climate change. If water temperature around a reef rises by more than about one degree Celsius for even a few weeks, corals begin to get sick."

"We all have a moral mission on earth to help make things better for people less fortunate than ourselves."

III

Where Do We Go From Here?

16

Why the World Needs More RenWomen

We are living at a time when change is happening at exponential rates, and adaptability and the capacity to handle an increasing array of input are essential. This is why having a Renaissance approach to life is invaluable. In the *Harvard Business Review* article "In Defense of Polymaths," author Kyle Wiens argues, "The problem with deep specialization is that specialists tend to get stuck in their own points of view. They've been taught to focus so narrowly that they can't look at a problem from different angles. And in the modern workscape we desperately need people with the ability to see big picture solutions."[100] Popular blogger Tim Ferris writes in his blog post "The Top Five Reasons to be a Jack of All Trades," "Was Steve Jobs a better programmer than top coders at Apple? No, but he had a broad range of skills and saw the unseen interconnectedness. As technology becomes a commodity with the democratization of information, it's the big-picture generalists who will predict, innovate, and rise to power fastest."[101]

Also important is the ability to manage the stresses of a shifting landscape. Interestingly, when it comes to stress, new research shows that men and women do not respond in the same way. Most people are well aware of the adrenaline-triggered "fight or flight" response to extreme stress. But according to UCLA social psychologist Shelley Taylor, who wrote an influential article (and later a book) on how women respond to stress, women do not go into fight or flight mode, instead they respond with a "tend or befriend" reaction.[102] This leads a woman to try and talk her way out of a stressful situation, or try to understand her opponent, thus potentially diffusing the threat. Taylor argues there are biological and evolutionary reasons for this difference, related to the care of offspring and the seeking of social support. According to Dario Maestripieri PhD, in his article for *Psychology Today*, "Gender Differences in Responses to Stress: It Boils Down to a Single Gene" there may even be a genetic marker that mediates the response.[103]

Linked also to this theory are recent studies on how men and women make decisions when under stress. According to a research article published in the journal *PLoS One*, the higher the stress, the more risk-taking men become, whereas under intense stress, women become more risk averse.[104] It is important to note that neither response is necessarily superior to the other. Under certain circumstances, more risk-taking can lead to greater rewards, but under other circumstances, it can lead to a potentially dangerous lack of caution. We noted in the introduction how much better companies do when they have both men and women in executive positions. These studies about stress responses are just further confirmation of how important it is to have a balance of men and women in key decision-making positions.

We are also living in a time of enormous conflict and turmoil throughout the world. Many have begun to question the patriarchal values that have brought us to this point and to wonder whether feminine values could offer us new and better options. As John Gerzema and Michael D'Antonio say in the introduction to their book *The Athena Doctrine* (in reference to their previous book *Spend Thrift*), "Most of the traits exhibited by the successful entrepreneurs, leaders, organizers and creators we profiled seem to come from aspects of human nature that are widely regarded as feminine."[105] This realization was what motivated the research that led to *The Athena Doctrine,* which, as previously mentioned, argues for the global need for the implementation of more female values.

There is an interesting and rather amusing story that illustrates these female values in action. When the U.S. government shut down for 16 days in 2014, while the men were saber-rattling and blaming their colleagues across the aisle, two women senators, Democrat Jeanne Shaheen and Republican Kelly Ayotte, decided to act. They hosted a pizza party for women senators from both parties to try to figure out how to resolve the situation. It was through their leadership that a compromise was finally achieved. Senator John McCain acknowledged, "It was the women's leadership that brought critical mass of Republicans and Democrats together."[106] Senator Mark Pryor stated, "Women in the Senate is a good thing. You see leadership. We're just glad they allowed us to tag along to see how it's done."[107] Although this was a somewhat tongue-in-cheek statement, there was clear admiration in it for how the women had succeeded in doing something the men couldn't. The feminine value of cooperation saved the day. Masculine values, of course, have their place. But, as we have said, it makes for a lopsided world when only one set of values prevails, and so the more women who share in leadership positions in society, the more balanced a world we will have.

What Still Needs to Change

The Renaissance women whom we have celebrated in this book, illustrate the amazing range of abilities that women have and that they will continue to develop. But we still live in a world where most Renaissance women (let alone women in general) do not have full access to their potential. In certain countries, women continue to be second-class citizens with very few rights and no access to education. This is a criminal state of affairs. But even in forward-thinking western countries, there is still important ground to cover.

Dana Manciagli, the corporate executive and career coach we cited in the Introduction, has certainly experienced high levels of success, but she acknowledges there is room for growth in the state of women in society: "There are still some serious barriers for women, as much as we're in the year 2015," she says. "Even the fact that we are still trying to get girls to believe they can excel in math and science is sad. It's sad that we're still talking about equal pay. It's sad that numerous male-dominated industries are lacking women at senior levels. And that female-dominated industries pay pathetically. Think of teachers and nurses! These are supposedly such prized professions. My sister was a teacher and she couldn't make ends meet!"

As noted by so many of our RenWomen, the key issue of the work-life balance is still largely unresolved and continues to place women in positions of having to make tough no-win choices. There is a reason why Anne-Marie Slaughter's article in *The Atlantic* entitled "Why Women Still Can't Have It All" caused such a stir! Slaughter served as Director of Policy Planning under Hillary Clinton at the State Department from 2009-2011. During this time, her husband and teenage sons remained in their hometown of Princeton. After her stint was up, instead of staying in Washington and pursuing other high-level government jobs, she chose to return to Princeton. Why? Because one of her sons was in crisis and although her husband had taken on the main responsibility of caring for the boys, she felt, at that moment, he needed her as well. She realized, with some consternation, that although she had always been a feminist who believed women could have it all, it was only in her previous jobs as a law professor and academic dean that she'd been able to manage it. Academia allowed her more flexibility in how she set up her schedule. But in the demanding work-around-the-clock position she held in Washington, "having it all" became an impossible concept. As she says, "The minute I found myself in a job that is typical for the vast majority of working women (and men), working long hours on someone else's schedule, I could no longer be both the parent and the professional I wanted to be—at least not with a child experiencing a rocky adolescence."[108] Slaughter notes that the onus has been put on women to make it to the top by being more ambitious, more driven, and certainly more sleep deprived. In other words, it is up to women to try to find ways to squeeze it all in, to be great at work *and* great at parenting, but the truth is, it's not always possible. Ultimately, the problem is a societal one—as long as we have a society in which care taking is denigrated or removed from the equation, the problem persists. As Slaughter later told *Business Insider*, "There's a tremendous loss of talent to businesses who cannot make room for their employees to attend to family responsibilities."[109] And she included men in this.

Indra K. Nooyi, the CEO of PepsiCo, when asked in *The Atlantic* whether women can have it all, answered in the following way: "I don't think women can *have* it all. I just don't think so. We pretend we have it all. We pretend we *can* have it all. My husband and I have been married for 34 years. And we have two daughters. And every day you have to make a decision about whether you are going to be a wife or a mother, in fact many times during the day you have to make those decisions. And you have to co-opt a lot of people to help you. We co-opted our families to help us. We plan our lives meticulously so we can be decent parents. But if you ask our daughters, I'm not sure they will say that I've been a good mom. I'm not sure."[110]

Dr. Sandra Loughlin, one of the women we spoke to while researching this book, was only the second woman to receive a PhD in neuroscience at UC San Diego. She was doing groundbreaking research on Parkinson's Disease and fetal cell transplants, when she made the choice to put family ahead of career. Her husband (whom she calls "just a terrific man") had made adaptations that allowed her to finish her PhD, but then she started having children at the same time as work became more demanding. As she says, "for a long time my husband and I had tried to have children. I finally gave up and adopted one and then adopted a second a couple of years later. About a week after that, I discovered I was pregnant! My research was going in wonderful directions, but I found it really difficult to continue. As I was wrapping up my bed-rest pregnancy, I came up for tenure, which meant I needed to work even harder to get grants renewed, to get papers published, etc. I ended up deciding to resign my position and give up my lab. I stayed home with my children until my youngest was in first grade." At that point, she went back to work in the field, part time. She is currently an administrator at UC Irvine. She feels that she has been able to have a satisfying and productive career in research and administration and, at last count, had 60 of her peer-reviewed publications referenced in nearly 3,000 published papers. She certainly does not regret her choices. But there are moments where she gets a little pang. She tells this story:

"At the 2014 UCI Commencement where President Obama

spoke, I had volunteered to help the faculty get into their regalia to do the procession into the stadium. I was there early in the morning and I enjoyed the whole thing, but a couple of people said to me, 'It was strange having you there and helping us and not being part of us, as we think of you as being part of us. When I got home, I found myself thinking, why *wasn't* I in that procession?

"So some days it feels like I 'have it all,'" Sandra continues. "Other days, I feel a bit remorseful to have not put more emphasis on my research, especially given all the training I received. But mostly I'm satisfied with the balance I have found between teaching, research, and parenting. And," she adds, "there's a lot of fulfillment in being a parent. There's a lot of pleasure and warmth and connectedness that comes from that."

There is little doubt that parenthood can be a deeply valuable and fulfilling experience, as can an intellectually stimulating and exciting career. The question is why does one so often have to be sacrificed for the other—either partially or completely? Despite many advances for women in the workplace, they are still frequently pulled between the two. There are those, of course, who find ways to have both, but it is never easy.

It is particularly difficult for women who have highly intensive jobs, like the government one Anne-Marie Slaughter had, that essentially do not allow for, or barely acknowledge their employee might have family responsibilities. These are the careers with long work hours, tight deadlines, heavy responsibilities, and, sometimes, lots of travel. As a number of our RenWomen have pointed out: considering that the period of time—one's late twenties to late thirties—when one is expected to put in the most time and dedication seeking growth and promotion in these jobs, is also the prime time for marriage and childbearing, the inherent dilemma is clear. For decades, men have been able to fully commit to long and brutal schedules as they build a career. Why? Because they had wives. Of course, they might hardly see their children, and that is a sad price many fathers (and many kids) have had to pay. Still, where are the "wives" for the women? When terms like "opting out" are used for women who leave these high-powered positions for the sake of children, this falsely implies far more choice in the matter than women actually have.

So, it is even more a testament to the persistence and fortitude of the RenWomen in this book that despite this ongoing struggle they have accomplished as much as they have! But one has to wonder, how many women are not able to take complete advantage of their gifts because of this dilemma? And why are policies like parental leave, flex hours, and workplace childcare still so lacking in America? To unlock the full potential of women, these issues need resolution. As Anne-Marie Slaughter says, "The best hope for improving the lot of all women. . .is to close the leadership gap: to elect a woman president and 50 women senators; to ensure that women are equally represented in the ranks of corporate executives and judicial leaders. Only when women wield power in sufficient numbers will we create a society that genuinely works for all women. That will be a society that works for everyone."[111]

17

CREATING FUTURE RENWOMEN

What about our future RenWomen? Those girls and young women who have the desire to realize a broad range of abilities? Those who are creative and independent thinkers and who see life as an adventure to be enthusiastically embraced? How do they see themselves living a 21st century version of a "Ren" life?

Well, for many of these young women, there are a number of opportunities for growth and flexible life choices that women of former generations didn't have. As already mentioned, the vast accessibility of knowledge from the buzzing "information highway" that is the World Wide Web cannot be underestimated in terms of how much more can be learned in less time. In "In Defense of Polymaths," young Kyle Weins points out: "In the digital age, learning has really never been easier—and not just for the geniuses that walk among us. Polymath status is accessible to just about anyone with a modem, a library card, and the desire to learn. Information is everywhere, and it's often free.

iTunesU gives your everyday Joe an opportunity to get a free, virtual Ivy League education from his couch. Khan Academy teaches people everything from beginning algebra to cosmology. Sign in to Google's Code University to learn programming languages in the moments snatched during lunch breaks or while the baby's napping."[112] Compare the vast accessibility of knowledge and learning now to what it was only a generation ago. And, as these articles point out, it can be done at one's pace and within one's schedule.

Entrepreneurship, using the Internet as a base of operations, is of course, another new flexible option. Take three successful young women business owners as examples:

Alexa von Tobel dropped out of business school to start LearnVest, an affordable financial advice website. In 2009, when she was only 24 years old, she launched her site, after recruiting advisors like the former CEO of the Huffington Post and former COO of DailyCandy and securing $1.1 million in funding. It is now going strong with a dedicated team of financial planners, behavior experts, and tech gurus to help everyday people learn how to best manage their money, with a particular focus on assisting young women to develop good financial habits early on in life.[113]

In 2007, at the age of 22, Lauren Bush and Ellen Gustafson co-founded the non-profit organization FEED, which manufactures and sells reusable bags that resemble feed bags with half of the proceeds going towards feeding the hungry. Their products have a number stamped on them that signifies the amount of meals or micronutrient packets provided with a purchase. Eight years later, they have built a movement which has provided over 87 million meals to hungry people worldwide.[114]

Then there is self-labeled "possibilitarian," Kelly Rae Roberts, mentioned by our RenWoman Alexandra Franzen, who gave up a career in clinical social work to launch a far riskier but eminently joyful life as an artist, writer, podcaster, and creator of the motivational website, "The Possibilitarian Project." Interestingly, as she fully committed to this new life that reflected all the parts of herself, success followed. Her licensed art has been featured in home décor and gift shops worldwide, her columns and articles have appeared in too many publications to count, and interview requests pour in. All while raising a toddler![115]

So the potential of online and home-based businesses is good news for the more entrepreneurial young RenWomen. Not only does it give them room to fully express themselves but it also allows them to manage the work-life balance a little better.

But what about those who are working or are planning to work in more traditional fields? How do they see themselves managing that balance? Many of these younger women observed their mothers frantically keeping balls in the air and wonder whether they want to do the same. Anne-Marie Slaughter, in "Why Women Still Can't Have It All," remarked that while talking to a group of 20-something Rhodes Scholars, she gave them a frank assessment of "how unexpectedly hard it was to do the kind of job I wanted to do as a high government official and be the kind of parent I wanted to be, at a demanding time for my children." The reaction she got may have been surprising. She recounts, "The audience was rapt, and asked many thoughtful questions. One of the first was from a young woman who began by thanking me for 'not giving just one more fatuous "You can have it all" talk.' Just about all of the women in that room planned to combine careers and family in some way. But almost all assumed and accepted that they would have to make compromises that the men in their lives were far less likely to have to make."[116]

Alex Espinoza, a young woman of 25 who holds down a

responsible full-time job, is working on an MBA, and hopes to eventually own her own business in the fashion industry, (and who, by the way, worked on the design of this book), talks about it this way: "At some point, you have to make the decision to put your career on hold and focus on having a family, if that's what you want for your life. My friends and I, as strong women, we want to focus on building careers in our twenties. Then, we want to get married before we are 30 years old. Then, for me, I want to start a family around the age of 33. Definitely before 35." But this sense of the importance of timing tends to be a strictly female consideration. And can they really determine what will happen when? "There is so much pressure," Alex says. "I was with a roommate who is turning 29 this year, and she was saying how depressed she was because she was finding it hard to meet guys she would want to marry. We were talking about how our biological clocks are ticking but for the guys, even though they are also getting older, there's no pressure, not in the same sense as we have it. If we want to have kids, we have to think about commitment no later than our thirties. Guys don't feel this way."

These are the questions that faced women of earlier generations. And despite much progress, these young women are facing them still.

It is little surprise, then, to see results like those listed in the *Business Insider* article "Why Women Vanish as They Move Up the Career Ladder," where the writer, Bob Sherwin, attributes this fall off to a number of factors, two of which are work-family balance and the greater domestic burdens placed on women. As he explains, "In many cases, the importance of work-family balance—especially motherhood—outweighs the leadership opportunities being offered by organizations." He adds, "Whether they want it or not, it's also clear that women end up with a double burden of responsibility in our society at large. If they work outside the home, studies show that more than 90% of them return home at night to assume the lion's share of the management of their own households."[117]

So the truth is, until there is a more equitable sharing of childcare and domestic responsibilities, as well as government-workplace support when it comes to childcare, parental leave and flexible hours, a young woman still must factor in how relationships, marriage, and children will influence the development of one or more careers. Although Sheryl Sandberg's influential book *Lean In* puts a lot of the burden on women to claim their right to "sit at the table," she also acknowledges the absolute importance of having a spouse who is willing to share 50/50 in childcare and household duties.[118]

Another important factor for young RenWomen in the making is the recognition and encouragement of their Renaissance-ness. Schools and society still have the tendency to try and steer young people into only one direction. The ubiquitous "What do you want to be when you grow up?" is a question that expects a single answer. It's about time to turn it from "choose one" to "all of the above."

In a blog on *elitedaily.com* entitled "On Being a Modern Day Renaissance Individual: This Is No Time to Be a One-Trick Pony," young woman writer Jenn Lee makes the following argument: "I am in a medical profession with a bachelor's degree in business and a penchant for art. I spent my free time in internships and hobbies that did not conform to a single 'career path.' This was often dismissed as being indecisive or noncommittal, but. . .I believe that innovation does not spark from something new, but rather, from a new perspective on something old. Art provides the creativity and out-of-box mentality that is fundamental for advancing in the fields of math and science.

"What we fail to realize is that the economy has shifted, and with continued globalization, this generation should not see specialization as the only option. We are in an age in which, if we so choose, we can be a Renaissance man or woman in the true sense of the word. There has been a revival of the art-science-technology movement and it is gaining traction.

"We need to expand our abilities and capabilities. There is nothing to lose by embracing a multitude of interests, but there is so much to gain."[119]

This could well be the manifesto of the 21st century young Renaissance woman. And those of us who are parents, teachers, and employers need to recognize and encourage these amazing young RenWomen in our midst, giving them the room to grow, expand and flourish!

CONCLUSION

Although all of the RenWomen featured in this book developed their own strategies for becoming who they are (and who they are still becoming), there are certain commonalities among them all.

Here are ten fundamental characteristics that all of our RenWomen share:

1) The Urge to Grow and Expand

In the book *Mindset* by Carol S. Dweck, PhD, the author defines the difference between what she calls a "growth mindset" and a "fixed mindset." A fixed mindset is the belief that "your qualities are carved in stone. . .[It] creates an urgency to prove yourself over and over. If you have only a certain amount of intelligence, a certain personality, and a certain moral character—well then, you'd better prove you have a healthy dose of them." The growth mindset, on the other hand "is based on the belief that your basic qualities are things you can cultivate through your efforts. . .everyone can change and grow through application and experience."[120] Well, our RenWomen all clearly have a growth mindset! For RenWomen, life is malleable and expandable. Alexandra Franzen had no trouble believing she could tackle both a helicopter's license and a massage license before launching into her other careers. Margaret Wertheim declared she wished she had "three lifetimes" to do everything that interests her. Marinela Gombosev has such an intense urge to grow and tackle challenges head on that when she is held back it deeply frustrates her. Lita Rawdin Singer, even as a young girl, never thought she could not do everything she wanted. Kathy Eldon's determination to "do more, be more, experience more, create more," says it all.

2) The Ability to Employ Flexibility, Adaptability, and Creative Problem Solving

This ability is an essential part of the RenWoman mindset. As we have already discussed, although the world is certainly improving, RenWomen still often encounter gender difficulties and the continual balancing act of work and family. Without flexibility, adaptability, and the use of creative solutions to problems, many women are left at the starting gate, or biding their time at mid-level jobs.

Our RenWomen often learned the art of flexibility as mothers. Every mother knows that the best laid plans for a day can be completely disrupted by a sick child or a most inconvenient tantrum. Barbara Lazaroff constantly invented new ways to be there for her kids, as well as her elderly parents, while building and maintaining a multi-million dollar business. At work, our RenWomen have often modulated their communication style depending on whom they are working with or what situation they are dealing with. Lydia Kennard learned to take a solid my-way-or-the-highway stand with her male personnel during the 9/11 crisis, while in other situations, she employed her consensus-building skills. Marinela used empathy when dealing with a disruptive team member and toughness and clarity when managing a sales team of all-male "cowboys."

Our RenWomen have displayed other unique forms of flexibility and creative problem solving. Lorie Karnath worked with the Chinese government to help advance education in China, while approaching the same challenge in Burma in an entirely different way (through the system of monasteries). When Jeanne Meyers, Rita Stern Milch, and Karen Pritzker couldn't get traction with their *My Hero* TV pilot, they adapted it to a new medium, the internet! Lydia Kennard was able to finance her first development deal as a young 26-year-old woman of color by hiring a prominent banking mortgage company to package the deal but not revealing at first that she was the developer. Dale Franzen raised enormous funds and did it at no cost, by using her opera voice and Dustin Hoffman's acting to turn each fundraising event into entertainment. Frances Hesselbein instigated highly innovative solutions to re-establish the relevancy of Girl Scouts of the USA. And Eva Haller? Hers was the most creative solution of all. She told a Nazi soldier she was too young and beautiful to die. And he let her go!

3) A Willingness to Buck the System

Women often like to "play nice." And certainly, our RenWomen approach life with kindness, consideration, and grace. But when they need to, they dig in their heels, draw a line in the sand, and fight the system with everything they've got. Lita Rawdin Singer did an end run around the good ol' boys of Wall Street to become a successful broker. Lydia Kennard, when pressured during 9/11 to open up the parking structures, insisted *no* loss of life was an acceptable risk. Hélène Cardona stood up to her father and the demands of an ossified academic structure to go her own way. Dale Franzen "went against the grain," choosing her own path at every turn, despite pressures to stick with the tried and true. Frances Hesselbein challenged the entire traditional structure of the Girl Scouts of the USA. The MY HERO team did not accept that positive stories had no place in the landscape of contemporary media. Margaret Wertheim has challenged the idea that science is only for the highly trained elite. Christine Wertheim challenges the very structure of language in her boundary-pushing poetry.

4) Abundant Curiosity and a Rage to Learn

Look through our profile chapters and see how often the words "curiosity" and "learn" come up. RenWomen are clearly driven by avid curiosity and an intense desire to learn. They look around, they ask questions, and they wonder. They seldom accept things at face value. For them, learning is not a chore, it is a delight. It is a way to expand, to celebrate the vast capacities of mind. Hélène Cardona describes her idyllic early school days as a time when the world was her "oyster." Lorie Karnath loved college so much that she says she felt like a "kid in a candy shop." (Later in life, she would pour all that curiosity into mind-expanding symposia.) Marinela Gombosev feels like the steeper the learning curve, the better. Alexandra Franzen advises to "lead with curiosity." Barbara Lazaroff followed her myriad interests in college to learn about theatre, dance, science, and medicine. Christine Wertheim was curious as to what would happen if she changed a crocheted mathematical model just slightly—a first step in opening up a vast new project for her sister and herself.

5) The Capacity to Embrace and Learn from Failure

This is a common theme among successful people everywhere. And RenWomen are no exception to this rule. For them, failure is not a stopping point, but rather a stepping stone to success. It is a source of lessons, and a means of improvement. Barbara Lazaroff proudly states that they may have made millions, but they lost millions too—at times, in fact, tottering on the brink of losing it all. But she says she learned more from her failures than her successes. Hélène Cardona needed to fail at trying to simultaneously please her parents and herself, an impossible task, before she learned to be true only to herself. Lita had to let go of a failing marriage to realize it had been impeding her ability to truly fly. Dale Franzen created, in the Broad Stage, a place where artists could fail, and thus also a place where they could experiment and thrive.

6) A Trust in the Power of One's Dreams and the Truth of One's Inner Voice

There are times when we wonder why we have dreams, especially when they seem impossible to reach. And yes, sometimes we don't reach them. Or in reaching for them, we are taken down an entirely different path that may even alter those original dreams. But RenWomen know there is power in dreaming; that a dream is a candle in a dark room, a sign post that points in the right direction. Dreams are intimately connected with our inner voice—what Eva Haller calls "our core" or what Kathy Eldon calls our "spark." There are so many other voices in our head, be they parental or societal, telling us to ignore that quiet voice, to let go of our dreams, to listen to everything and everyone but ourselves. RenWomen know otherwise. It is a lesson that has sometimes been hard-earned. Hélène Cardona had a nervous breakdown and a collapse from exhaustion before she finally listened to that voice within. Eva's heart longed for love, but tragedy made her believe it would only lead to loss, until a loving man helped her believe again. Marinela was driven to reach the next milestone and the next, even when people warned her to slow down or she would burn out. (She hasn't yet!) Lydia Kennard never let being a woman of color slow her down. She knew who she was, and she wasn't going to wait for anyone else to see it; she just proved it. Kathy's Eldon's life has been about following her vision of celebrating the legacy of her son by supporting the work of creative activists.

7) The Desire to Nurture, Inspire, and Serve Others

RenWomen do not hold their abilities and their wisdom close to the vest. They share them. Wherever they can they encourage, guide, and support others, whether it is their life purpose, as is the case with Kathy Eldon, and Jeanne, Rita, and Karen of The MY HERO Project, or whether it is simply a part of their lives. Marinela, as young as college-age, was bringing fellow students and industry together, and has continued to organize and inspire as a member of the C200 Scholars Program. Alexandra Franzen is inspiration in action with every word she writes on her motivational website and in her articles and books. Lita nurtures growth and transformation in her therapy clients, and inspires readers through her two insightful books. Eva Haller is a mother figure and mentor to countless young people and nonprofits. Frances Hesselbein is one of the most innovative and inspirational leaders this country has produced, and she sums up her personal philosophy by saying "To serve is to live."

8) A Willingness to Take Risks and Jump into the Unknown

You cannot grow unless you take risks. RenWomen know this well. It is not that they are fearless but that they face their fears head on, knowing the absolute validity of the expression "nothing ventured, nothing gained." The MY HERO ladies risked believing that they weren't the only ones who wanted to celebrate heroes. Lydia Kennard risked life and limb by guiding LAX through the 9/11 crisis. Dale Franzen leapt headlong into the founding and financing of a multi-million dollar arts complex, even though she had never done something like that before. Her daughter, Alexandra, gave up a secure and promising job to launch herself as an online entrepreneur. Lorie Karnath, as an explorer, took often perilous expeditions to the far corners of the earth. Kathy Eldon risked her own safety as a journalist while living in Kenya and when she returned to the site of her son's death in Somalia. Eva Haller's early life was one harrowing risk after another. Frances Hesselbein took a chance with a revolutionary new vision for Girl Scouts of the USA. Margaret and Christine Wertheim risked the disapproval of the scientific community by showing the value of art, aesthetics, and female handicraft as other avenues into scientific "knowing."

9) A Need to Make a Difference in the World

This wider view, this need to help improve the world we live in, is a key hallmark of a RenWoman. Jeanne Meyers, Rita Stern Milch, and Karen Pritzker work tirelessly to promote unsung heroes, who, every day, are changing people's lives. Kathy Eldon turned the worst tragedy a mother could experience into the impetus for an organization that uses the power of media and arts to build social movements that impact the world. Margaret and Christine Wertheim have combined science, math, and art to crochet a colorful coral protest against global warming. Barbara Lazaroff supports countless charities, with a special emphasis on hunger, children's causes, and AIDS. Lorie Karnath builds schools where schools have never been, and brings cutting edge ideas to the world through symposia. Eva Haller champions, mentors, and participates on boards of groundbreaking and world-transforming non profit organizations.

RenWomen do not live self-centered lives. Despite their time spent on developing so many skills and passions, they always find room to give back, in large ways or small.

10) A Broader Definition of "Success"

When looking at the question of success, our RenWomen see it as so much more than money, power, or renown. They know that each person must define for herself what success is, and the definition is linked to both how she chooses to *be* in this world and what she wants to leave behind. For Frances Hesselbein, it is about creating leadership that is ethical, collaborative, and values based. For Lita, it is pointing the way to the spiritual core of life and relationships. For Lydia, it is about moving past societal barriers through hard work, confidence, and strength. Christine and Margaret value the beauty of art and science, the contribution of women to both, and the necessity to work toward saving the environment. Barbara Lazaroff contributes much creatively and philanthropically to the world and particularly wants to be remembered as a good mother. Eva Haller is driven to guide and support burgeoning non-profit organizations that, among other things, tackle the terrible suffering among war-torn and poverty-stricken people. Dale and Alexandra deeply believe in following their own iconoclastic visions and inspiring others to do the same. Jeanne, Rita, and Karen want to point to, promote, and celebrate the good in this world. Marinela wants to keep exploring and evolving, while urging women to embrace their own drive and ambition. Hélène pours an abundance of creativity into her many artistic expressions and encourages others to be faithful to their true selves. Lorie seeks to bring education in all its forms to the world. Kathy fosters world-changing creative activism and seeks to ignite the creative spark within all of us to make a positive difference in this world.

Of course, many of our RenWomen have also achieved recognition, influence, and monetary rewards. But that is not their priority. They know that there are many dimensions to life—intellectual, emotional, and spiritual—and they have the wisdom to honor them all.

Ultimately, a RenWoman is like a beautiful oak tree. Her branches spread out in many directions. And her roots go deep.

END NOTES

1. Lobenstine, Margaret. *The Renaissance Soul: Life Design for People with Too Many Passions to Pick Just One*. New York: Broadway Books, 2006. p. 47-8.

2. Greenemeier, Larry. "Remembering the Day the World Wide Web Was Born." *Scientificamerican.com*. 12 March 2009. Web.

3. Meister, Jeanne. "Job Hopping Is the 'New Normal' for Millennials: Three Ways to Prevent a Human Resource Nightmare." *Forbes.com*. 8 Aug. 2014. Web.

4. Angelou, Maya. Interview by Lucinda Moore. "Growing Up Maya Angelou." *Smithsonianmag.com*. April 2003. Web.

5. "About Tao." *Taoporchon-lynch.com*. 2015. Web.

6. "About Gloria Steinem." *Gloriasteinem.com*. Web.

7. Fisher, Anne. "Boys Vs. Girls: What's Behind the College Grad Gender Gap?" *Fortune.com*. 27 March 2013. Web.

8. Adler, Roy D. "Profit, Thy Name Is … Woman?" *Psmag.com*. *Pacific Standard*, 27 Feb. 2009. Web.

9. McKinsey & Company. "Gender Diversity: A Corporate Performance Driver." *Mckinsey.com.* 2007. Web.

10. "Closing the Gap." *Economist.com. The Economist,* 26 Nov. 2011. Web.

11. Enskog, Dorothee. "Women's Positive Impact on Corporate Performance." *Credit.suisse.com. Credit Suisse,* 23 Sept. 2014. Web.

12. Massachusetts Institute of Technology. "Collective intelligence: Number of women in group linked to effectiveness in solving difficult problems." *Sciencedaily.com.* 2 Oct 2010. Web.

13. Hadary, Sharo, and Henderson, Laura. "Why Women Should Lead Boldly." *Smartblogs.com. Smart Blogs on Leadership,* 3 Dec. 2012. Web.

14. Gerzema, John. "'Feminine' Values Can Give Tomorrow's Leaders an Edge." *Hbr.org. Harvard Business Review,* 12 Aug. 2013. Web.

15. Scholasticus, Socrates, de Valois, Henri, and Walford, Edward. *The Ecclesiastical History of Socrates, Surnamed Scholasticus, or the Advocate: Comprising a History of the Church, in Seven Books, From the Accession of Constantine, A.D. 305, to the 38th Year of Theodosius II., Including a Period of 140 Years.* London: H. Bohn, 1853.

16. Gottfried of Disibodenberg and Theodoric of Echternach. Qtd in Dronke, Peter. *Women Writers of the Middle Ages.* Cambridge: Cambridge University Press, 1984. p. 145.

17. Ruether, Rosemary Radford. *Visionary Women.* Minneapolis: Augsburg Fotress, 2002. p. 10-11.

18. Madigan, Shawn. *Mystics, Visionaries and Prophets: A Historical Anthology of Women's Spiritual Writings.* Minnesota: Augsburg Fortress, 1998. p. 96.

19. Marek, George R. *The Bed and the Throne: The Life of Isabella d'Este.* New York: Harper and Row Publishers, 1976. p. ix.

20. Tudor, Mary. Qtd in Castor, Helen. "Elizabeth I: Exception to

the Rule." *Historytoday.com*. Web.

21. Ibid.

22. "Elizabeth Tilbury's Speech." *Bl.uk. The British Library Board.* Web.

23. "Elizabeth I Tudor: Quotes." *Goodreads.com*. Web

24. "Margaret Fuller: Quotes." *Goodreads.com*. Web.

25. Roosevelt, Eleanor. "On the Adoption of the Universal Declaration of Human Rights." United Nations. Paris, France. 9 Dec. 1948.

26. Roosevelt, Eleanor. *The Autobiography of Eleanor Roosevelt.* New York: Harper and Brothers, 1961.

27. Roosevelt, Eleanor. *You Learn by Living: 11 Keys to a Fulfilling Life* New York: Harper and Row, 1960.

28. "51 Wonderful Quotes by Eleanor Roosevelt." *Quotesigma.com*. 25 Feb. 2015. Web.

29. *Brainyquote.com* and *Goodreads.com*.

30. Clinton, Hilary Rodham. "Remarks in Recognition of International Human Rights Day." Palais de Nations. Geneva, Switzerland. 6 Dec. 2011.

31. Fonda, Jane. Interview by Hilton Als. "Queen Jane, Approximately." *Newyorker.com. The New Yorker,* 9 May 2011. Web.

32. Ibid.

33. Beaumont-Thomas, Ben. "Jane Fonda: Hanoi Jane Photo was a 'huge mistake.'" *Theguardian.com*. 20 Jan 2015. Web.

34. "Jane Fonda Center." Emory University. *Janefondacenter.emory. edu*. Web.

35. Fonda, Jane. Interview by Mickey Rapkin. "The One and Only Jane Fonda." *Dujour.com*. Web.

36. Ibid.

37. Fonda, Jane. "Life's Third Act." TedxWomen. Dec 2011.

38. Huffington, Arianna. *Thrive: The Third Metric to Redefining Success and Creating a Life of Well-Being, Wisdom, and Wonder.* New York: Harmony Books, 2014. p. 1.

39. Ibid., p. 12.

40. Huffington, Arianna. "Arianna Huffington's Best Advice." *Harpersbazaar.com.* 5 July 2014. Web.

41. Huffington, Arianna. *The Fourth Instinct: The Call of the Soul.* New York: Simon & Schuster, 1994.

42. Russakoff, Dale. "Lessons of Might and Right: How Segregation and an Indomitable Family Shaped National Security Advisor, Condoleezza Rice." *Washington Post Magazine,* 9 Sept. 2001.

43. Rice, Condoleezza. Interview by Katie Couric. "Condoleezza Rice Tells Katie Couric, 'I Don't Miss Washington Very Much'." *Glamour.com.* 5 Oct. 2010. Web.

44. Dodd, Brian. "27 Leadership Quotes and Lessons from Condoleezza Rice – Chick-Fil-A Leadercast." *Briandoddonleadership.com.* 11 May 2013. Web.

45. Antoniacci, Mandy. "10 Empowering Leadership Quotes From Women's Golf." *Inc.com.* 11 Jun. 2015. Web.

46. Eldon, Kathy. Interview by Xenia Shin. "Women Transforming Media." *Myheroblog.com.* 8 March 2015. Web.

47. "Creative Visions." *Creativevisions.org.* Web.

48. Eldon, Kathy. *In the Heart of Life.* New York: Harper One, 2013. p. 13.

49. Ibid., p. 120.

50. Ibid., p. 34.

51. "Dan Eldon Biography." *Daneldon.org.* Web.

52. Eldon, Kathy. *In the Heart of Life.* New York: Harper One, 2013. p. 246.

53. Eldon, Kathy. "The F-Word Revolution." Tedx Orange Coast. 17

Oct 2013.

54. Ibid.

55. Haller, Eva. Interview by Xenia Shin. *Myheroblog.com*. 8 March 2015. Web.

56. "Video Volunteers." *Videovolunteers.org*. Web.

57. Hesselbein, Frances. *My Life in Leadership: The Journey and Lessons Learned Along the Way*. San Francisco: Jossey-Bass, 2011. p. 12.

58. Ibid., p. 16.

59. Ibid., p. 20.

60. Ibid., p. 14.

61. Ibid., p. 25

62. Ibid., p. 50.

63. Ibid., p. 52.

64. Ibid., p. 57.

65. Hesselbein, Frances. Interview by Colleen Leahey. "Learning from Peter Drucker and the Girl Scouts." *Fortune Online*. November 9, 2011. Web.

66. Hesselbein, Frances. *My Life in Leadership: The Journey and Lessons Learned Along the Way*. San Francisco: Jossey-Bass, 2011. p. 75.

67. Ibid., p. 91.

68. Ibid., p. 92.

69. Hesselbein, Frances. Interview by Colleen Leahey. "Learning from Peter Drucker and the Girl Scouts." *Fortune Online*. November 9, 2011. Web.

70. Drucker, Peter F. "What Business Can Learn from Nonprofits." *Harvard Business Review*. July-August 1989.

71. Hesselbein, Frances. Interview by Colleen Leahey. "Learning from Peter Drucker and the Girl Scouts." *Fortune Online*. November 9, 2011. Web.

72. Hesselbein, Frances. *My Life in Leadership: The Journey and Lessons*

Learned Along the Way. San Francisco: Jossey-Bass, 2011 p. 142.

73. Ibid., p. 144.

74. Ibid., p. 158.

75. Helgesen, Sally. "Frances Hesselbein's Merit Badge in Leadership." *strategy+business* magazine. May 11, 2015.

76. Karnath, Lorie. *Architecture in Burma: Moments in Time.* Berlin: Hatje Cantz, 2013.

77. Oldham, Jennifer. "Chief of LAX a Calm Voice Amid Shouting Over Safety." *Los Angeles Times.* 12 Nov. 2001.

78. Villaraigosa, Antonio. Interview by Jennifer Oldham. "Airport Agency Chief Has Steered LAX Out of Turbulence." *Los Angeles Times.* 13 Nov. 2006.

79. Horowitz, Joy. "'Look Who's Talking' Suit On Plagiarism Is Settled." *The New York Times.* 14 June1991.

80. "Moment 24: Meeting Mattie Stepanek." *Oprah.com.* Web.

81. Pritzker, Karen. *My Hero: The My Hero Project.* New York: Free Press, 2005. p. xxi.

82. Singer, Lita Rawdin. *Cancel the Pity Party: Five Steps to Creating Your Best Life.* Bloomington: IUniverse, 2015. p. 96.

83. Ibid., p.36, citing: Benson, Herbert. *The Relaxation Response.* New York: William Morrow, 1975.

84. Singer, Lita Rawdin. *Cancel the Pity Party: Five Steps to Creating Your Best Life.* Bloomington: IUniverse, 2015. p. 51.

85. Ibid., p. 73.

86. Ibid., p. 97.

87. Ibid., p.107.

88. Ibid., p. 108.

89. Ibid., p. 105.

90. Ibid., p. 110.

91. Singer, Lita Rawdin. *Adam Was Trapped, Eve Was Framed: Five*

Steps to Relationship Freedom. New York, Bloomington: IUniverse, 2008. p. xii.

92. Wertheim, Margaret. "The Beautiful Math of Corals." TED Talk. Feb. 2009.

93. "Crochet Coral Reef." *Crochetcoralreef.org*. Web.

94. Wertheim, Margaret. Interview with K. L. Mulholland. "Crocheting in hyperbolic space." *Blog.ted*.com. TED Blog. Web.

95. Ibid.

96. Wertheim, Margaret. "The Beautiful Math of Corals."

97. Ibid.

98. Ibid.

99. Wertheim, Margaret. Interview by Krista Tippett. "The Grandeur and Limits of Science." *Onbeing.org*. *OnBeing*, 23 April 2015. Web.

100. Wiens, Kyle. "In Defense of Polymaths." *Hbr.org*. *Harvard Business Review*, 8 May 2012.Web.

101. Ferriss, Tim. "The Top 5 Reasons to Be a Jack of All Trades." *Fourhourworkweek.com*. 14 Sept. 2007. Web.

102. Taylor, Shelley E. "Tend and Befriend Theory." *Handbook of Theories of Social Psychology*. Sage Publications. 2012.

103. Maestripieri, Dario. "Gender Differences in Responses to Stress: It Boils Down to a Single Gene." *Psychology Today*. 17 March 2012.

104. Gorlick, Marissa A., Lighthall, Nichole R., and Mather, Mara. "Acute Stress Increases Sex Differences in Risk Seeking in the Balloon Analogue Risk Task." *PLoS One*. 1 July 2009.

105. D'Antonio, Michael, and Gerzema, John. *The Athena Doctrine, How Women (and the Men WhoThink Like Them) Will Rule the Future*. San Francisco: Jossey-Bass, 2013.

106. McCain, John. "Women in Politics." *Makers: Women Who Make America*. PBS. PBS SoCal, California. 4 Nov. 2014. Television.

107. Pryor, Mark. "Women in Politics." *Makers: Women Who Make America*. PBS. PBS SoCal, California. 4 Nov. 2014. Television.

108. Slaughter, Anne-Marie. "Why Women Still Can't Have It All." *The Atlantic*. July/August 2012.

109. Slaughter, Anne-Marie. Interview with Richard Feloni. "The Woman Who Told 2.7 Million Readers 'Women Can't Have It All' Explains How She's Changed Her Mind." *Businessinsider.com*. 15 Oct. 2015. Web.

110. Nooyi, Indra K. Interview by Conor Friedersdorf. "Why PepsiCo CEO Indra K. Nooyi Can't Have It All." *Atlantic.com*. 1 July 2014. Web.

111. Slaughter, Anne-Marie. "Why Women Still Can't Have It All." *The Atlantic*. July/August 2012.

112. Wiens, Kyle. "In Defense of Polymaths." Hbr.org. Harvard Business Review, 8 May 2012. Web.

113. "Learnvest." *Learnvest.com*. Web.

114. "About FEED." *Feedprojects.com*. Web.

115. "The Possibilitarian Project." *Kellyraeroberts.com*. Web.

116. Slaughter, Anne-Marie. "Why Women Still Can't Have It All." *The Atlantic*. July/August 2012.

117. Sherwin, Bob. "Why Women Vanish as They Move Up the Career Ladder," *Businessinsider.com*. 27 Janurary, 2014. Web.

118. Sandberg, Sheryl. *Lean In: Women, Work, and the Will to Lead*. New York: Alfred A. Knopf, 2013.

119. Lee, Jenn. "On Being a Modern Day Renaissance Individual: This Is No Time To Be a One-Trick Pony." *Elitedaily.com*. 29 April 2014. Web.

120. Dweck, Carol S. *Mindset: The New Psychology of Success*. New York: Ballantine Books, 2008 p. 6-7.

ACKNOWLEDGMENTS

We want to express our heartfelt gratitude to Dale's husband, Greg Stamos, and to her son, Alec Stamos, for their unerring patience with Dale's long hours and intense schedule while she was working 24/7 writing this book. We're grateful to Alec Stamos and to Jacinta Marasco, for transcribing the interviews; to Katey Dager, for the first proofreading pass; and to Jordan Shelby and Lisa Raub, for a final proofing and fine-detail edit. We are indebted to Alex Espinoza for her diligent involvement in many aspects of this project, from the design and production, to working closely with Scott on the brand development and marketing direction. We are thankful for the help of Scott's close friend and fellow professor in the MBA program at Pepperdine University, John Buckingham, an early champion and supporter, and for the invaluable aid of Emmanuel Itier, an enthusiastic advocate and opener-of-doors throughout our process. We have unending appreciation for all the extraordinary RenWomen in this book, who allowed us into their lives and trusted us with their stories. Particular nods go to Barbara Lazaroff, a special lady, who was our first subject and who provided valuable inputs that helped put more wind in our sails, and to Eva Haller, who joined our promotion efforts from the beginning, recognizing that *RenWomen* is much more than a book, it is a movement.

Dale is grateful to her dedicated and unswerving collaborator and twin brother, Scott, who conceived of the idea for this book as well as the brand "RenWomen," while cajoling and persuading her to write it. He spent long hours with Dale as they talked, brainstormed, formed and reformed the structure and vision of the book. Scott is grateful to Dale for then "taking the ball and running with it," pouring her heart and soul into interviewing our RenWomen, and capturing in prose their remarkable and transformational life stories.

Finally, our thanks go out to all RenWomen everywhere, those in full flower and those still blossoming, inspirational in their own right, as they aspire to embrace their greatness.

ABOUT THE AUTHORS

Dale Griffiths Stamos

Dale Griffiths Stamos is a professional playwright, poet, screenwriter, and producer; as well as a teacher, story consultant, and editor. She is the recipient of multiple awards and recognitions—including the Heideman Award from Actors Theatre of Louisville, *Writer's Digest* Stageplay Competition top ten winner (twice), The Jewel Box Theatre Prize, and an Emmy nomination for her story contribution to a CBS after school special. Her plays have been produced throughout the country. Her short films have been official selections at a number of festivals, garnering two Audience Awards and one Jury Award. Her feature-length screenplay *One White Crow* has been an official selection in the screenwriting component of two film festivals, as well as a finalist and semifinalist in two prestigious screenwriting competitions. Her poetry has been published in numerous journals and magazines. She occasionally dons a producer's hat through her company, Venice Sky Productions, producing or co-producing both theater and film projects. As a teacher, writing consultant, and presenter, she holds a yearly workshop in "Story Structure for All Genres" at the Santa Barbara Writers Conference, is a private manuscript consultant/editor and has spoken about writing to groups such as the Southern California Writers Association, the Writers Club, the Alliance of Los Angeles Playwrights, and Stage Day LA. Dale started out as a linguist, getting a master's degree in Romance languages and literatures from UCLA, and she speaks French, Spanish, Italian, and even a bit of Greek! A musician and songwriter as well, she plays keyboard and guitar.

W. Scott Griffiths

Scott Griffiths has been building companies and directing successful brands for twenty years, including for Paul Mitchell ("Mitch for Men"), House of Blues, Crystal Cruises, Nokia, and Vertu just to name a few. He is the CEO and Founder of 18/8 Fine Men's Salons (www.EighteenEight.com) an international chain of upscale salons designed for men, with 400 stores operating and in development. He has led or was on the leadership team of twenty start-ups and early stage companies. After attending Chapman University, Mr. Griffiths graduated as a scholarship student from Art Center College of Design, where he later served as President of the Alumni Board. He also went on to pursue his MBA from the UCLA Anderson School. He is a past member of the Harvard Business School Association of Orange County, where he helped direct the marketing of the annual Entrepreneurs Conference for 12 years. He has served as marketing advisor to the UCLA Anderson Economic Forecast, taught at Chapman University Business School, and presently teaches at Pepperdine University Graziadio School of Business and Management. He also sits on the Board of Directors for the Surfing Heritage & Cultural Center. Scott is the co-author/producer of five books published by Random House, Doubleday, and Little Brown. Two of his books: *Air Powered* and *America's Best Beers* were best sellers.